CW01081662

200 Years of Royal Arch Freemasonry in England 1813-2013

(A Compendium of the Order)

200 Years of
Royal Arch Freemasonry
in England 1813-2013

(A Compendium of the Order)

by Yasha Beresiner

DEDICATION to JIMMY SALTIEL

This book is dedicated with all my heart and love to Jimmy, who has been a blood brother throughout our lives, rather than the uncle that he is. May he long enjoy his bridge and his swimming and his friends and his family as we enjoy him.

200 Years of Royal Arch Freemasonry in England 1813-2013
(A Compendium of the Order)

This impression 2013

ISBN 978 0 85318 439 3

All rights reserved. No part of this book may be reproduced or transmitted in any form or by any means, electronic or mechanical, including photocopying, recording or by any information storage and retrieval system, without permission from the Publisher in writing.

© Yasha Beresiner 2013

Published by Lewis Masonic

an imprint of Ian Allan Publishing Ltd, Hersham, Surrey KT12 4RG.

Printed and bound by CPI Group (UK) Ltd, Croydon, CR0 4YY

Distributed in the United States of America and Canada by BookMasters Distribution Services

Visit the Lewis Masonic website at www.lewismasonic.co.uk

Copyright
Illegal copying and selling of publications deprives authors, publishers and booksellers of income, without which there would be no investment in new publications. Unauthorised versions of publications are also likely to be inferior in quality and contain incorrect information. You can help by reporting copyright infringements and acts of piracy to the Publisher or the UK Copyright Service.

All images reproduced by kind permission of The Library and Museum of Freemasonry, London, unless otherwise stated.

"The Royal Arch is not a separate entity, but the completing part of a Masonic legend, a constituent ever present in the compound body, even before it developed into a degree ... If the Royal Arch fell into desuetude, the cope-stone would be removed, and the building left obviously incomplete"

Dr W J Chetwode Crawley
in Caementaria Hibernica, 1895

Contents

About the author

Yasha was born in Turkey in 1940 and is a Law Graduate of the Hebrew University of Jerusalem (1968). He moved to England in 1969 and after an extended career as a legal consultant was appointed a Director of Stanley Gibbons Ltd, the stamp magnates. In 1983 he set up his own international collectors' company, thus named InterCol London (**www.intercol.co.uk**). He is a City of London Guide (Editor of their quarterly publication) and a Past Master (2001/2) of the Worshipful Company of Makers of Playing Cards, founded in 1628. He is an accredited NADFAS lecturer and the author of a dozen books, of which the present volume is the 5th on Freemasonry. He has also written many articles in various specialised publications throughout Europe and the Americas. He was initiated in London in 1975, exalted to the Royal Arch in 1978 and is a Grand Officer in both, as he is in the Mark degree. He is active and an honorary member in many jurisdictions and Orders in England, Scotland, Israel, Belgium, Romania and the USA. In 1992 he was invited to become a full member of the Quatuor Coronati Lodge No. 2076, the Premier Lodge of Masonic Research, serving as Master in 1998/9. In 2009 he was nominated a member of the prestigious American Society of the Blue Friars.

By the same author

The Paper Tiger, (with Art Buchwald & Uri Ben-Yehuda), Eichenberger 1968

Colombian Currency, Stanley Gibbons 1973

The Story of Paper Money, (with C Narberth), David & Charles 1974

A Collectors' Guide to Paper Money, Andre Deutsch, 1977

British County Maps, ACC 1983

The Ortiz-Patiño Collection of Playing Cards, InterCol 1995

Masonic Curiosities, ANZMRC 1999

Royal Arch: the 4th degree of the Antients, Supreme Grand Chapter of England 2000

City of London – a Masonic Guide, Lewis 2007, (reprinted 2011)

Masonically Speaking, Lewis 2008

Freemasons' Handbook of Toasts, Speeches and Responses, Lewis 2009

Taken by Surprise, Lewis 2012

Preface and Credits

The publication of this book coincides with the celebratory Convocation of the Supreme Grand Chapter of England on Wednesday 16 October 2013. The event commemorates the 200th anniversary of the inclusion of the Royal Arch in the Articles of Union between the Moderns' and Antients' Grand Lodges wherein it is declared that 'pure Ancient Masonry consists of three degrees and no more, viz., those of the entered apprentice, the fellow craft and the master mason, including the Supreme Order of the Holy Royal Arch'. The more observant amongst the readers may correctly point out that the appropriate date for the bicentennial celebrations of the foundation of the Royal Arch would be on 18 March 2017. There was, after all, a four-year hiatus after 1813 and it was not until 18 March 1817 that the so-called 'United' Grand Chapter of England was founded, grand officers appointed and a committee formed to provide regulations to govern the Order. The year 2017, however, as well as being the 200th anniversary of the formation of the United Grand Chapter of England, is also the year of the 300th anniversary of the foundation of the premier Grand Lodge of England. Great celebrations are planned for the latter and in order to ensure that the Royal Arch is given its well-deserved independent credit and attention, and not lost in the midst of Grand Lodge Craft activities, the earlier date was agreed on as suitable and appropriate. The Craft union of the two Grand Lodges is separately celebrated in December 2013.

For clarification, the pertinent dates are:

24 June 1717	The premier Grand Lodge of England (Moderns) is founded
17 July 1751	The Antients' Grand Lodge begins to be founded (the term 'Antients', is the archaic spelling of 'ancient' and is used when referring to 'The Grand Lodge of England According to the Old Institutions')
22 July 1766	The Supreme Grand Chapter of England is founded
25 November 1813	The Articles of Union between the Moderns and Antients are signed and sealed (accepting the Royal Arch as part of pure Ancient Masonry)
1 December 1813	The same articles are 'ratified, confirmed and further sealed'
27 December 1813	The Grand Lodge celebrates its union
18 March 1817	'United' Supreme Grand Chapter of England is founded

It is not possible to consider the last 200 years outside the context of the several decades that led to the establishment of the Royal Arch as part of pure Ancient Masonry. Nor can the Royal Arch be isolated and distanced from the Craft. It is only a Craft Freemason, after all, that can become a Royal Arch Mason. Thus, part I of this book considers the period leading up to the union of December 1813. This period is of utmost and direct relevance to the Royal Arch, because it brought about the emergence of the Order and culminated in the dissolution, without a replacement, of the Supreme Grand Chapter, with only a minimal mention of the Royal Arch in the Articles of Union of 1813.

In order to give a complete picture of the Royal Arch within the context of Freemasonry as a whole, the period taken into account starts in 1717. Particular consideration is given to the emergence of the Antients' Grand Lodge in 1751 and its approach to the Royal Arch, the single occurrence which finally led to the union of 1813. This union created those very special historic circumstances that make English Craft Freemasonry's relationship with Royal Arch effectively unique in the world of Freemasonry. These circumstances have been explained so far as possible, and a number of controversial subjects relevant to the Royal Arch are also discussed:

- The Ancient's Grand Secretary and Deputy Grand Master Laurence Dermott's position vis-à-vis the Royal Arch
- The coincidence of the wording in the Antients' minutes of July 1752 with those used by Fifield Dassigny in his publication almost a decade earlier in 1744
- John Rawdon Dashwood's (1889-1961) theories of a falsification in the Charter of Compact
- An analysis of the physical Articles of Union documents that have survived
- The Duke of Sussex's revival of the Restoration Chapter No. 1

The second part is an innovation for this type of book, which I hope the reader will approve of and enjoy. It covers the single day of celebrations of the union on 27 December 1813. This second part is presented in the form of a novella. Whilst, clearly, a great deal of imagination has been used in composing the text, every effort has been made to use as many actual known names as practicable and correct dates and data.

Part III is a chronological account of Royal Arch and related events treated in the manner of a lodge or chapter history of the Supreme Grand Chapter. The chronology is not intended to be, nor could it be, comprehensive. Certain key events during this period are emphasised and covered at some length. The historic annotations to each year, chosen at random, are intended to place the text in the context of contemporary events.

Due to the abbreviated format of a celebratory book such as this, it has not been possible to incorporate many of the historical aspects of the Royal Arch, such as, for example, the close association of the Royal Arch to the Order of the Knights Templar. References to the important involvement of Scotland and Ireland in English Craft affairs during this period have also been omitted. They are well emphasised in John Belton's recent publication, 'The English Masonic Union of 1813 - A Tale Antient and Modern' (Arima Publishing 2012).

This book on the Royal Arch is meant to be enjoyable and an 'easy read', not an academic or scholarly study of the subject. Endnotes have been omitted. The sources used are mentioned in the body of the text and an extensive bibliography has been included to accommodate those wishing to pursue the subject further. Every effort has been made to assure the accuracy of the content.

I here express my gratitude to Diane Clements, Director of the Library and Museum of Freemasonry, Martin Cherry, the librarian, Susan Snell, the archivist, Peter Aitkenhead, assistant librarian, and to the remainder of the excellent staff for their unstinting help. They have been a tower of strength and support, not to mention patience, and I never cease to be amazed at their knowledge and dedication to assist readers. I would also like to acknowledge the outstanding professional editorial assistance given me by Harriet Sandvall; it has proven to be invaluable. John Belton has been a friend beyond all my expectations. He read through the manuscript and gave me excellent advice. Andreas Rizopoulos, my long standing (fifty years or more) friend and colleague, has to be thanked for looking through my text and usefully commenting on it. This, notwithstanding his incapacity and discomfort at the time of writing. I wish him health and long life. Keith Tallon's expertise in Royal Arch ritual matters is without parallel and I have been the beneficiary of his helpful views. Companion Douglas Burford has been a mentor to me since my appointment, in his footsteps, as the Batham Lecturer in 2000. I acknowledge his wise and knowledgeable guidance which I have fully adopted. I am also grateful to my colleague John Acaster for his incisive and knowledgeable editorial corrections, and to my friend Emanuele Minotti for his care and encouragement. All of the illustrations for the book have been very kindly provided by The Library and Museum of Freemasonry, London, and my particular thanks go to Mark Dennis, Curator and Andrew Tucker, Assistant Curator, for their invaluable help in sourcing and photographing the images. Finally, Martin and Pip Faulks have been inspirational supporters and backed me throughout the rather brief period that I was given to complete the book.

This book does not – and is not intended to – resolve the perennial question of the exact standing of the Royal Arch under the English Masonic system. That is a subject that remains open to further debate. As already mentioned, the subject of the Royal Arch in England since 1813 cannot be detached from the Craft. To appreciate the development of the Royal Arch in the 19th and 20th centuries, parallel activities and decisions of the United Grand Lodge of England have to be taken into consideration. Let it be emphasised, one more time, that a companion of the Royal Arch has to be, by force of circumstance, a qualified brother in the Craft. The part played by the Duke of Sussex (1773-1843) in establishing single-handedly, so to speak, the standing of the Royal Arch in 1813, is the most manifest aspect of this dependence of the Order on the United Grand Lodge of England. Thus Supreme Grand Chapter activity, in all its aspects, will reflect that of the Craft.

The success of the Order is guaranteed, if for no other reason than the fact that the membership consists entirely of dedicated Freemasons seeking further light. Had the companions concerned not been enthusiastic they would not have furthered their Masonic education by joining an additional Order beyond the Craft. Thus the companions of a Royal Arch Chapter are a 'converted and captive' group. This is reflected in the warm and friendly ambiance to be encountered in the naturally smaller gatherings of chapter meetings.

*   *   *   *   *

Part I

The Royal Arch – From Birth to Union (1717-1813)

Background

The premier Grand Lodge of England was founded on St John the Baptist's Day, 24 June 1717 by four lodges that met at the Goose and Gridiron tavern in the City of London. It was the start of organised Freemasonry. The emphasis is on the word 'organised'. Clearly lodges existed prior to that date and speculative, for the want of a better word, Masonic activity in England is in evidence before the Civil War, with the initiation of Elias Ashmole (1617-1692) in 1646 as the iconic Masonic event of that century, if not in the history of Freemasonry as a whole. This was not true, of course, of operative Masonry. The Masons Company of London are recorded as being represented on the City Court of Common Council in 1375 and, almost 20 years earlier in 1356, the Mayor and Alderman of the City passed rules and regulations relevant to the comportment of the Masons. These documents are deposited in the archives of the City of London Corporation. The perennial question 'did the speculative masons originate from the medieval operatives?' has still not been satisfactory answered. Our origins remain a mystery. Even events in 1717, which were totally ignored by the contemporary press, have no source of reference before James Anderson's (1680-1739) 'Constitutions of the Antient and Honourable Fraternity of Free and Accepted Masons' published in 1738. This second edition of the constitutions of the Freemasons remains the primary source as to what is purported to have happened when the four London lodges met and 'formed themselves into a Grand Lodge' on 24 June 1717.

The newly created 'Society of Free and Accepted Masons of England' prospered well beyond the expectations of its founders. The recruitment of nobility into its leadership, within the first decade of its existence, popularised the organisation. In the first half of the eighteenth century it became fashionable to be a Freemason. It is generally accepted that there is no evidence of the Royal Arch in this early period and that at best, some terms then used may be found in later established Royal Arch proceedings. In this context the evidence given by John Coustos (1703-1746) under interrogation by the Inquisition in April 1744, is the most frequently cited example. The relevant documents are reproduced and analysed by J R Dashwood in *AQC*, 66, 1952, pp. 107-123.

Exposures

The only disruption to the harmony of events was the advent of the exposures that were intended to disclose the 'secrets' of the Society. The earliest known English exposure, an untitled catechism of the ritual in the form of an anonymous letter, later named 'A Mason's Examination', appeared in the 'Flying Post' or 'Post Master' dated 11-13 April 1723. By then there had already been several written attacks on Freemasons, all on record. The most important and consequential exposure, however, was the thirty-two page pamphlet entitled 'Masonry Dissected' by Samuel Prichard, who claimed to be a 'late member of a Lodge' and about whom there is very little information. The first edition of this exposure appeared on 20 October 1730. By the 31 October in the same year no less than four editions of the pamphlet had been printed, probably not reflecting the curious interest of the general public but rather the enthusiasm of contemporary Freemasons. It was they who were purchasing copies of the exposure, no doubt to assist with their learning of the ritual. The indirect benefit of these publications was to spread knowledge of freemasonry far and wide, although the publications were also to take their toll on the Society's standing in due course. It has been suggested that these publications were not exposures and were instigated by Grand Lodge, targeted at the Brethren in an endeavour to standardise the ritual at a time when written versions would have been strictly prohibited. (See Jan Snoek 'Oral and Written Transmission of the Masonic Tradition' Grande Loge Reguliere de Belgique Acta Macionica Volume 8 (1998) p44 & p47). In any case, these detailed disclosures of the ritual as practiced by Freemasons in the first half of the eighteenth century do not hint at anything resembling the Royal Arch.

Nobility

Meanwhile, the interest shown by the nobility in what, even then, appeared an historic and ancient Craft grew unabated. The Reverend John Theophilus Desaguliers (1683-1744), third Grand Master, was as instrumental as any other single person in bringing Freemasonry to the attention of the academic aristocracy of the period, and amongst members of the Royal Society in particular. Desaguliers was an intellectual Huguenot of rank and stature. A respected scientist, well known as an experimental philosopher, he was elected a member of the Royal Society in 1714. He was soon appointed the curator of this most important scientific body. But what was it that induced Desaguliers to join the Craft in the first place? It is possible that the establishment of the Masonic fraternity, with its peculiar secrets restricted to members only, attracted the attention of the Royal Society membership. These secrets of Freemasonry have always consisted of not much more than the words and signs associated with the various degrees. There appears to be little evidence that freemasons have had any secrets associated with hermetic philosophy, the kabala or other similar mystical schools of thought, notwithstanding the element of spirituality most members are able to enjoy and interpret in their own individual manner. It is possible that these same simple and limited Masonic secrets, unknown to the profane, attracted the curiosity and subsequent membership of the intelligentsia of the period towards joining our fraternity. Members of the Royal Society, led by John Desaguliers and others, intrigued and engrossed by hermetic and alternative philosophy, as was then being studied in such academic circles, had to be initiated into Freemasonry in order to discover that there was nothing of scientific consequence in the Masonic secrets, founded on the concepts of 'brotherly love, relief and truth'. These laudable concepts alone, however, may have been of sufficient value to men of high moral standing to induce them to continue and encourage the praiseworthy activities of Freemasonry. Rather ironically, those very circumstances that had so encouraged the speedy prosperity of the Craft, namely the recruitment of the nobility and aristocracy into its midst, were also to prove to be the cause of the beginning of a temporary decline in the Society's fortunes.

The origins of the Royal Arch

By the 1740s, things were not going particularly well for the premier Grand Lodge. The anti-Masonic exposures mentioned, *Masonry Dissected* (London: J. Wilford, 1730) and other similar articles, led to the clandestine making of masons who were thus enabled to apply for Masonic charity. This caused mayhem in the corridors of Grand Lodge. The long standing Grand Secretary (1734-56) of the premier Grand Lodge, John Revis, later to become Deputy Grand Master (1757-63), proved to be ineffectual in his duties, albeit a staunch and loyal Freemason. Not surprisingly, the Grand Masters appointed from the aristocracy, acting effectively as figureheads during the first half of the eighteenth century, were unable or, more likely, unwilling to attend meetings of Grand Lodge which, in any case, was not meeting regularly. The twenty-five-year-old William, 5th Lord Byron (1722-98), appointed Grand Master in 1747 for a five-year span, is often cited. In the whole time of his tenure he did not attend a single meeting, nor did he take any action whatever with regard to new appointments in the Grand Lodge. Meanwhile, there was an element of resentment in Masonic circles on the part of Irish brethren who had migrated to England following the Irish famine of 1740-41. They found it difficult, to put it mildly, to be welcomed or accepted as joining members of English lodges. Freemasonry in England was at its lowest ebb and the eventual emergence of a new and competing Grand Lodge was not surprising.

It was in this ambiance of general anxiety in English Masonic circles that the Royal Arch first surfaced in the 1740s as a separate degree of Freemasonry. There is as little information on the origins of the Royal Arch as there is of the Craft. Theories abound. Bernard Jones (*Freemasons' Book of the Royal Arch* London, George Harrap, 1957) divides researchers into two fields: those who believe the Royal Arch to have some origin in the earliest fabric of freemasonry, and those who believe the Royal Arch to be a mid-eighteenth-century innovation.

One clear mistake of many students of the Royal Arch is to fail to differentiate between 'origin of' and 'source to'. The former denotes a continuous lineal descent. Not so with sources, which are isolated islands of recorded information, often in the distant past such as the Bible, the single source for much of Masonic ritual and practices. We can hardly claim however, that any biblical legends are the origins of Freemasonry. With this distinction in mind, an excellent and acceptable possibility of a source behind the Royal Arch legend of the crypt is expounded by Ian Thorpe in his article 'The Origins of the Royal Arch Degree: A personal view' (*The Square*, December, 2012, p19). In a clearly written and convincing article, Thorpe traces the source of the Royal Arch legend, as used in today's chapters, to a ninth-century manuscript volume in the Bodleian Library, Oxford. This is an excellently researched article and appears to establish an undisputed source for the Royal Arch, previously mentioned in the preface to Bernard Jones' book cited above. It is not, however, in any way to be seen as the origins of Freemasonry, which would imply a direct link and continued pedigree from the ninth century to the ritual of the present day.

Though only speculations, among the most popular and credible explanations of the origins of the Royal Arch is the possibility that the third degree was fragmented after the introduction of the Hiramic legend (familiar to all Master Masons) in the late 1720s. Chronology favours the association of the Hiramic legend to the first Temple in 957 BC, which is then followed by the content of the Royal Arch ritual and its relevance to the Second Temple of 516 BC. The suggestion that the Royal Arch may have been instigated by masons belonging to the Moderns Grand Lodge has not been substantiated. In practice, there is no link between the third degree and the Royal Arch. Harry Carr, in his paper entitled 'The relationship between the Craft and The Royal Arch' (*AQC*, 86, 1974, pp. 35-86), shows that the oft-quoted concept that the substituted word in the third degree is found in the Royal Arch ceremony is quite erroneous. In the Master Mason's ceremony the word may not be uttered because of the death of Hiram and the need of the presence of three for the word to be pronounced. The word in the third degree, therefore, is not lost and the ritual does not state or even suggest that it is lost. Thus, the word that is found in the exaltation ceremony of the Royal Arch and referring to an event taking place four centuries later, is not the same word purportedly lost and now rediscovered. It is a totally new and un-associated word.

Another popular theory, expounded, *inter alia*, by Bernard Jones cited above (p24), is that the three Craft degrees, having been introduced to the continent by Irish and Scottish military lodges under travelling warrants, were found to be lacking in content and colour. In simple terms, they were boring. Thus the French, it is theorised, took the initiative to improve matters, extend the legends and composed a new ritual, which was then re-imported into England. It has also been suggested that an unidentified English Mason, an innovator, adopted one of the many existing European rituals and introduced it to England.

A more original approach has been suggested by Douglas Knoop, that the content of the Royal Arch ritual, viewed from a spiritual or esoteric point of view, can be found in Craft practices in the early eighteenth century. Some credence is to be given to the concept that the emergence of the Royal Arch in these early decades of the eighteenth century is fragmented and needs identification in order to be interpreted in current Royal Arch terms. In this context the Scots or Scottish Master degree, which has nothing to do with Scotland, may be relevant. In any case, it would appear that the seed for the Order can be identified as having being spread among Freemasons sometime before 1740.

There is, however, no dispute as to the authenticity of the earliest mention of the words 'Royal Arch' in a Masonic context, namely a report in the minutes of the Irish Lodge No. 21, which states that a 'Royal Arch' was carried in a procession by 'two Excellent Masons' through Youghal, Ireland, in December 1743. The Royal Arch, as we recognise it today, is mentioned for the first time by Fifield Dassigny (1707-44). It occurs in his *A Serious and Impartial Enquiry into the cause of the present decay of Free-Masonry in the Kingdom of Ireland* (Dublin: Edward Bate, 1744). Toward the end of the publication, under the heading 'Remarks', the relevant text reads:

> Now as the landmarks of the constitution of Free-Masonry are universally the same throughout all kingdoms, and are so well fixt that they will not admit of removal, how comes it to pass that some have been led away with ridiculous innovations, an example, of which, I shall prove by a certain propagator of a false system some few years ago in this city [Dublin], who imposed upon several very worthy men under a pretence of being Master of the Royal Arch, which he asserted he had brought with him from the city of York; and that the beauties of the Craft did principally consist in the knowledge of this valuable piece of Masonry. However he carried on this scheme for several months and many of the learned and wise were his followers, till at length his fallacious art was discovered by a Brother of probity and wisdom, who had some small space before attained that excellent part of Masonry in London and plainly proved that his doctrine was false; whereupon the Brethren justly despised him and ordered him to be excluded from all benefits of the Craft [...] (Dassigny, 1744, p. 11)

Masters' Lodges

Before looking at the emergence of the Antients Grand Lodge in 1751, this is an appropriate opportunity to raise an unresolved question about the Royal Arch in relation to 'Masters' Lodges'. What was their purpose and did they promote the cause of the Royal Arch in its earliest days? The subject has been discussed, *inter alia*, in two important papers which have been published in the Quatuor Coronati Transactions, namely John Lane's *Masters' Lodges* in *AQC*, 1, 1886/88, pp. 167-179, and Bernard E Jones's *Masters'*

Lodges and Their Place In Pre-Union History published in *AQC*, 67, 1954, pp. 13-28. A list of lodges, found in the Bodleian Library in Oxford and compiled in 1733 by Dr Richard Rawlinson (1690-1755), mentions Lodge No. 116 (erased in 1736) and refers to it as a 'Masters' Lodge'. Not as a 'Past Masters', nor an 'Installed Masters', but simply as a 'Masters' Lodge'. Rawlinson, an active Freemason and Fellow of the Royal Society, bequeathed a sizable and important collection of documents, many relating to freemasonry, to the Bodleian Library in 1755. A great deal of research has already been undertaken on the significance of these Masters' Lodges, but there is no final conclusion as to what the exact function of a Masters' Lodge was.

The 1729 edition of the Engraved List of Lodges was the first one with allocated lodge numbers. Until then the lodges were identified by the sign of their meeting place. The 1733 engraved list, as an example, names Lodge No. 116, meeting at the King's Arms in the Strand, as 'Master Masons' Lodge'. This lodge, and many subsequent ones in later editions of the Engraved Lists, is attached to a named parent lodge, it is not an independent lodge. Unlike their parent lodge, these Masters' lodges invariably met on Sundays, with reasonable frequency. Those references that have been identified as relating directly to these lodges refer only to the relationship between the Masters' Lodge and its parent Craft lodge.

On the surface the almost obvious function of a Masters' Lodge appears to be the conferment of the third degree. This would be supported by the timing of the appearance of the Masters Lodges coinciding with the emergence of the Hiramic legend as a separate third degree. This theory is persuasively argued by Bernard Jones, in his paper 'Masters' Lodges (3°) and their place in pre-Union history' mentioned above. There is still no evidence to support this logical theory.

After a twelve-year gap and without warning, so to speak, Masters' Lodges emerge again in the Engraved List of Lodges for 1750 and they now continue to appear until the union in December 1813. Why this renewed need for Masters' Lodges after 1750? One of the possible answers is that the re-emergence of the Masters' Lodges occurred to accommodate the recent rise in the popularity of the Royal Arch amongst members of the premier Grand Lodge, the Moderns. Despite the objections of the premier Grand Lodge, meetings of the new order appear to be held both in Craft lodges, as well as in separate, specially-convened, Royal Arch 'chapters'. It may have been this objection by their Grand Lodge that led to the re-establishment of Masters' Lodges after 1750: an ambiance for companions of the premier Grand Lodge to practice the Royal Arch beyond the scrutiny of their own Grand Lodge. Again we face a possible and logical theory, but without any solid evidence. This feasible theory generates as many new questions as it resolves. For instance, the Society of Royal Arch Masons was formed under the authority of The Excellent Grand and Royal Chapter on 10 July 1765. A year later, on 22 July 1766, the Charter of Compact was signed by Cadwallader, 9th Lord Blayney (1720-75) and senior members of the Royal Arch. At last, members of the premier Grand Lodge could practice Royal Arch masonry openly and formally without hindrance. Had the function of the Masters' Lodges been the covert practice of the Royal Arch by members of the Moderns Grand Lodge the need for such Masters' Lodges would have been superfluous. And yet Masters' Lodges continue to appear as active lodges, listed as before, well past 1766.

In addition to this mystery, what were the further and additional functions of Masters' Lodges, which justified their continued existence from 1766 till 1813? One possible explanation has a strong Royal Arch link. It is that Masters' Lodges continued after 1750 until the union of 1813 to confer one single and very special type of degree: that of the Constructive, or Virtual Master. In earlier days, both the Antients' Grand Lodge and the members of the Supreme Grand Chapter required all Royal Arch Masons to be Past Masters of their respective Craft lodges. This caused one major problem in that there simply were not sufficient Masons qualified as Past Masters to become Royal Arch companions. In order to resolve the problem and facilitate the increase in numbers among Royal Arch masons, the Constructive or Virtual Master's degree was invented. Brethren of Craft lodges, who were Master Masons but had not yet attained the chair, were made Past Masters in a shortened ceremony during which they were symbolically installed by being placed in the Master's chair for a brief moment. The ceremony, although it did not grant them the status of a Master, enabled them to join the Royal Arch. This may have been the ceremony conducted in Masters' Lodges at the period leading up to the union in December 1813.

The Antient Grand Lodge and the Royal Arch

Meanwhile in London, on 17 July 1751, five lodges, whose membership consisted exclusively of Irish Freemasons, met as a General Assembly at the Turk's Head tavern in Greek Street, Soho, and began the formation of 'The Grand Lodge of England According to the Old Institutions'. They became known as 'The Antients'. The minutes refer to this body as 'The Grand Committee', and it remained active under that title until 5 December 1753, the date on which the first Grand Master, Robert Turner Esq, was installed. Ironically, members of the premier Grand Lodge, founded in 1717, were dubbed 'The Moderns'. These terms of reference (the Antients and the Moderns), remain prevalent to this day. It has long been established that the foundation of the Antients was not a schism or secession from the premier Grand Lodge. However, the Antients were formed as a rival body to the existing Grand Lodge. Their strong Irish origins led them to diverge toward a ritual and practice which was distinctly different and quite innovative compared to that worked in the lodges under the premier Grand Lodge.

The two Grand Lodges saw each other as irregular and illegal. This outlook was to continue to the end of the century when finally the potential benefits of a union were recognised by both parties, not least due to the adverse repercussions on the Craft of the Unlawful Societies Act of 1799. Although the Royal Arch was adopted as the fourth degree by the Antients Grand Lodge, all records show that the number of Royal Arch masons who had actually taken the fourth degree was sparse at best. The Register of Members of the Royal Arch (Antients) dated 1783 lists, on page five, just thirty-seven names of qualified Royal Arch masons covering the period from 1746 to 1783. Five columns are headed: *Time/Names/No/Where Admitted/ Remarks*. The first entry is dated 1746, naming Laurence Dermott (1720-91), DGM (Deputy Grand Master) admitted in Lodge No. 26, Dublin, under *Remarks* it states *Dead*. It also states '*Dead*' for the next entry, that of John McCormick, a Past Master of Lodge No. 6, who was admitted in 1754 in Lodge No. 27, London. There are also entries for John Richardson and Thomas Self. These four names are the only Royal Arch members recorded for the period leading up to 1765. Thereafter and up to 1783, thirty-three additional brethren were made Royal Arch Masons in 12 lodges. Whilst too much reliance should not be placed on the completeness of this first page of the listing, the overall indication remains apparent, namely that in 1783, when the Register was begun, there was a significantly small number of Antient masons who could be identified from London as members of the Royal Arch.

In considering Royal Arch activities within individual Antients' lodges, we need to bear in mind again that the exaltation, often referred to as 'admission' in early records, took place in Craft lodges as a fourth degree. It was not worked in independent separate chapters. The records in the 'Register of Members of the Royal Arch' are of the names of Royal Arch Masons taken from the returns made by the various Craft lodges. The dates in the Register reflect that of the return and not necessarily that of the exaltation of the individual Mason. The Register cannot be regarded to be comprehensive and there are obvious errors and omissions. Nonetheless, the Register shows that nearly one hundred and seventy Antients' lodges made returns relevant to the Royal Arch between 1784 and the time of the union in 1813. The frequency of Royal Arch activity is reflected in the returns submitted from 1779 onward when one or more of the lodges report on the Royal Arch almost every year up to 1813. The returns for 1797, for instance, record thirteen lodges and those for 1802 record eleven. On several occasions lodges cease their Royal Arch chapter activities to resume them at a later date.

It has always been understood that the Royal Arch and indeed, many other orders beyond the Craft, were practiced in Antients' lodges by the authority of their Grand Lodge. There has never been a satisfactory explanation as to where such authority, if it existed, came from. There is the distinct possibility that lodges took on their extracurricular activities, conferring degrees beyond the Craft, without any authority. Had authority been granted, one would expect it to be incorporated into the Antients' lodge warrants. There are, in fact, no warrants emanating from the Grand Lodge of the Antients authorising lodges to work the Royal Arch or any other degree. A viable explanation, as regarding the implied authority granted by the Antients' Grand Lodge to its subordinate lodges, may be derived from the influence that Ireland had on the Antients' Grand Lodge. The oldest Irish warrant extant, for a lodge to meet at Mitchelstown, is dated 1 February 1731 *(See<<<http://www. munsterfreemason.com/1st_Lodge_of_Ireland.htm>>>* accessed 27 May 2013). The almost identical text, which has been used on subsequent Irish warrants since, states:

> We do hereby give and grant (to the Lodge members) [...] to make such laws, Rules and Orders as they from Time to Time shall think Proper and Convenient for the well being and Ordering of the said Lodge [...]. *(property of First Lodge of Ireland, Cork, A Time Immemorial Assembly on display at The Masonic Hall 27, Tuckey Street, Cork. Ireland).*

Thus every Irish lodge was authorised to confer any degree by the authority of its warrant, having created the necessary rules and regulations in lodge. The close association of the Antients with the Grand Lodge of Ireland may well have led to the presumption, first that no special authority was required for a lodge to work degrees beyond the Craft and, furthermore, that rights that applied to Irish lodges had also been conferred, from the start, on lodges under the jurisdiction of the Antients' Grand Lodge. In practice, it is only with the rules and regulations of 1794 that official authorisation is given for Antients' lodges to confer the Royal Arch degree under the authority of their Craft warrants. The first two clauses of the Grand Lodge minutes for 3 December 1794 state:

> ANCIENT MASONRY consists of Four Degrees. - The Three first of which are, that of The APPRENTICE, The FELLOW CRAFT, and the Sublime Degree of MASTER; and a Brother being well versed in these Degrees, and having discharged the Offices of his Lodge, particularly that of Master, and fulfilled the Duties thereof with the Approbation of the Brethren of his Lodge, is eligible, if found worthy, to be admitted to the Fourth Degree, The HOLY ROYAL ARCH.

and

> It follows, therefore, that every regular Warranted Lodge possesses the power of forming and holding lodges in each of those several degrees; the last of which, from its pre-eminence, is denominated among Masons a Chapter. [London, Library and Museum of Freemasonry (LLMF), Antients' Grand Lodge Proceedings, BE 140 GRA (ANT)]

These two statements, that Antient Freemasonry consists of four degrees and that every Craft lodge may exalt Royal Arch Masons, is here promulgated for the first time as the policy of the Antients' Grand Lodge. There is no earlier mention among the Antients of the Royal Arch as the fourth degree in any document or source material until the publication of these rules and regulations.

York

In this context, attention should be drawn to the instance of a Royal Arch exaltation in York at a much earlier date. Although the event was not associated in any way with the Antients' Grand Lodge, it may be seen as the cause of some misunderstandings. It would appear that Dermott did his best to associate the Antients with York Freemasonry in an endeavour to give his Grand Lodge a semblance of antiquity. In 1725 a time immemorial lodge in York assumed the standing of a Grand Lodge and became known familiarly as the York Grand Lodge. It was effectively inactive from about 1740 but it renewed its Grand Lodge status in 1761. During the period of its 'revival, as described by Gilbert Yorke Johnson, librarian of York Lodge No. 236 at the time, in his article in AQC, 57, 1944, pp. 196-255, a Royal Arch lodge was warranted, meeting at the Sign of the Punch Bowl in Stonegate. The first minutes of this lodge, dated 7 February 1762, recorded the presence of four candidates, namely John Burton, John Palmer, John Tasker and John Dodgson, who 'petition'd to be raised to the 4th Degree of Masonry Commonly call'd the Most Sublime or Royal Arch'. The minute book further records that the candidates were duly made and paid 11/6 for advancement to the 4th degree. This lodge survived for just two years. A Royal Arch chapter, however, was also chartered in York and worked from 1768 to 1772. This chapter was revived in 1778 through the effort of a number of companions who had been members of the chapter. On being re-established, it proclaimed itself to be a Grand Chapter known as 'York Grand Chapter' or 'Grand Chapter of All England'. This was not a break away from the Supreme Grand Chapter established two years earlier in London, and it was certainly not considered as competing with, or trying to usurp, the authority of the Grand & Royal Chapter in London. The *raison d'être* of the York Grand Chapter was to be responsible for Royal Arch activities in the City of York and its surroundings. A total of five Chapters were constituted by the Grand Chapter in York (and its predecessor the Royal Arch Chapter) before it finally closed its doors forever in 1781. The early mention of the 4th degree in this instance cannot be attributed in any way to the Antients, though the misleading association between the Antients and the Grand Lodge at York may have led to such wrong conclusions.

Dassigny

There is a curious apparent coincidence, still unresolved, regarding Dassigny's entry in his 'A Serious and Impartial Enquiry' referred to above, and Dermott's record in the second minutes of the Antients' Grand Lodge proceedings, from 4 March 1752 (LLMF, MS Minutes of the Antients' Grand Lodge BE 140 GRA (ANT) 5th February 1752 - 24th June 1761). It is in these minutes that the Royal Arch is mentioned for the first time by the Antients. The full text of the relevant entry reads:

Grand Committee at the Griffin Tavern Holborn - March 4. 1752
Brother John Gaunt Master of No. 5. In the Chair

The following Brethren viz. Thomas Figg of No. 5. Laurence Folliot of the same
Lodge, Samuel Quay of No. 2. Richard Price of No. 3 & Henry Lewis of No.
4. Made formal complaints against Thomas Phealon and John Mackey, better
known by the name of the leg of Mutton Masons. In course of the examination
it appear'd that Phealon and Mackey had initiated many persons for the mean
consideration of a leg of Mutton for dinner or supper, to the disgrace of the
Ancient Craft. That it was difficult to discover who assisted them if any, as
seldom met twice in the same Alehouse. That Macky [sic] was an Empiric in
phisic; and both impostors in Masonry. That upon examining some brothers
whom they pretended to have made Royal-Archmen, the parties had the least
Idea of the secret. That Dr Macky (for so he was called) pretended to teach the
Masonical Art by which any man could (in a moment) render himself Invisible.
That the Grand Secretary had examined Mackey at the House of Mr James
Duffy Tobacconist in East Smithfield who was not a Mason and that Macky
appear'd incapable of Making an Apprentice with any degree of proprerty. Nor
had Mackey the least Idea or knowledge of Royal Arch Masonry. But instead
thereof he had told the people whom he deceived, a long story about 12 white
Marble stones &c &c and that the Rain Bow was the Royal Arch with many
other absurdities equally foreign and Ridiculous. The Grand Committee
Unanimously agreed and ordered that neither Thomas Phealon nor John
Mackey be admitted into any Ancient Lodge during their natural lives.

Thus, the first mention of the Royal Arch in the available records of the Antients'
Grand Lodge, is of two men involved in the making of Royal Arch Masons without
authority. There is one very striking aspect to this report. It is the coincidence of the
circumstances and wording of these minutes with the words used by Dr Fifield
Dassigny quoted above. In his *A Serious and Impartial Enquiry* […], in referring to
the Royal Arch in 1744, Dassigny says:

> […] some have been led away with ridiculous innovations […] by a certain
> propagator of a false system […] under a pretence of being a Master of the
> Royal Arch […] his fallacious art was discovered by a Brother of probity and
> wisdom […] whereupon the Brethren […] ordered him to be excluded from
> all benefits of the Craft […]

It appears that these two earliest recorded mentions of the Royal Arch in what are two
totally separate instances eight years apart refer to extraordinarily similar circumstances.
In considering this comparison we need to bear in mind that the Antients derived

their inspiration from Ireland and that the Antients' minutes referred to above were written by Laurence Dermott. Dermott, the indefatigable and dedicated Secretary of the Antients since 1752, had also subscribed to the 1744 edition of Dassigny's 'Enquiry'. It is also worth noting that Dermott quotes Dassigny verbatim in the first edition of *Ahiman Rezon* the Constitutions of the Antients published in 1756. The title *Ahiman Rezon* still defies definition, as evidenced by the papers and comments on the subject; see for example 'Ahiman Rezon - a look at the Hebraic terms and prayers used by Dermott' by the late Walter Sharman (*AQC,* 105, 1992, pp. 49-68).

There is no evidence, however, to support the view that the Antients earnestly adopted the Royal Arch from the start of their Grand Lodge in 1751. The earliest date that can be applied to the formal adoption of the Royal Arch as part of the Antients' Craft is the date of the publication of the first edition of *Ahiman Rezon* in 1756. There is surprisingly little material relating to the Royal Arch in this or any of its several future editions. There are obvious opportunities to mention the Royal Arch that are missed. The title page, for instance, is crowded with details of content. It mentions 'Prayers used in the Jewish [. . .] Lodges', yet it omits to mention the Royal Arch. Dassigny's *Serious and Impartial Enquiry […]* is quoted at some length by Dermott with only a single, brief and incomplete reference to the Royal Arch. There are extensive and lengthy discourses, addresses, charges, prayers, rules, regulations and songs in the two hundred pages of the first edition of *Ahiman Rezon*, yet less than three pages in total are devoted to the Royal Arch. The prayer entitled 'Ahabath Olam (Eternal Love) - A prayer repeated in the Royal-Arch Lodge in Jerusalem', has only the title to link it to the Royal Arch. However, there is a bracketed quote explaining that the author believes the Royal Arch to be 'the root, heart, and marrow of masonry.' (The archaic definition of marrow is 'inmost' or 'essential' part). This has become an iconic statement but the available evidence indicates that the degree was not practiced in London by the Antients before at least 1766 and probably only after December 1771.

In the intervening period, Laurence Dermott single-handedly kept the Royal Arch in the minds of his Brethren. He did so by intermittent reference but no practical action. A good example is the incident involving Thomas Phealon and John Mackey which, in my interpretation, is an incident either entirely contrived by Dermott, at best exaggerated by him. Dermott used Dassigny's *A Serious and Impartial Enquiry* […] as a source, as an inspiration. Phealon and Mackey may well have pretended to have made 'Royal-Archmen' in addition to having initiated many persons 'for the mean consideration of a leg of Mutton for dinner'. After all, if an additional fee could be charged for an additional degree, why not? This illicit making of 'Royal-Archmen' however, was only later discovered by Dermott personally, after he had 'examined Mackey at the House of Mr James Duffy Tobacconist in East Smithfield'. Duffy, it should be noted, was not a Mason.

It is important to emphasise that Dermott was a formidable, assertive and enterprising man and Mason. The possibility, unlikely as it may seem, that Dermott actually invented that part of the incident relating to the Royal Arch by embellishing an otherwise true event, must be given consideration. By March 1752, Dermott must have reached a stage where it was necessary to acknowledge the existence of the Royal Arch, in spite of it not being practiced by the Antients. Here was an opportunity to record the existence of the additional degree almost in passing: what better example could there be of the first mention of the Royal Arch among the Antients than circumstances so strikingly similar to the first mention of the Royal Arch as a whole in 1744? The coincidences are too many to be dismissed as insignificant.

Laurence Dermott was born in Ireland and initiated in Dublin in Lodge No. 26 (erased in 1801) on 14 January 1740. In June 1746 he is recorded as being installed Master of the same lodge and made a Royal Arch Mason. He was a truly extraordinary Mason and man. He totally devoted his life to Freemasonry, in particular to the cause of the Antients' Grand Lodge. He served as its Secretary for nearly 20 years and in 1771 was appointed Deputy Grand Master for the first time. He served in the same post again from 1783 to 1787. He was the driving force behind the Antients and the author of *Ahiman Rezon*, the Constitutions already mentioned, first published in 1756. It is my opinion, that despite the many statements and declarations that Royal Arch was an integral part of Antients' Freemasonry from 1751, Dermott deliberately arrested the advance of the Royal Arch as the fourth degree of the Antients' Grand Lodge. The simple reason being that he had his hands full with the formation of the new competing Antients' Grand Lodge. Although clearly, the Royal Arch proved a helpful device to emphasise the significant differences between the Antients and the Moderns, the additional fourth degree did not give any practical advantage to the cause of the Antients' Grand Lodge and would have been a distraction. It is certain that the premier Grand Lodge, though tolerant, wished to have nothing to do with Royal Arch or anything beyond the Craft degrees of Freemasonry. It was thus expedient for Laurence Dermott to declare the Royal Arch to be a landmark of Antients' Freemasonry and simultaneously deride the Moderns for refusing to recognise it as such. He did not do so, however, from the start and not until well into the second half of the century.

Spirited Royal Arch activity amongst the Antients becomes prevalent only after the independent 'Grand and Royal Chapter of the Royal Arch of Jerusalem', consisting entirely of Modern masons, was ratified by a Charter of Compact on 22 July 1766. There is no mention of the order or the fourth degree in any of the relevant early documents of the Antients, such as Morgan's Register. The Grand Lodge Minutes and *Ahiman Rezon* make minor, if any, reference to the Royal Arch, implying a lack of Royal Arch activity amongst the Antients' Grand Lodge. The one celebrated mention of the Royal Arch in the minutes of the Antients' Grand Lodge before 1760 is a reference of an indirect nature, frequently quoted and publicised. It is written by Dermott and appears as a footnote to the minutes of the emergency meeting of Grand Lodge on 16 December 1759. This footnote follows the report in the minutes where a petition was heard from one William Carroll, a certified sojourner in distress. Dermott's memorandum, in the form of a postscript to the minutes, states:

The private collection made for Carroll above mention'd amounted to five Guineas: It appeared that William Carroll a Certified freemason of Dublin petitioned the Modern Masons (not knowing any difference) and that Mr Spencer then Secretary to the Modern Society sent out the Answer to Carroll's petition in the following words viz. 'Your being an Ancient Mason, you are not entitled to any of our Charity the Antient Masons have a Lodge at the five Bells in the Strand, & their Secretary's name is Dermott. Our Society is neither Arch, Royal Arch or Antient so that you have no Right to partake of our Charity'. The petitioner Carroll delivered the original paper written by Mr Spencer to Mr Dermott G S in whose custody it remains.

This 'original paper written by Mr Spencer delivered to Mr Dermott' is now lost. Clearly it has not been quoted in full in the minutes. Its exact content, considering Dermott's attitude toward the Moderns, may well reveal more than can be deduced from Dermott's minutes or his quotation from the letter in the later editions of *Ahiman Rezon*.

Lastly and significantly, with regard to the lack of Royal Arch activity among the Antients, the first two anonymous exposures published since the appearance of Prichard's *Masonry Dissected* in 1730, namely *Three Distinct Knocks; or the Door of the Most Ancient Free-Masonry* and *Jachin and Boaz; or An Authentic Key to the Door of Free-Masonry* in April 1760 and March 1762 respectively, refer to the ritual workings of the two Grand Lodges. *Three Distinct Knocks [...]* claimed to be written by 'W****O***V****n Member of a Lodge in England at this Time', implicitly states in the introduction that the content of the pamphlet is the actual ritual as practiced by the lodges of the Antients. The content is described in the title page:

The Three Distinct Knocks; or the Door of the Most Ancient Free-Masonry Opening to All Men, Neither Naked nor Clothed, Bare-footed nor Shod, &c. being An Universal Description of all its Branches from Its First Rise to this Present Time as it is delivered in all Lodges: Giving an exact account of all their Proceedings in the making of a Brother, with the Three Obligations or Oaths belonging to the First, Second, and Third Degrees of Masonry, viz. The Entered-Apprentice, Fellow Craft, and Master-Mason; with the Obligation belonging to the Chair and the Gripe and Word. Also, full Discriptions [sic] of the Drawing upon the Floor of the lodge, with the Three Steps and a Prayer used at the making of a Brother; with Songs to be sung after grave Business is done, and the Examination of a brother whereby he may get Admittance into a Lodge, without going through the Obligations.

There is no mention of the Royal Arch anywhere in the exposure. This work, published nine years after the formation of the Grand Lodge of the Antients, is an accurate account of the working of the Antients. It gives details of the ritual working of the three degrees and the installation ceremony. There is no explanation or reason for the exclusion of the Royal Arch from 'Three Distinct Knocks' unless the author was unaware of the existence of the degree because it was simply not being universally practiced. It is a viable explanation to what would otherwise be an extraordinary omission and is further evidence that the degree was not functional in Antients' lodges as late as 1762.

The first Grand Chapter 1765

Notwithstanding the lack of Royal Arch activity by the Antients, its very existence and pronouncements by Dermott, recognising it as part of Ancient Masonry, remained an irritant to those members of the Moderns Grand Lodge that had adopted the Order and practiced it covertly, by force of circumstances. What choice did these companions now have? The option to leave their own Grand Lodge and join the Antients, in order to enjoy a full-fledged degree, was out of the question. The only alternative left to them was to form their own separate and independent Royal Arch Order, which is exactly what happened in the spring of 1765.

Records of Royal Arch activity in what is today's Supreme Grand Chapter start with the entry in the first minute book of the unnamed 'Excellent Grand and Royal Chapter' dated 22 March 1765. The meeting were held at the mysterious and still unidentified Mr Inge's premises, until the move to The Turk's Head in Gerrard Street, Soho on 12 June of the same year. The records show the more than dual role that Grand Chapter played from the start until 1795, during which time it was both a regulatory body chartering new chapters, and an ordinary chapter undertaking exaltations, holding rehearsals for ritual work and receiving lectures. In 1769 several chapters were chartered by the Supreme Grand Chapter, of which the first was the Restauration [sic] Lodge or Chapter of the Rock Fountain Shiloh No. 1. Because of the importance of this Chapter No. 1, and a document that has newly come to light in the Library and Museum of Freemasonry, the chronology and history of the Chapter No. 1 is followed here to its end (past the union of 1813) and in detail.

Chapter No.1

Chapter No. 1 was conceived on 13 January 1769 when Brother John Brooks, acting as Haggai in Grand Chapter, moved that '*a Constitution might be granted to himself and other Companions to meet privately as might be convenient*'. This was unanimously agreed to. The Chapter was chartered several meetings later on 14 July at the Turk's Head, when '*the following Warrants of Constitution passed the Seal of the Chapter, viz. No 1 to our M. E. Companion Br Brooks PZ empowering him to hold a Chapter in his own House by the title of 'The Restauration Lodge or the Chapter of the Rock Fountain Shilo* [...]'. Although a Lodge name was given in addition to that of the Chapter, the *'Lodge of Restauration'* never existed. The 'Restauration Chapter' was so named in 1795, when it was revived by Grand Chapter. The word 'Restauration', the archaic form of 'Restoration', is so spelt in the original minutes but not in all of the subsequent entries. There are no records of the activities of Chapter No. 1 after its foundation until 1795. Meanwhile the dual role taken on by Grand Chapter, both as an administrative body and undertaking exaltations, was the cause of a great deal of confusion and dissension until the resolution in Grand Chapter, on 17 December 1795, that:

> ' [...] in order to conciliate, and do away every remaining jealousy, and
> uneasiness (if such exists) among the several Chapters, or any of them - that a
> Committee be now appointed - consisting of the present Officers of the Grand
> Chapter - to consider of the precise mode of separating the business of that
> Chapter - and a Chapter for the purpose of exalting Master Masons to this
> sublime degree &c [...] so that Chapter No. 1 be revived for that purpose.'

On 22 April 1796, at a special meeting, the proposal for the revival of Chapter No. 1 was adopted and the three Grand Principals of Grand Chapter were nominated the Officers "*for that Chapter*" and were elected. The meeting dates and times were established to coincide with those of Grand Chapter and it was agreed that members of Grand Chapter were to constitute the membership of Chapter No. 1. Clearly this was to be a chapter within a Chapter. However, it was decreed that separate books would be kept, to sort finances out and that no further exaltations would take place in Grand Chapter except in the case of Nobility. Thus the Committee revived Chapter No. 1, which was now '*open for Business*'.

The only available evidence of any further activity by Chapter No. 1 is to be found in the names of those brethren attending Grand Chapter as visitors. As an instance, a Captain William Gill and Sir John Earner attended and signed in as visitors from Chapter No. 1, on 13 May 1796. These two gentlemen were proposed for exaltation in Grand Chapter before the agreement to revive Chapter No. 1 was reached. Thus their registration as visitors from Chapter No. 1 is significant. The Chapter again disappeared until 5 February 1811, when a member of Caledonian Chapter No. 2, Companion Charles Pidgeon, presented to Grand Chapter the original charter of the '*Royal Arch Chapter of Restoration* [sic] *or the Rock and Fountain of Shiloh, No. 1*' and he was thanked for preserving it against loss.

In January 1812 the same charter was re-issued, at his own request, to the Duke of Sussex who, contrary to various accounts by historians, revived Chapter No. 1, for a short period of time. (Companion A R Hewitt, in 'Supreme Grand Chapter of England 1966 Especial Convocation' booklet on page 26 says: '[...] 5th February

1811 [...] No more is heard of the Chapter or its charter and it is suggested that [...] the Duke wished to 'kill' the Chapter [...]' and Brother John Dashwood in 'The 2nd and 3rd Minute Books of Grand Chapter' *AQC,* 62, 1949, p. 68 states: '[... Duke of Sussex's] Grand Master's own private Chapter [...] but no such Chapter ever came on the books.'

The evidence for this revival lies in the surviving minute of the Restoration [sic] Chapter, No. 1, which show it to be vibrant again, as the Duke of Sussex's effective personal Chapter. The manuscript minutes are housed in the Library and Museum of Freemasonry (former Ref:, BE 366 RES, now archives Ref: GBR 1991 ECM/700 A19882) and were recently moved from the library to the archives. They consist of six quarto pages handwritten on both sides of the paper, bound in a soft card cover. They record on the first page, a list of the twenty members of the Chapter and their addresses. The members are all Officers of Grand Chapter, headed by HRH The Duke of Sussex shown as MEZ, John Dent, MEH, the Rev John Austin MEJ, Richard Spencer as PS, J C Burckhardt, Treasurer, Rev D Hemming as E, William H White as N and William Lowndes, Organist. The entries that follow are a record of the four consecutive meetings of the Chapter, held at Freemasons Tavern (none held in Kensington Palace) between April 1813 and September 1815. The first minutes record the meeting on 30 April 1813 attended by 20 members and no visitors, when nine senior Freemasons - three Provincial Grand Masters, four Past Senior Grand Wardens, a Grand Chaplain and the Rev David Lewis - are proposed by the MEZ, the Duke of Sussex, and exalted.

The Chapter held its second meeting on 28 January 1814. It was attended by sixteen members taking office, headed by HRH the Duke of Sussex and sixteen visitors. They included: John Aldridge of Grand Chapter, the Rev G A Browne, Grand Orator and His Excellency The Count de la Gardie. HRH the MEZ proposed four candidates for exaltations, namely: Bros Dr Von Heys [sic] of the Grand Lodge of Hamburg; the Rev Giese, WM of Pilgrims Lodge; William Meyrick, Grand Registrar and, at the special request of the MEZ, Sir George Nayler, Grand Director of Ceremonies who was unable to attend his exaltation at the St James's Chapter No. 60 at their 28 January meeting.

The date of the third meeting of Chapter No. 1, on 2 July 1814, should be noted as it coincided with the final day of the protracted meetings of those attending the International Compact negotiations in Great Queen Street, London. The importance of this meeting justifies a full account of events. The Duke of Leinster (1791-1874), Grand Master of Ireland; Lord Kinnaird, Grand Master elect, Scotland; the Earl of Rosslyn, Past Grand Master, Scotland; Thomas, 1st Lord Dundas, Deputy Grand Master, England, and Lieut. Gen Sir John Doyle, Provincial Grand Master, Guernsey, are proposed for exaltation by HRH The Duke of Sussex, MEZ in the Restoration Chapter No. 1 at Free Masons Tavern, London. In attendance are twenty officers and companions of the Chapter as follows:

Comp	HRH The Duke of Sussex	MEZ
	John Aldridge	as MEH
	Revd John Austin	MEJ
	Richard Spencer	PS
	J C Burckhardt	Treasurer
	Revd Dr Hemming	E
	William H White	N
	H J Da Costa / William Meyrick	Ass Sojourners
Comp	Sir George Nayler	
Comp	Simon Mc Gillivray	
Comp	Dr I Cooke	
Comp	William Wex	
Comp	Revd Dr Coglan	
Comp	W Lowndes	Organist
	Hon W Shirley	
	Colonel S Stewart	
	James Deans	
	Arthur Tegart	
	William Williams	

There were present in addition six visitors, namely: The Earl of Donnoughmore , Dr Von Hoyse [sic], James Parry, James Agar, Thomas Harper and Isaac Linde.

The fourth and last recorded meeting of the revived Restoration Chapter No.1 took place on 14 September 1815, again at Freemasons' Tavern, attended by twelve members who took office headed by HRH The Duke of Sussex. The minuted records appear unfinished with the statement '*The Chapter was opened in Ancient and Solemn Form. The Minutes of the last Chapter were read and confirmed*'. Nothing more.

Although there appear to be no further records of meetings of Chapter No.1, the Hon. Washington Shirley, the British Royal Navy officer and amateur astronomer, of Vineyard Cottage, Fulham, listed as a member of the Chapter, offers his services as a Steward at the Festival of Grand Chapter in May 1818, citing Chapter No. 1 as his 'mother' Chapter. So does Brother William H White (1777-1866) joint Grand Secretary, a year later, on 12 May 1819. In the November 1821 list of '*Chapters which have conformed to the Regulations of the United Grand Chapter, and attached themselves to the Lodges specified by Numbers*' the Restauration Chapter is listed as No. 43 (i.e. attached to Lodge No. 43). This is Alpha Lodge No. 43 [previously No. 76], which amalgamated with the Red Apron Royal Lodge No. 210 [313] to become Royal Alpha Lodge No. 16 in 1824. There are no names of members of Chapter No. 1 in the 1817 Register and Chapter No. 1 does not appear in the 1852 Register (LLMF, Archives, Royal Arch Membership Register, GBR 1991, SGC, 3/2/9, 1817-1852). There appear to be no further records of the

Chapter after 1821. Chapter No. 1 is not to be confused with the present Grand Master's Chapter No. 1 which was only chartered in 1886.

Returning to the 1765 minute book that recorded the first meeting of the 'Excellent Grand and Royal Chapter', three new Royal Arch Masons, 'pass'd the Arch' i.e. were exalted, reflecting the expediency of the Grand Chapter at the time. The entry in the minute book, a volume very handsomely bound in leather by Sandorski and Sutcliffe of London, is attributed to the first Scribe Ezra Francis Flower. The short eight-line entry reads:

22 March 1765
The Most Excellent Grands & Brethren met at Mr Inge's
Brother Bourcard, Br Pakin & Br Vander Upwich pass'd

the Arch & paid the fine of one Guinea each....................	3	3	-
Bro Williamson passed the Arch and paid a fine of	-	5	-
Rec'd of Bro Inge the Balance in his hands.....................	-	12	-
	4	-	-
Expences &c for that Night	1	14	2
Balance in Hand	2	5	10

Additional minutes on the same page, separated by a single drawn line from the entry quoted above, record meetings on 8 April, again at Mr Inge's, when seventeen members were present to witness Bro Reek Jnr and Bro Rouby passing the Arch; on 15 May 'at the Chapman's Coffee House' and on 3 June, again at the unidentified 'Br Inge's', when Bro Galloway is 'desired' to provide the robes for the three 'Excellent Grands'.

The next meeting is the crucial key meeting of 12 June 1765 at The Turk's Head in Gerrard Street, Soho. Notwithstanding the importance of this meeting, and not wishing to forego the income due, five brethren 'passed the Chair and paid the fine of one guinea each', before the real business of the evening was proceeded with. A list of the thirty-four members present is followed by a second 'List of the Members 12 June 1765 (10 July members subscribed)' now showing a total of 51 names with addresses. Six senior members were chosen as officers 'until the first meeting after the Feast of St John the Evangelist'. It was now that the 'Companions of the E.G. & R.C. commonly called The Royal Arch . . . in full Chapter assembled' agreed to a series of resolutions, formally adopted as the bye laws. They are signed on the fourth page of the minutes in a disorderly sequence, indicating that the signatures were not all applied contemporaneously but many at subsequent meetings. These five pages, dated 12 June 1765, have been placed at the start of the minute book, followed retroactively, so to speak, by the earliest minutes of 22 March 1765 referred to above. This would indicate that the tidily written minutes is a 'clean copy' of notes taken previously and dispensed with after having been neatly copied. Thus 'The Society of Royal Arch Masons' was formed under the authority of 'The Excellent Grand and Royal Chapter'. However, it still needed the authority of a Charter.

Charter of Compact 1766

It is on 11 June 1766 that the 'Society of Royal Arch Masons' is formed under the 'Excellent Grand and Royal Chapter'. In the presence of twenty-seven 'brethren' [sic] and a visitor, the Grand Chapter was opened by the Three Grands: Bro Galloway, Bro Maclean and Bro Dunckerley, respectively. At this meeting, 'the Right Hon[ble] & Right Worshipful Grand Master Lord Blayney passed the Royal Arch and became a member of the Excellent Grand and Royal Chapter'. This event in itself was a major coup for the members of the Royal Arch. After all, Lord Blayney was Grand Master of that very same premier Grand Lodge that refused to recognise the Royal Arch. Better was yet to come. On the same day of his exaltation, Lord Blayney agreed to enter into an alliance with the companions of the order. This alliance manifested itself in 'The Charter of Compact', a most crucial document, under the authority of which chapters still meet today. It was to be signed and executed just a few weeks later on 22 July 1766. At the next meeting of the Grand Chapter on 2 July 1766, Lord Blayney was installed as Prince Zerubbabel and took his seat as the First Grand Principal of 'The Excellent Grand and Royal Chapter of the Royal Arch of Jerusalem'. He was subsequently, in 1767, elected to continue as 'Grand Master of the Most Excellent Chapter or Fourth Degree'. This was the first Grand Chapter in the world. Lord Blayney continued in his post as Prince Zerubbabel of the Grand Chapter at the meeting on 22 July. Significantly, this date appears on the Charter of Compact, although the Charter is not mentioned in the minutes of this Convocation. He also presided at the next meeting on 30 July 1766, after which he appears to take no further interest in Royal Arch affairs.

There is an element of controversy regarding the dating of the Charter of Compact that may be fittingly discussed and determined here. This beautifully engrossed and illuminated document is dated 22 July 1766. However, until 1951 it was thought that the date was 1767. In 1951, John Rawdon Dashwood pointed out the delicate alterations that had been applied to the original 1766 date on the document making it appear to be 1767. In an article entitled 'The Falsification of the Royal Arch "Charter of Compact"' (*AQC*, 64, 1951, pp. 137-137), Dashwood claimed that the changes had been carried out in order to avoid embarrassment to the premier Grand Lodge when Lord Blayney, their Grand Master, was appointed First Grand Principal of the newly formed Royal Arch Order, as detailed above. Lord Blayney was due to step down as Grand Master of the premier Grand Lodge in 1767. Thus the deferment of the date on the Charter, Dashwood argued, would imply that Lord Blayney had acted in a private capacity rather than as the Grand Master of the Grand Lodge.

It is my view that Dashwood's theory is erroneous, and that the changes to the Charter of Compact, far from being a falsification, were legitimate alterations, carried out with the knowledge and approval of those aware of the changes being made at the time (LLMF, Typescript, Convocation minutes CN: A85TWE, SGC, 11 February 1998). As already mentioned, on 11 June 1766 Lord Blayney was exalted into the Royal Arch and entered into an alliance with the companions of the order to be signed and sealed with a Charter of Compact at the convocation on 22 July 1766. This is the date at which the Charter was expected to be executed as a legal document. There were additional alterations made to the Charter, including intricate changes to the dates on the jewel devices along the borders of the document. There is also a change to the title of 'Lord Blayney Grand Master' where the letter 'P' has been inserted in front of the word 'Grand' to read 'Lord Blayney P Grand Master. My contention is that Dashwood's theory is weak and illogical. How could the changes to the date of issue possibly appease contemporary members of the premier Grand Lodge, when the Charter was privy to Royal Arch members only, and they only would be aware of the significance of such changes? The Grand Chapter consisted entirely of members of the Moderns Grand Lodge. Lord Blayney remained the most prominent figure amongst them and many of his respected colleagues and officers were Royal Arch Masons who are mentioned by name on the Charter of Compact. They would not have needed any appeasement. Dashwood's theory of falsification suggests that the changes to the document reflect the deliberate delays in the execution of the Charter as a legal document. There is, however, no record, apart from the Charter itself, to support this theory. In fact there is no direct reference whatsoever to the Charter of Compact in any of the minutes of Grand Chapter, with the sole exception of the accounts for 30 July 1766.

I believe that it was somewhat optimistic for the companions, in their enthusiasm, to propose the 22 July 1766, five short weeks after Lord Blayney's exaltation, as the date for the formal acknowledgment of the Charter of Compact. There would not have been sufficient time to have a sophisticated and complicated document legally drafted, drawn and illuminated. I contend that the Charter was simply not ready for the Quarterly Convocation held on 22 July 1766. This would explain why the Charter of Compact is not mentioned in the minutes of 22 July or 30 July 1766 or thereafter. It would appear that the Charter did not come into force as a legal document, a process that necessitated the ratification of all the companions named in the body of the document, until the last signature was obtained sometime in 1767. It was only then that the date and other details were altered to reflect the true date of the completed document. Those present at such a meeting would have unanimously agreed to such alterations which, even if unrecorded (as indeed, so many other events of consequence had been), had the tacit approval of the membership of the Order.

The entry in the Accounts for 30 July 1766 which shows: 'By Cash for Mr Parkinson for engrossing the Charter £2.2.0' would support a theory of the Charter not being ready for 22 July. 'Engrossing' does not encompass all aspects of the 'execution' of the document. Since the Scribe also acted as Treasurer, there is the possibility that the sum was only approved for disbursement, not payment, on 30 July. It was, in my view, circumstances that necessitated the implementation of a well-intentioned alteration to a wrongly recorded date: a simple change, to reflect events as they occurred.

The 'Antients' Grand Chapter' 1771

The proclamation of the new independent Order of Royal Arch Masons in 1766 by the companions, all members of the Moderns Grand Lodge, pulled the carpet from under Dermott's feet, so to speak, and took the Royal Arch initiative away from him. He was now no longer able to claim the Royal Arch to have supremacy over the Craft degrees. The contrary was true. The establishment of a Supreme Grand Chapter by his opponents had relegated Dermott's Royal Arch to the mere fourth degree of the Craft. The new 'Supreme Grand Chapter', meanwhile, could boast to be a sovereign body, an independent Order, far higher in status than a paltry fourth degree. Laurence Dermott had to take some action and decided that the establishment of an Antients' Supreme Grand Chapter would be the solution.

As Deputy Grand Master, in 1771 he introduced the subject of the Royal Arch to be debated at the 4 December Convocation of the Antients' Grand Lodge, when he informed the Grand Lodge of the proceedings of the Royal Arch meeting

> [. . .] and expatiated a long time on the scandalous method pursued by most of the Lodges (on St John's day) in passing a number of Brethren through the Chair on purpose to obtain the sacred Mystry's *(sic)* of the Royal Arch and proved in a concise manner that those proceedings were unjustifiable; therefore moved for a regulation to be made in order to suppress them for the future (LLMF, MS, Minutes of the Convocation of the Antients' Grand Lodge, 4 December 1771, un-catalogued at the time of writing).

The same Convocation minutes record how Dermott queried whether Grand Lodge was a suitable forum to debate Royal Arch matters. He claimed that Grand Lodge could not be a suitable venue because brethren who were not Royal Arch Masons would always be present. Other Royal Arch matters were consequently ' [. . .] referred to the Royal Arch Chapter with full authority to hear, determine and finally adjust the same.' These were acknowledged on 27 December 1771 when:

> [. . .] the D Grand Master gave the Brethren (present) to understand that it was to be strictly observed in their respective Lodges – and that a Grand Chapter was to be held on the first Wednesday in January next to finally

settle that part of the minute referred by the Grand Lodge to said Chapter. (LLMF, MS, Minutes of the Convocation of the Antients' Grand Lodge, 27 December 1771, un-catalogued at the time of writing).

So came into existence the so-called 'Grand Chapter of the Antients', that great incongruity in our Masonic history. In reality, this supposed separate ruling body of the Antients was no more than a committee of Royal Arch-qualified members of the Antients' Grand Lodge. At the next communication of the Antients' Grand Lodge on 27 December 1771, these resolutions were again raised and confirmed and they were formally adopted at a later General Chapter meeting, held on 3 January 1772. These several references to 'General Chapter' and the Antients' 'Grand Chapter' are misleading at best. The minutes of Antients' Grand Lodge show that the Grand Chapter met on a number of occasions. At times, the minutes are even headed 'Grand Chapter', but separate minutes of an Antients' Grand Chapter have never been found. Clearly and logically, a Grand Chapter of the Antients could not have existed. After all, to the Antients the Royal Arch was part of Craft Masonry, the fourth degree implemented in Craft lodges. There was no such concept as separate chapters among the Antients, so how then could there be a Grand Chapter? The improbable phenomenon seems to have sprung from necessity for Dermott to combat the establishment of the new Supreme Grand Chapter by the Moderns' members by giving a semblance of the existence of a separate Antients' Grand Chapter.

On 5 November 1783 the resolutions of 1771 relating to the Royal Arch were confirmed at a special meeting of Royal Arch Masons. These minutes mentioned above, all manuscript documents elaborately illuminated with Lawrence Dermott's designs, are attached to the Grand Chapter Register (LLMF, MS, Antients' Grand Chapter Minutes, GBR 1991, SGC, 3/2/1, 5 November 1783). This isolation of the minutes from the remainder of the bound and chronological reports emphasises Dermott's effort to establish an Antients' Grand Chapter to appear as a separate and independent body. The minutes begin with the opening statement: 'A General Chapter or Grand Lodge of Royal Arch Masons was held in the Chamber or Room of No. 5'. These are followed by a re-iteration of the earlier resolutions of Grand Lodge in 1771 and 1772 and the passing of nine new resolutions for the government of the Order. The eighth of these resolutions is of particular interest in this context. It confirms the absence of any superior Grand Chapter body in stating: 'a copy of the resolutions adopted at this meeting will be respectfully laid before the General Grand Lodge upon the first Wednesday in December 1783'. These were approved at the meeting of the Grand Lodge on 3 December 1783. These minutes are the only ones bound in with the register, and are followed by a hand-drawn frontispiece by Lawrence Dermott depicting a vault holding the Ark of the Covenant followed by the elaborate title page headed in Hebrew:

Sefer Haneala Rabim –
The Register of Excellent Masters
! in the Supreme Degree !
Of Free – Masonry:
Commonly called the Royal Arch

All of the decisions and the code of Regulations of the Grand Chapter that were first published in 1783 had to be approved by the Antients' Grand Lodge before being promulgated. It was only with the publication of the Laws and Regulations of the Antients in 1794 that the Royal Arch was established on a firm footing as the fourth degree in Freemasonry. Only now, forty-three years after their establishment as a grand lodge, was formal retroactive authority given for Antients' Craft lodges to confer the Royal Arch degree: the fourth degree of Craft Masonry. There was no acknowledgment, and there never has been, of an independent Grand Chapter of the Antients.

Preston's Harodim

In 1788, the second edition of *The Sufferings of John Coustos for Freemasonry* lists a total of fifty-five Chapters in England and Wales (Birmingham: M Swiney, 1788 p. 259). The Order of Harodim, launched by William Preston (1742-1818) in January 1787, may be seen as of negligible importance to the Royal Arch in general but is, nonetheless, a notable one. 'Harodim', denoting the supervisors of the Temple builders, is a Hebrew term meaning 'strong'. The term 'Harodim' is also used to denote the Order of Knight Templar Priests, where one of the degrees is entitled 'Made Free from Harodim'. (The term is not to be confused with the 'Rose Croix of Heredom', which is the title of the 18th degree of the Ancient and Accepted Rite, or the first degree of the Royal Order of Scotland, the 'Heredom of Kilwinning').

This separate and new 'Grand Chapter of Harodim' was meant to be a revival, according to Preston, and constituted a five-degree system with the Master of Arts and the Royal Arch as the fourth and fifth degrees respectively, following on directly from the three degrees of the Craft. The Order appears to have been no more than a School of Instruction. It did not survive for long and it never conferred any degrees. A Harodim Lodge No. 558, founded in 1790, was amalgamated in 1794 with Preston's own Lodge of Antiquity No. 2. Colin Dyer (1910-1987), in his authoritative biography of William Preston (William Preston and his Work, London: Lewis Masonic,1987, p. 101), is convinced that Preston used the Antients' practice of accommodating the Royal Arch as the fourth degree as his source for the fifth degree of the Harodim. Dyer also reaches the conclusion that this is sufficient evidence, without need for further proof, that Preston may have been a Royal Arch mason. The Order is mentioned in the minutes of Supreme Grand Chapter from 30 December 1790, where it is recorded that 'the Order of Harodims [sic] returned their thanks for the use of our organ etc' (LLMF, MS, Royal Arch Membership Register, GBR 1991, SGC, 1/1/1/2, 1776-1806). This may be interpreted as some kind of 'recognition' of the Order.

Ancients' Committee 1797

By 1800, a half a century after the foundation of the Antients' Grand Lodge, attitudes toward the historic conflict between the two rival grand lodges were mellowing. The new generation of freemasons of the late eighteenth century were mostly unaware, and certainly uninvolved, in past unpleasantness. They were aware, however, of the increasing superfluity of two grand lodges running side by side. Members of both grand lodges were ready to meet with each other, inter-visiting was on the increase, and brethren from opposing camps were beginning to join each other's lodges. These included many prominent masons.

The first and earliest initiative toward reconciliation of the two grand lodges was taken by the Antients on 6 December 1797. At the Quarterly Communication on that day, Brother Morton of Lodge No. 63 moved, and Bro Gilvery, Past Master of Lodge No. 3 seconded, that

> [...] a Committee be appointed by this R W Grand Lodge to meet one that may be appointed by the Grand Lodge of Modern Masonry and with them to effect an Union. The previous question was thereupon moved and carried almost unanimously. (LLMF, MS, Quarterly Communication of the Ancients' Grand Lodge, 6 December 1797, un-catalogued at the time of writing).

The fact that the motion was 'carried almost unanimously' is notable and may be an indication of a lack of conviction on the part of some members of the Antients' Grand Lodge. Nonetheless, the resolution is on record. The lack of response by the Moderns' Grand Lodge frustrated any of the good intentions that the Antients may have had. It is a curious thought to consider the later delays on the part of the Antients, when healthy negotiations began to take place in the approach to the union. Could these have been prompted by a sense of revenge? Eighteen more years were to pass before a final union was to be achieved.

Unlawful Societies' Act 1799

It was, ironically, the consequences of the French Revolution, raging in Paris since 1789, that were finally to bring matters to a head for Freemasonry in England. One of the natural consequences of the French Revolution was the emergence all over Europe of hundreds of politically-motivated clubs and societies. Some of these associations demanded an oath of allegiance and secrecy from their members, a requirement that was of concern to the authorities. In England, in a direct effort to prevent potentially subversive societies from becoming active, an Act of Parliament (39 Geo. 3 c. 79) was passed on 12 July 1799 'for the more effectual suppression of Societies established for Seditious and Treasonable purposes', commonly referred to as the 'Unlawful Societies Act 1799'. The implications of the Act were of immediate concern to every individual member of a Craft lodge and Royal Arch chapter. The Act does not mention 'companions' or 'chapters' separately. Its repercussions on companions of the Royal Arch, however, were, logically, as significant and disconcerting as they were on members of the Craft. The law was intended to prevent attendance at secret meetings, and the taking of oaths was now considered illegal. For Freemasons to comply with the law would mean the cessation of the meetings of all lodges and chapters in England. There is no doubt that the potential repercussion of the Act brought together the Moderns and Antients, as well as the Grand Lodge of Scotland, who were all able to appreciate the common good that would ensue from a joint effort in confronting it.

The premier Grand Lodge acted through its Hall Committee. On Tuesday 30 April 1799 it convened 'to consider what could be done to avert the danger with which the Society was threatened if the Bill passed into a Law' (LLMF, Rough minute book of the Moderns Grand Lodge Hall Committee, GBR 1991 FMH Minutes:/2 18 April 1795 - 22 December 1801). This Hall Committee, though its *raison d'être* was related to the physical building in which Grand Lodge was housed, extended its remit well beyond such matters. The various entries of its minutes show that the Hall Committee acted as an equivalent to the present Board of General Purposes by taking on responsibilities beyond their original mandate. The meeting on 30 April was presided over by Francis Edward Rawdon-Hastings, Earl of Moira (1754-1826). Present was also John Dent (1761-1826), banker, MP and a member of the Hall Committee, who was requested to arrange a meeting with the Prime Minister, William Pitt, to receive a deputation of the Society, 'in order to explain the nature of it [Freemasonry] to him' (London, Library and Museum of Freemasonry, op. cit.). The deputation of nine members that was appointed for that purpose was headed by the Acting Grand Master the Earl of Moira, the Senior Grand Warden Sir John Garner, the Grand Secretary James Heseltine (1745-1804) and two more MPs from County Durham: Sir Ralph Milbanke (1747-1825) and Rowland Burdon (1757-1838). Differences were set aside and a joint body of Moderns' and Antients' masons was agreed upon. On 2 May 1799, the Earl of Moira and the Duke of Atholl, Grand Master of the Antients' Grand Lodge, with a retinue of senior masons from both grand lodges, met with William Pitt, the Prime Minister, in Downing Street, with a view to presenting the case for the exemption of Freemasons from the parliamentary bill about to be passed. It was as a result of this meeting that the special exemption clauses V and VI were inserted into the Act.

Freemasons were also exempted from a further and similar Seditious Meetings Act

(57 Geo. 3 c. 19) passed in 1817. The main result of these laws was that lodge secretaries had to make annual returns which had to be deposited with the local Justices of the Peace, the Magistrate and, later, the local police. As mentioned above, the law did not make specific reference to the Royal Arch, nonetheless chapters had to comply with its requirements. An instance of such compliance is to be found in the Royal Arch minutes of the Chapter of Paradise No. 139 Sheffield, dated 19th January 1812 which record, with reference to the annual subscription: 'Those companions who would not pay the subscription and sign those resolutions ceased to be members. and their names would not be registered at the Clerk of the Peace's office.' (John Tokes, 'The History of Royal Arch Masonry in Sheffield', Sheffield, 1922, p37). Although theoretically the law was not rescinded until enactment of Section 13 (2) of the 1967 Criminal Law Act, the practice had long fallen into disuse and it appears to have never been properly monitored from the start.

Thomas Harper's Expulsion

The period of approach to a happy union was not without incident and misunderstanding. The Earl of Moira's intervention, as crucial and vital as it was, caused misgivings not least due to his perceptible naiveté, if not ignorance. He appears, rather surprisingly, not to have appreciated that the foundation of the Antients' Grand Lodge in 1751 was an independent act. He considered it a secession of some brethren from the premier Grand Lodge of England, as had later been advocated by William Preston. Accordingly his ill-timed invitation, as well-intentioned as it was, for the Antients to 'return to the fold', antagonised the brethren of the Antients' Grand Lodge. Likewise, though clearly supportive of a union between the two English grand lodges, a great deal of effort was applied by the Earl of Moira to promote what has been referred to as his failed 'Grand Design', namely a union not between the Antients and the Moderns but one between the premier Grand Lodge of England and the Grand Lodge of Scotland.

A major incident that threatened the preparations for the union began on 20 November 1801. Thomas Harper (1735-1832) and four others were summoned before the Committee of Charity of the premier Grand Lodge to answer charges that they regularly attended meetings of lodges under the Antients' Grand Lodge. Thomas Harper was also later accused of being too frequently absent from the Charity Committee, the equivalent of the current Board of General Purposes, of which he was a member. Harper had been initiated under the premier Grand Lodge and was a member of several lodges under its jurisdiction, for example the influential Lodge of Antiquity No. 2 (1792) and Globe Lodge No. 23. He had also been a Grand Steward in 1796. However Harper was also well entrenched in the Antients' camp. Not only had he served as Junior and Senior Grand Warden (1786 and 1787/9) and joint Grand Secretary (1792-95) becoming Deputy to Robert Leslie two years later, in 1801 he was also appointed Deputy Grand Master of the Antients, a post he held until the union of 1813.

(His namesake Edwards Harper followed in his footsteps as Deputy Grand Secretary to Robert Leslie (1801) and joint Grand Secretary with William White, after the Union).

The complaint against Harper and the others was initiated by one Francis Columbine Daniel. Daniel, who had recently himself been excluded from the Antients' Grand Lodge, invoked a regulation enacted in 1777 by which anyone attending lodges in England other than those constituted by the premier Grand Lodge would be subject to expulsion. At the meeting of the Committee on 5 February 1802, James Heseltine, Grand Treasurer, reported that he had met with Harper and James Agar (Past Deputy Grand Master of the Antients 1790-4) to discuss the possibility of a union. He suggested that the charges against Harper be set aside until a decision on the union had been taken. Since no further progress was made in the matter of the union, Harper was expelled from the premier Grand Lodge in 1803. Douglas William Burford, in his Lecture 'The Anomalies of the Royal Arch - Craft Connection' (*Batham Royal Arch lecture series*, London: privately printed, 1993) sees an element of hypocrisy on the part of the Moderns' Grand Lodge, when comparing Harper's position to that, for instance, of the Duke of Kent, whose loyalties were also equally divided between the Antients and the Moderns at this period of time. The repercussions and tensions that followed continued for the best part of seven years, until the Committee of Charity on 2 February 1810 reinstated Harper, a decision that was confirmed in Grand Lodge on 11 April of the same year. Clearly, it was duly appreciated that Harper, having a foot in each camp, would be particularly well placed to act as the leading negotiator for the Antients. Harper did become involved in the preparation of the Articles of Union, and was a signatory to them in 1813. He remained a regular attendee at the United Grand Lodge until his death in 1832.

On 5 September 1810 the Antients' Grand Lodge required that all resolutions regarding the 'Union' be printed and circulated throughout the Craft. In a rapprochement to the needs of the Moderns, the Antients' Grand Lodge passed a few more resolutions on 4 December 1812: first, that the period of time that a Mason needed to be in the Craft before being elected Worshipful Master be at least twelve months and that the privileges of a Past Master were not to be enjoyed until a brother had served as Worshipful Master for twelve months; secondly, that the two installation meetings a year hitherto held in Antients' lodges should be trimmed down to one, and thirdly, and of importance here, that no emblem of the Knights Templar or any other order of Knighthood be worn at the Craft festival. In the Moderns' camp, these concessions were welcome and warmly received.

The Lodge of Promulgation 1809-1811

The commitment by the members of the Moderns to bring about a union with the Antients is manifest in the decision by the Committee of Charity on 7 April 1809 to recommend a change that had been a continuous complaint of the Antients against the Moderns since their foundation. Grand Lodge declared that it was 'not necessary any longer to continue in Force those Measures which were resorted to, in or about the year 1739, respecting irregular Masons, and do therefore enjoin the several Lodges to Revert to the Ancient Land-Marks of the Society' (LLMF, MS, Committee of Charity Minutes, 7 April 1809, un-catalogued at the time of writing).

The decision was put into practice a few days later. The 'Measures' of 1739 referred to the changeover of the first and second degree penalties by the Moderns, that had been applied in order to protect the brethren from impostors. It was a direct result of the publication of Samuel Prichard's exposure *Masonry Dissected* in 1730 which had enabled outsiders to gain access to lodges. (However, see Jan Snoek 'Oral and Written Transmission of the Masonic Tradition' op.cit.). In due course the Antients were to claim that these protective changes had been a major deviation from true masonry. The premier Grand Lodge's decision in 1809 to change the password back to that used originally, was a direct reconciliatory response to such claims. This led to the establishment by the Moderns of the Special Lodge of Promulgation warranted by the Earl of Moira on 26 October 1809. Unusually, the lodge was given an end-date for its existence. It was to conclude its activities and functions by 31 December 1810. The Special Lodge of Promulgation was to be the model for the much later Royal Arch Chapter of Promulgation of 1835, discussed in Chapter III (*vide* 1835).

The Lodge of Promulgation was composed of a Worshipful Master, his two Wardens and twenty-three elected members, eleven of whom ranked as either Past Grand Wardens or Provincial Grand Masters. The remaining nine were ruling Masters of lodges. These, rather curiously, included the Duke of Sussex by virtue of his being the Master of the Time Immemorial Lodge of Antiquity No. 2. The first meeting of the Lodge of Promulgation was held on 21 November 1809. It considered its purpose as being to finally determine the exact 'landmarks' of each of the Societies, to consider the differences between them, and to promulgate an accord. These landmarks, which should be 'carefully preserved', are mentioned in the General Regulations of the 1723 Constitutions and they are not mentioned again until 1913. They have never been defined or formally adopted by the Grand Lodge of England. They comprise essential rules, such as a belief in a Supreme Being, the exclusion of women from regular Freemasonry, the presence of a Volume of the Sacred Law in an open Lodge, the ban of discussion of politics or religion at meetings and so forth. Bro Harry Carr stated that a Landmark is something in Freemasonry which if removed, it would materially alter the basis of Freemasonry. This definition has had wide acceptance among scholars. Dr Albert Mackey (1807-1881), the erstwhile prolific American author, has suggested twenty five such landmarks but his list has not been well received. (See John H Hamill 'The Landmarks of Masonry', London Grand Rank Association Quarterly Bulletin No 200, May 2013 pp. 8-11).

This Moderns' lodge's *raison d'être* was thus to 'Promulgate the Ancient Landmarks of the Society and instruct the Craft in all such matters and forms as may be necessary to be known by them [...]', as stated in the warrant (LLMF, MS, Warrant of the Lodge of Promulgation, un-catalogued at the time of writing, 26 October 1809). This was a subtle but delicate retreat. After all the Moderns had, for a long time, been attacking and criticising the Antients and a total and sudden turnaround may be seen as being hypocritical. Interestingly, in the months that were to follow, almost every procedural and administrative change that was decided upon by this Moderns' Lodge of Promulgation favoured the working of the Antients. The meetings were frequent, initially every week with a long five-month summer break from May till October 1810. They were often followed by a festive board with speeches and toasting. The recorded decisions, though curtailed by the need for discretion, were frequent and consistent. Some of the outstanding items discussed and resolved include the crucial matter of the deacons and the installation of the Master. On 13 December 1809 it was 'Resolved that Deacons (being proved on due investigation to be not only Antient but useful and necessary officers) be recommended'. This had been a practice in all Antients' lodges and just a few Modern ones. A far more important practice among the Antients was the installation ceremony of a new Master, which had been totally neglected by the Moderns. On 19 October 1810 it was 'Resolved that it appears to this Lodge that the ceremony of Installation of Masters of Lodges is one of the two Landmarks of the Craft and ought to be observed'. It should be noted that the word 'two' is generally accepted to have been a misspelling for 'true'. (See, *inter alia*, Jones op. cit. p181)

At the meeting on 14 December 1810 a request presented to the Grand Master to extend the warrant of the Lodge of Promulgation by two months was granted. It allowed the Earl of Moira to be formally installed in the newly recommended ceremony, as the Acting Grand Master in Grand Lodge, on 6 February 1811. The prescribed installation ceremony was formally reported upon and approved by the Lodge of Promulgation at its meeting on 5 March 1811. The lodge had played an important part in preparing the way for a union. It may have deviated, concentrating on irrelevant and unimportant issues, and it may not always have had the full backing of the Grand Master, nonetheless its membership had consisted of a total of thirty-nine brethren each of whom, at one time or another, had been active members.

Lodge of Reconciliation

Whilst the Lodge of Promulgation endeavoured to assure a smooth union of the two grand lodges, it also laid the foundation for the far more effective Lodge of Reconciliation, warranted by each of the two grand lodges in 1813; the Antients on 1 December and the Moderns on 7 December. The lodge, as conceived in Article V of the Articles of Union of 25 November 1813, was to consist of nine expert Master Masons and Past Masters representing both grand lodges. The members included the respective Grand Secretaries, Edwards Harper (d.1859) for the Antients and William Henry White (1777-1866) for the Moderns. The Revd Dr Samuel Hemming D.D.

(1767-1832), a Moderns' Mason, was nominated Worshipful Master, and William Meyrick and William Shadbolt were appointed Wardens. The lodge was formed in order to obligate and instruct ruling Masters, Past Masters and brethren of both grand lodges. Inexplicably, considering their experience, only five members of the former Lodge of Promulgation were invited to join the Lodge of Reconciliation. Although the lodge held meetings on many occasions (with alternating Masters at each meeting), the ritual to be performed at the union celebrations remained an outstanding issue to the last: the committee members of the Lodge of Reconciliation, specially seated in the hall, famously withdrew during the actual ceremony of the union on 27 December to consider the modes of recognition and other matters, after which they returned and reported to the assembled brethren that the agreed obligation could at last be formally pronounced. In 1814 ten additional members were appointed. The lodge closed its doors in 1816. Its activities are considered in further detail in Chapter III (*vide* 1816).

Sussex's Exaltation and more

The Royal Arch meanwhile, since the foundation of the Order in 1766, was progressing with noteworthy success. As reflected in its minutes, the 'Supreme Grand and Royal Chapter of Royal Arch Masons of England' was acting as the Supreme authority of the Order, while also simultaneously exalting brethren into the Royal Arch. The most important of these exaltations took place on 10 May 1810 when the Duke of Sussex, in what must be recorded as the speediest progression ever achieved, was proposed, 'introduced', elected and installed as First Grand Master of Royal Arch Masons, all within the space of a few hours:

Supreme Grand Chapter
Grand Chapter of Communication
Free Masons Tavern Great Queen Street
Thursday 10 May 1810

Earl of Moira   Z
R W Wright   H
Aldridge   J
22 other [named] officers/members
29 visiting Companions
[...]
Most Excellent Zerubbabel proposed that the ceremony for the ballot for HRH the Duke of Sussex to become an associated member of the Grand Chapter be dispensed with and that HRH be requested by the unanimous

voice of the Grand Chapter to become a member thereof which proposal was
approved without any dissented voice.

Companions Burckhardt Grand Principal Sojourner and Da Costa were
commissioned to examine HRH and their report being in all prospects
satisfactory they were also desired to introduce him which was accordingly done.
The Most Excellent Zerubbabel proposed to the companions present that our
companion the Duke of Sussex should be requested to accept the office of
the 1st Grand Master of Royal Arch Masons of England for the ensuing year
which was unanimously agreed to by the acclamation of all the companions
present and HRH signified his acceptance of the same.

[. . .]

HRH the Most Excellent Zerubbabel than proceeded to appoint his officers

[. . .]

All business being ended the Supreme Grand and Royal Chapter was closed
according to Antient form and the day concluded in Festivity and Harmony.
(LLMF, MS, Excellent Grand and Royal Chapter meeting minute book GBR
1991 SGS 1/1/1/3 10 May 1810.)

According to E Comp A R Hewitt, in his pamphlet mentioned above and entitled 'The
Bi-Centenary celebrations of Supreme Grand Chapter Especial Convocation held on
1st July 1966', refers to the statement that the Duke of Sussex was "introduced" [which]
presumably means he was exalted'. This view of Brother Hewitt has been accepted,
though there is no precedence or other evidence to support or deny it. It must be
presumed that the 'introduction', if it was indeed intended to replace the ceremony of
exaltation, entailed a shortened version of such a ceremony, similar to the 'making' of
Royal and Noble Freemasons 'at sight' in 'Occasional Lodges'. One possible alternative is
that the Duke of Sussex, among the many degrees and Orders he was bestowed with in
Berlin, under the jurisdiction of the Grand Lodge of Prussia, may have also received an
Order that, at the time, was sufficiently acceptable to Supreme Grand Chapter to have
him 'introduced', without further ceremonies. It is interesting to note that today Brethren
of the Scandinavian jurisdictions from the VIth degree upwards are qualified to attend
Royal Arch convocations in England. (The degrees and Orders taken by the Duke of
Sussex as a member of the Grand Lodge in Prussia are listed in Part II.)

It is clear that these minutes date from a time without a standardised Royal Arch
nomenclature. The First Principal is here referred to variously as '1st Grand Master of
Royal Arch Masons of England', 'Most Excellent Past Master Zerubbabel of the Order',
'Grand Master Zerubbabel' and 'Most Excellent Zerubbabel', while the present
standardised form requires the three Principal Grand Officers of the Supreme Grand
Chapter of England to be known as the First, Second and Third Grand Principals. From
1766 ,when Supreme Grand Chapter was established, until 1817 these Grand Officers
were also referred to respectively as Grand Master Zerubbabel, Grand Master Haggai

and Grand Master Joshua. The Antients on their part were referring to the Grand Principals as the Grand Chiefs. Grand Chapter membership appears to be achieved by joining or exaltation. There was no obligation on senior companions to join Grand Chapter, and attendance records show a series of joining members as well as senior Royal Arch Masons who were not members. An example is Thomas Dunckerley (1724-1795), a past Grand Zerubbabel and, famously, Grand Superintendent of the Royal Arch in no less than twenty eight Counties (in addition to being the Provincial Grand Master of eight), signing in, in Grand Chapter, as a 'visitor' on 22 May 1778.

On 10 March 1812 a very distinguished group of politicians was exalted in Grand Chapter, reflecting the popularity of the Order: Richard Wellesley (1760-1842), 1st Marquess Wellesley, brother of Arthur, 1st Duke of Wellington, and two Members of Parliament: George Canning (1770-1827, Prime Minister 1827) and John Dent (c.1761-1826). The last exaltation in Grand Chapter took place on 2 May 1832. (*vide* Part III). Meanwhile, new chapters were being regularly chartered, reaching one hundred and twenty new chapters in 1813 alone. The business of running the Order was being competently handled by an active and enthusiastic group of Grand Chapter Officers. Considering the fact that the membership of the Royal Arch consisted entirely of Modern masons, it was natural for these administrators of the Society to remain aware of, though effectively uninvolved in, the activities taking place in the Moderns' Grand Lodge relating to the approaching union.

Henceforth, events leading to the union began to move with considerable speed. The decision on 2 February 1810 for the Moderns' Grand Lodge to rescind their 1803 expulsion of Thomas Harper was accompanied with the resolution of the Antients, a month later ,'that a Masonic Union on principles equal and honourable to both grand lodges, and preserving inviolate the Land Marks of the Antient Craft would [. . .] be expedient and advantageous to both'. Much activity took place behind the scenes, and not everything was going according to plan. The Moderns' enthusiasm for progress was frustrated by the Antients' need to refer all decisions, without exception, to their grand lodge. The Moderns, on the other hand, led by the Earl of Moira, Acting Grand Master since 1790, had full power to negotiate to the end. Special efforts were made to resolve issues, most especially through the untiring efforts of Moira. Clearly the earlier failed and missed opportunities for a union, in 1798, 1802 and 1810, were not to be repeated in 1813.

Sussex made Grand Master

On 7 April 1813, as the final steps were being taken toward the union, HRH the Prince of Wales (1762-1830, from 1820 becoming King George IV), appointed Prince Regent in February 1811, 'signified his pleasure to decline, upon the present election the situation of Grand Master'. The Duke of Sussex was elected and 'was pleased to express his willingness to accept the high and important trust' (LLMF

Ref: BE 140 UNI, 7 April 1813). On 12 May 1813 the Duke of Sussex was installed Grand Master of the premier Grand Lodge of England.

Sussex, in a long and active Masonic career, had already been appointed a Past Grand Master in 1805 on his return to England from Berlin where he had been initiated and introduced to Freemasonry as well as to many degrees and Orders beyond the Craft. He joined the Prince of Wales Lodge, now No. 259, and became its permanent Worshipful Master as was traditional for a mason of royal blood. A few years later he joined the Lodge of Friendship, now No. 16, again attaining the chair as permanent Master. In 1808 he joined the Lodge of Antiquity No. 2, in which he also became permanent Master. In 1810, as described above, he was exalted and made First Grand Principal of the Grand and Royal Chapter, all in one day. His undiminished interest in Freemasonry is reflected in his later (1820) joining a fourth lodge, what is now the Royal Alpha Lodge No. 16.

In 1812 he assumed the duties of Deputy Grand Master, being promoted to Grand Master just a few months preceding the union. At the installation, his elder brother Edward Augustus, Duke of Kent, soon to be elected Grand Master of the Antients, acted as Deputy Grand Master. Sussex as Grand Master took an active role from the beginning. He ensured that he was present at as many meetings as possible, appointing his own Grand Officers and creating new offices. On 17 May 1813 he appointed the Revd George Adam Browne, eventually to acquire repute as the creator of the current Royal Arch ritual, to the new post of Grand Orator. On 23 June 1813, the last entry in the Moderns minute book confirms:

> Duke of Sussex Grand Master
> HRH the Grand Master having expressed his anxious wish that a Union of the two societies of Masons in England should be effected upon terms equal and honourable to both parties [...]. Resolved that HRH be fully empowered to take such measures as to him may seem most expedient for arranging a Union between this Grand Lodge and the society of Masons under His Grace the Duke of Atholl and if necessary to agree and conclude the same [...] and to convene such members of the GL as he may think fit to be a committee to assist in effecting this object [...]

Atholl Resigns

On Monday 8 November 1813 'An Especial Grand Lodge' of the Antients was held at the Crown and Anchor Tavern with Thomas Harper, Deputy Grand Master, in the Chair. A letter from the Duke of Atholl was read which expressed his desire to resign the office of Grand Master in favour of the Duke of Kent, the acceptance of which was resolved unanimously. Thomas Harper, Deputy Grand Master, was placed in the Chair until the appointment and installation of a Grand Master. It was agreed that the Installation was to take place on 1 December 1813.

It would appear that no Quarterly Communications of the premier Grand Lodge took place after 23 June 1813, and the Articles of Union therefore constitute the first official document of material relevance available on the subject. In private correspondence Douglas Burford, a senior companion of the Royal Arch and the 1993 Batham Lecturer, wrote:

> The prime object of the Act of Union was to acknowledge the fact that the two Grand Lodges had settled their differences on matters of principle in order that they could merge, which had nothing whatever to do with the Royal Arch; in reality, all that the Act did, so far as the Royal Arch was concerned, albeit in a somewhat clumsy and almost incomprehensible fashion, was to enable one Grand Lodge whose constituent Lodges worked Four Degrees to merge, at grass root level, with those of the other Grand Lodge working only three degrees. In so doing it also paved the way for the Exaltation of Master Masons.

Kent and Moira

The events on 1 December 1813 were set in an overt ambiance of reconciliation. The Duke of Kent, elder brother of the Duke of Sussex, replaced as Grand Master of the Antients' Grand Lodge, the Duke of Atholl. Prince Edward Augustus, Duke of Kent and Strathearn (1767-1820), fourth son of George III and father of Queen Victoria had been initiated on 5 August 1789 in the *Loge l'Union des Coeurs* founded in 1768 in Geneva, Switzerland (the lodge is still active today under the Rectified Scottish Rite). Generally, the function of the Duke of Kent in the proceedings leading to the union has been seen as simply symbolic. John Belton, however, has shown that Kent supported the Antients' cause a decade earlier and was well aware of the significance of the approaching union (op. cit. p.19). It was by his own choice that he declared his allegiance to the Antients' Grand Lodge and presented himself as an Antient Mason before being invited to act as Provincial Grand Master for Lower Canada. This was confirmed by a warrant issued in London in March 1792. On his return to London his closeness to the Antients was confirmed when the Duke of Atholl, Grand Master of the Antients, appointed the Duke of Kent to represent him in meetings with the Moderns' Grand Lodge following the Special Communication of the Antients' Grand Lodge on 18 May 1813, six months before the union. Quite clearly the Duke of Kent was well qualified and had proven his enthusiastic support for the Society well before his appointment as Grand Master of the Antients on 1 December 1813.

By April 1813, when more than fifty brethren gathered to wish the Earl of Moira *'Bon voyage'* on his way to India (taking up his post as Governor of Bengal and Commander-in-Chief of the military forces there), he had brought Masonic matters in England to a satisfactory stage through his indefatigable efforts, securing the cooperation of all the leaders involved. Moira's impressive Masonic activities are comprehensively dealt with by John Hamill in 'The Earl of Moira, acting Grand Master 1790-1813, England' (*AQC*, 93, 1980, pp. 31-48). He had been appointed Assistant Grand Master in 1790, and his indispensable intervention in cooperation with the Antients' Grand Master, the Duke of Athol, averted the total collapse of the fraternity following the Unlawful Societies Act in 1799. He was equally active in Scotland and was responsible for the restoration of cordial relationships between the respective two Grand Lodges of England and Scotland. His efforts for a union between the Antients and Moderns were untiring, and he would undoubtedly have felt a sense of satisfaction at the forthcoming celebrations, even if unable to attend the final ceremonies. He continued his active participation in proceedings until this very last moment, and was presented on the eve of his departure with a patent appointing him 'Acting Grand Master of Royal Arch Masons for the whole of British India'. Brother Alexander Fraser, present at the event, took handwritten notes later published in his contemporary book *An Account of the Proceedings at the Festival of the Society of Freemasons on Wednesday the 27th of Jan 1813 given to their M W A G M The Right Honourable The Earl of Moira [. .]* (LLMF Ref: BE 68 (MOI) GRA 1813). Fraser goes into great detail reporting on all aspects of the proceedings.

Invitations to the union celebrations, planned for 27 December 1813, were sent out well in time to the two sister jurisdictions. Although Scotland sent its congratulations following an extraordinary meeting of Grand Lodge on 20 December 1813, their representatives did not attend the union a week later and their apology from their grand secretary R W Brother Lawrie was read out at the proceedings. The Grand Lodge of Ireland had granted recognition to the Antients long before it recognised the premier Grand Lodge of England. Ireland too failed to send representatives to the celebrations of the union and, in a similar extraordinary meeting of Grand Lodge on 13 December 1813, expressed their regrets, which were also read out from a letter by W Brother W F Graham, Deputy Grand Secretary of the Grand Lodge of Ireland, during the proceedings on 27 December. The reasons and circumstances for these events are carefully analysed by John Belton in his recent publication *The English Masonic Union of 1813 [...]*, mentioned above.

The Articles of Union and the Royal Arch

The Articles of Union were not meant to declare the official recognition of the Royal Arch, nor did they define the Order. They only stated that the Royal Arch was 'the completion of pure Ancient Freemasonry', nothing more (Supreme Grand Chapter,

Especial Convocation, 30 November 1813). Nonetheless, as indicated below, article II materially changed the historic and functional standing of the Royal Arch in England forever. It was meant to bring about the immediate cessation of the activities of Supreme Grand Chapter and its subordinate chapters, as well as the cessation of activities of the Royal Arch Masons of the Antients' Grand Lodge. Most importantly, the Articles of Union did not provide for the creation of an alternative body to cater for the needs of Royal Arch Masons. It created a void so far as the Order was concerned, and chapters tottered on, acting independently and without control, until 18 March 1817.

The union was formally celebrated on 27 December 1813, in accordance with Article I of the Articles of Union, which stated:

> I. There shall be, from and after the day of the festival of Saint John the Evangelist next ensuing *[i.e. 27 December 1813]* a full, perfect and perpetual union of and between the two Fraternities of Free and Accepted Masons of England [...] represented in one Grand Lodge, to be solemnly formed, constituted and held, on the said day [...] (LLMF, Articles of Union BE 105 ACT fol.).

The word 'celebrated' needs emphasising. The union had in fact been 'consummated', so to speak, on 25 November 1813 and 'ratified' and confirmed on 1 December 1813. These three key dates – 25 November, 1 and 27 December - have caused some confusion among historians.

The 'Consummation' of the Union 25 November 1813

On 25 November 1813, the Grand Masters of both grand lodges met at Kensington Palace with six deputies representing both Grand Lodges. The purpose of the meeting was the signing of two identical Articles of Union, one for each grand lodge. The original document belonging to the Antients is extant in the Library and Museum of Freemasonry in London. It measures 324x205mm, and consists of a total of ten pages with text on both sides and with the last three pages left blank. The document is signed on page seven by the eight dignitaries present and each signatory's wax seal has been added, under the legend: 'Done at the Palace of Kensington, this 25th Day of November, in the year of our Lord 1813, and of Masonry, 5813'. The signatories are:

[On the left hand side for the Antients' Grand Lodge:]

Edward	G M	(HRH Edward, Duke of Kent & Strathearn)
Thos Harper	DGM	(Thomas Harper Deputy Grand Master)
Ja Perry	PDGM	(James Perry Past Deputy Grand Master)
Jas Agar	PDGM	(James Agar Past Deputy Grand Master)

[On the right side, for the Moderns' Grand Lodge]:

Augustus Frederick	Grand Master (HRH Duke of Sussex Installed 12 May 1813)
Wright, Waller Rodwell	Pro GM Ionian Isles (Provincial Grand Master of the Ionian Islands)
Arthur Tegart	PJGW (Past Junior Grand Warden)
J Deans	PJ Grand Warden (James Deans Past Junior Grand Warden)

Although the Duke of Kent was only Grand Master Elect at this time, it would have been felt that he was qualified to sign the document as 'Grand Master'.

The signatures follow twenty-one articles, visible alterations having been made to Article II only, as was discovered by Douglas Burford, who reported his conclusions in his 1997 Batham Lecture (op. cit. p.9). It is worthy of quotation in full. He states:

> In Article 2, the word 'three' obviously replaces a word which has been completely erased, but as the space each side is slightly less than elsewhere, it is not unreasonable to deduce that the original word may have been 'four'. Likewise, there is an 'ampersand' squashed in before 'the Master Mason' whereas elsewhere 'and' is written in full. The word 'including' after 'Master Mason' has been distorted in order to fit it into the space left by the word or words erased which, in all probability, were 'and also' or similar.
>
> The word 'Order' was clearly 'degree' before the changes were made, as parts of the original word are still visible. The only other difference between the manuscript Preliminary Articles and the fair copy signed and sealed on the 27th December 1813, is the absence of the 'comma' in the former after the words 'Master Mason' which was no doubt an oversight when 'four' was changed to 'three' and 'including' took the place of 'and also'. There is a distinct possibility therefore, that when Article 2 was originally drafted, it read as follows:
>
> It is declared and pronounced, that pure Antient Masonry consists of 'four' degrees, and no more, viz. those of the Entered Apprentice, the Fellow Craft, the Master Mason 'and also', the Supreme 'Degree' of the Holy Royal Arch.

The most significant changes were to the words 'four degrees' being altered to read 'three degrees' and the words 'Supreme Degree' in the next line being altered to read 'Supreme Order'. The definition of the two terms 'Degree' and 'Order' and their significance relevant to the Royal Arch has been the cause of much of the confusion and lack of definitions that have persisted in the last two centuries.

In simplistic terms, the first sentence of the article as finally set down may be read as: 'pure Ancient Masonry consists of three degrees and no more, including the Supreme Order of the Holy Royal Arch', allowing the Royal Arch to be a 'spiritual mantle', so to speak, to the three Craft degrees, but no more.

The event of 30 November 1813

Meanwhile, on Tuesday 30 November 1813 at Free-Masons' Tavern, London, the Supreme Grand Chapter of Royal Arch Masons of England gathered for an 'Especial Convocation', presided over by Grand Principals Dent, Aldridge and Austin (LLMF EG & RC Meetings minute book GBR 1991 SGC 1/1/1/3 30 November 1813). Austin stated that the Grand Lodge of England under the Grand Master, HRH the Duke of Sussex, had entered into preliminary articles with the grand lodge now under HRH the Duke of Kent, for a union of those two grand lodges under one Grand Master. The preliminary Articles of Union were read, and commented upon in the following manner:

> By those Articles the Order of the Royal Arch was acknowledged as the Perfection of the Master's Degree; and, the articles approved and this Chapter convened by HRH Sussex for purposes of submitting the subject for consideration and in order that such measures be adopted
>
> 'Resolved that as Grand Lodge has agreed to acknowledge the Royal Arch, this Grand Chapter considers a Union of this Order with the Grand Lodge highly proper and desirable'.
>
> 'Resolved that HRH the Duke of Sussex be invested with full powers to negotiate and conclude a Union on behalf of this Supreme Grand Chapter with the Grand Lodges under their Royal Highnesses the Duke of Sussex and the Duke of Kent, in such a way as may appear to HRH most conducive to the general interest of Masonry. The Chapter was closed in due form. (op. cit.)

The 'Ratification of the Union' 1 December 1813

Returning to the amendments in the Articles of Union, these were 'ratified' by each Grand Lodge separately at the 'Especial Grand Lodge' meetings, which followed the Duke of Kent's installation and sumptuous dinner on 1 December 1813. The proceedings were reproduced by William James Hughan on pages 18-26 of his *Memorials of the Masonic Union of A D 1813*, revised edition, Leicester in 1913.

Wednesday 1 December 1813 must have been a busy day for all masons involved in the union, and especially for the Duke of Sussex. During the course of the day (probably in the morning, and at any rate before the start of proceedings at noon) the Duke of Sussex and others were admitted as Ancient Freemasons at the Crown and Anchor Tavern. To quote the records:

> His Royal Highness the Duke of Sussex, Grand Master of the other
> Fraternity of Masons, together with several others of his Grand Officers,
> having been made Ancient Masons in the Grand Master's Lodge, No. 1 (in a
> room adjoining), took their places in the Procession, which entered the Grand
> Lodge [. . .]. (Hughan op. cit. p.19)

In the midst of the impressive procession, the banner of the Royal Arch was prominent. Behind it marched the 'Grand Principal of the Holy Royal Arch' (Hughan op. cit. p. 19), though who this Antient Companion may have been has remained a mystery. The final issued 'Laws and Regulations for the Instruction and Government of The Holy Royal Arch Chapters under sanction of the Grand Lodge of England according to the Old Institutions' state:

> That, agreeably to established custom, the Officers of the Grand Lodge, for the
> time being are considered as the Grand Chiefs; the Grand Secretary and his
> Deputy for the time being shall act as Grand Scribes; and the said Grand Officers
> and Grand Scribes are to preside at all Grand Chapters, according to seniority.

The Antients' Grand Master on this occasion was of course the Duke of Kent, Grand Master-elect, and thus otherwise engaged in the day's proceedings! One must presume that in their-efforts to give a semblance of authority to the Royal Arch, the Antients nominated a senior companion to act as Grand Principal for the purpose of the procession alone. Could it have been M W Brother James Agar, Past Deputy Grand Master of the Antients?

HRH the Duke of Sussex followed his brother, HRH the Duke of Kent, at the end of the procession. The elaborate ceremonies that followed will have lasted into the late evening. As astonishing as it may sound, the two grand lodges, following the dinner, retired to prepare for the separate opening of their respective grand lodges. The circumstances of the extraordinary events are recorded in detail by the Swedish freemason, aristocrat and diplomat Count Jacob Pontusson De la Gardie in his diary. The diary entries and much more are quoted verbatim by Y Åkerrén in his article *London in December 1813: The Place and Time of a Momentous Encounter of English with Swedish Rites (AQC, 115, 2002, pp.184-204.)* De la Gardie presented himself as the 'Grand Master of the First Lodge of the North' (although not so qualified) and joined the Duke of Sussex for the remainder of the proceedings on the evening of 1 December. The members of the premier Grand Lodge retired to Freemasons' Hall in Great Queen Street and the Antients remained at the Crown and Anchor Tavern. The purpose of these two grand lodge communications was to validate the Articles of Union as mentioned above. The respective proceedings of each grand lodge show parallel decisions being taken by both grand lodges. The original document signed by the Moderns' on the 1 December is missing. The Antients' original copy survives, deposited in the Archives of the Library and Museum of Freemasonry (un-catalogued at the time of writing).

It was now time to prepare for the celebrations of 27 December. Two large and engrossed manuscript facsimile copies of the original Articles of Union were produced, with a view of their being ceremoniously carried into Grand Lodge and signed during the proceedings. They were to be deposited into the Ark of the Covenant, a chest-like piece of ceremonial furniture designed for the occasion by the newly appointed Grand Superintendent of Works, the architect Sir John Soane. The Ark was later destroyed, together with Thomas Sandby's magnificent Masonic Hall, in a fire in 1883. It must be presumed that by this time, the facsimile copies had been removed from the Ark and deposited with the library in Grand Lodge. Both copies of these facsimiles survive and are housed in the archives of the Library and Museum of Freemasonry in London (un-catalogued at the time of writing). As facsimile copies of the Articles, they include both date-legends that appear on the original, namely: 'Done at the Palace of Kensington, this 25th Day of November, in the year of our Lord 1813, and of Masonry, 5813' and : 'In Grand Lodge this first day of December A.D. 1813, Ratified and Confirmed, and the seal of the Grand Lodge affixed'. These facsimile copies have no legal value or standing. The facsimiles of the Act of Union were copies made for symbolic use only and were not signed in full, nor were any seals attached to them. Their purpose was to act as a substitute for the original documents on the day of the union.

The facsimile copy of the Articles of Union belonging to the Antients was subsequently selected for use as the 'Master' or official document of the union and was accordingly handsomely bound in a decorated and embossed velvet cover. The copy was signed by the four signatories of the Antients (it is presumed the Moderns never bothered to sign this document or may never have been asked to, nor was it necessary for them, or the Antients, to do so) and, until recently, it was carried into Grand Lodge at each Quarterly Communication in the special satchel still in use today and on display at the Museum of Freemasonry.

The facsimile belonging to the Moderns' Grand Lodge has an interesting pedigree, as reported to the author in private correspondence by Susan Snell, Archivist and Records Manager at the Library and Museum of Freemasonry and a former British Records Association (BRA) archivist. She writes that the document concerned, accessioned as 'BRA 1607' together with a large quantity of other unrelated documents, was deposited with the BRA on 12 August 1968 from the College of Arms via the Historical Manuscripts Commission (HMC) as a gift. The British Records Association acts as an archives clearing house for London solicitors' papers and other records of potential historical interest. On 16 January 1976, Janet Foster, then the BRA archivist, wrote to the United Grand Lodge and the document was subsequently delivered to James Stubbs, Grand Secretary at the time, at Charterhouse where he was residing. The receipt of the document 'despatch number 1662' is acknowledged with thanks in a letter from the United Grand Lodge of England addressed to the BRA dated 5 February 1976. The relatively late discovery of the document may explain why it has not been referred to by several authors who have written on the subject, and who may have reached different conclusions had the existence of a Moderns' version of the facsimile copy been known to exist.

Finally

The Royal Arch is conspicuous by its absence in much that took place in the events leading to 27 December 1813. The small role it did play, by being mentioned in the Articles of Union, had enormous repercussions still felt today. 23 December 1813 is the date of the last entry in the minute book of the Antients' Grand Lodge. It records the presence of Thomas Harper as the Deputy Grand Master, and the Duke of Sussex, 'Grand Master of the other fraternity', is also shown to be present. The record confirms the minutes of the special Grand Lodge held on 1 December and the installation of the Duke of Kent as Grand Master. It ends by thanking the Duke of Kent

> [. . .] for negotiating the Union with the Fraternity of Masons of which the Duke of Sussex is Grand Master'. Grand Lodge is closed in due form and 'adjourned unto St John's Day now next ensuing to meet at Freemasons' Hall Great Queen Street at the hour of ten o'clock in the forenoon. (LLMF Ref: BE 140 UNI, 23 December 1813.)

The details for the proceedings having been agreed upon by the Lodge of Reconciliation, nothing now remained but to conclude with the happy celebrations of the union.

*   *   *   *   *

Part II
A Day in the
Life of a Duke
27 December 1813

Kensington Palace, London
27 December 1813

*T*hree distinct knocks on the bedroom door woke HRH the Duke of Sussex from a sleepless night. Norman and Gilbert, his two trusted valets, entered the palatial room in unison. Norman approached the Duke, who was gently lifting himself to a sitting position, the adrenalin flowing through his system overriding his tiredness. 'Good morning, your Grace' greeted him, Norman with outstretched arms, offering him the dressing gown he had picked up from the plush chair. Meanwhile, Gilbert approached the large French windows and drew the curtains to reveal the morning sky beginning to spread its light over the vast parterre and Vanbrugh's magnificent Orangery. 'It is going to be a cold but beautiful day, your Grace'. Gilbert could not have been aware of the impact his few words had on the Duke's speedily awakening consciousness. It felt to the Duke as if he had been waiting an eternity for this 'cold but beautiful day' and now, as he slipped his arms into his favourite fur–lined banyan, he relished the prospect of the historic hours that lay ahead.

Today, on St John the Evangelist day, Wednesday 27 December 1813, was the day that the Union would be celebrated and the new Grand Lodge launched. Today was the day when the final consolidation of the two Grand Lodges would take place and he, Augustus Frederick, the Duke of Sussex, would be declared Grand Master of the new United Grand Lodge of England. As importantly, thought the Duke optimistically, today the Royal Arch – that deep thorn that had penetrated his skin almost a decade ago – would finally be removed. The Royal Arch was about to find its way to becoming established, firm and forever, as an integral part of . . . or was it? Thoughts were racing through the Duke's troubled mind as he approached the bathroom door and shut it behind him. Had he really resolved the Royal Arch issue? Was he compromising the total trust the members of the Supreme Grand Chapter had placed in him? What was to become of the Royal Arch in the next months and years? He had to make a forcible effort to stop the spiralling sensation in his head. Everyone concerned, he reminded himself, knew full well the significance of this great day of Masonic unity. He had to clear his mind and concentrate on the fast approaching events of the day.

Within a half hour the portly Duke of Sussex was washed, shaved and regally clothed, ready to face the arduous day. He stood firm and tall in front of the mirror and looked himself up and down with satisfaction. He proudly followed the latest fashion, newly launched by 'Beau' Brummell, a popular friend of the Prince Regent. The Duke's dark coat and full–length trousers, so recently replacing the knee breeches now discarded by the aristocracy, well fitted his form and had been tailored to perfection. His immaculate linen shirt and cravat complemented the outfit.

Though his health left much to be desired, he felt good. He had done all that could be done to reach this epic Masonic day: first the signing of the Articles of Union had already taken place on 25 November – an event that had taken place in a clinical ceremony in the royal apartments here in Kensington Palace, and then the mutual agreement of the union affirmed by both parties a week later … a bizarre thought flashed before the Duke's mind: if things were to go wrong today, even if the event was to be cancelled … the 'marriage' would remain intact .. it had taken place on 25 November and the honeymoon 'consummated' on 1 December … there was no going back! In an effort to dismiss further macabre thoughts of anything going wrong, he shook his head vigorously sideways, his flabby cheeks flapping on his face.

The Duke had had to step on many toes to reach his goals, not least on those of his fellow Companions in the Supreme Grand Chapter of England. It was, after all, only just over a decade since his initiation into Freemasonry, and it was his Royal status, he knew, that gave him the power to implement decisions without excessive consultation. The intrigues and machinations needed to bring the current state of affairs to a satisfactory conclusion suited his nature perfectly. Approaching his 41st birthday, just a month away, the Duke, sixth son and ninth child of King George III, had had a life of controversy at best. It was not just his two illegal marriages, quickly dissolved by his father when informed that his renegade son was again breaching protocol, but his whole career to date. Cursed by ill health, he failed to follow in family tradition in the armed forces. Instead, he energetically pursued Whig politics and dabbled in social reform. Fortunately for the fraternity, his many interests in charitable causes – in addition to his fine achievements as a patron of the fine arts, architecture and science – included Freemasonry. He recalled his introduction to the Craft with considerable pleasure and satisfaction – travelling back in time, his mind placed him in situ:

Berlin, Kingdom of Prussia
17th December 1798

'My dear Prince, it is a true privilege to approach you on behalf of the Masonic Fraternity of this Kingdom, to invite you to join us as a member of our great and universal institution'. The speaker was Brother Gustav Fessler, the Deputy Grand Master of the Grand Lodge Royal York of Friendship of Prussia. A tall man with angular features matching his physical stature, Fessler stood erect and stiff, reflecting his respect in addressing so prominent a man as the son of a British King. Although Fessler had been a fellow student of the premier German University of Göttingen which the Prince attended before his move to Berlin, he had never been addressed by Fessler personally. 'The Most Worshipful Protector of our Craft, His Royal Highness August Ferdinand the Prince of Prussia himself has authorised me to speak with you', continued Brother Fessler, surprised to be made to feel so much at ease by the Prince's affable smile. 'He asked me to state how honoured we would be by your acceptance to become a Freemason here in our capital City of Berlin'.

The concept of being initiated into the society of Freemasons was not novel to the Prince. He was aware of the long-standing tradition of his family and ancestors as patrons of the Craft in England: five of his six Brothers were Freemasons, as were numerous royal uncles and relatives. He was confident that his joining the fraternity would be well received at home. There was no need for further consultation with England. 'Thank you, my friend' the Prince extended his hand in a gesture of friendship. 'I will be happy to accept'. Brother Fessler clutched the Prince's hand with enthusiasm in an involuntary Masonic grip.

The significance of his acceptance to become a Prussian Freemason dawned on the English Prince almost abruptly. He recalled his cousin and godparent, the Duke of Saxe-Gotha-Altenburg, proudly talking of the achievements of Prussia. How it had shaped the history of the whole German nation, with Berlin as its capital since 1451. The Kingdom had been proclaimed in 1701. Now under the rule of Frederick William III, Prussia was the dominant force in Germany, overshadowing its rival Austria. The relationship with England, particularly the respective Royal families, had been close, those of allies, very cordial in all respects. Indeed, his father George III held the title of Duke of Brunswick and Lüneburg, Arch Treasurer and Prince-Elector of the Holy Roman Empire. The Duke's own University in the City of Göttingen had been founded in 1734 by his grandfather, George II, King of Great Britain and Elector of Hanover. He felt it a privilege, even for a member of the Royal family such as himself, to be invited to be part of the traditions of this respected Kingdom. His thoughts were suddenly interrupted by the now familiar voice of Bro Fessler 'Our Grand Lodge of Prussia, you may know, is also named Royal York of Friendship Lodge and was only founded earlier this year (1798). We were honoured by the initiation of your uncle, your father's younger Brother, Edward Augustus, Duke of York here in Berlin, in the Lodge of Friendship, in 1765 and we gave his name to our Grand Lodge to commemorate his presence'.

Brother Fessler felt it unnecessary to explain that the Grand Lodge of Prussia was originally founded by the Grand Orient of France in 1752 and had, in fact, not worked in German until 1778. In 1796, under the guidance of Brother Fessler himself, thorough reforms had been undertaken, leading to the establishment in June 1798 of Royal York of Friendship Lodge as a Grand Lodge, with the command over three subordinate 'blue' lodges. Thanks mostly to Fessler's exertions, within the next three years the number of Lodges had increased to sixteen. The Prince knew of his uncle's trip to Berlin but was not aware of this Masonic connection. The thought of the family proximity warmed his heart.

Again, his mind placed him back to that December day in Berlin and to Fessler's speech. 'If you are prepared to proceed, my Lord' continued Brother Fessler 'I will introduce you even today to our veteran Freemason, Most Worshipful Brother Jürgen Amelang, a member of my own Frederick William Lodge dedicated to Crowned Justice'. The concept of each Lodge's name being dedicated to a virtuous cause was customary among several continental Saxon Grand Lodges. 'You may then proceed, the day after tomorrow, to Lodge Urania dedicated to Immortality. There on 19 December you will be duly proposed by Brother Klaus Basset as an initiate and a vote can be taken, which if proved favourable – and we have no doubt it will – will allow you to be initiated, on the Wednesday 20th December, in the lodge dedicated to Victorious Truth by the Right Worshipful Master, Brother Wolfgang Formey' concluded Brother Fessler, with a sense of

58

satisfaction and almost out of breath. 'That seems a rather cumbersome route of initiation. Is this normal Prussian Masonic practice?' queried the Prince somewhat naively. 'Not at all' came the rapid response. 'We feel so privileged at having you join us' explained Fessler 'that in order to avoid the tensions which would undoubtedly be generated by a discussion as to which Lodge is to receive you, we decided that if you were to take each step in a different Lodge we would all be very satisfied. Thus you will also be receiving your second Fellow Craft Degree and that of Master Mason in new Lodges' concluded Brother Fessler. 'I trust this meets with your approval?' Although only 25 years old and inexperienced in Masonic matters, the Prince had heard of the 33 and other quaint and enticing names and titles of Masonic Orders. 'What about all the additional degrees I have heard of? Am I to attend 33 different Lodges for the 33 degrees in other Orders?' he asked. Fessler was unable to restrain a chuckle 'I can assure you that is not the case'. Fessler swiftly clarified the confusion. 'We do not have that number of Lodges in the whole of Berlin! Our plan, with your agreement, is to confer the three degrees of the Craft on you as soon as possible. We already have allocated the 19th January next year to pass you as a Fellow Craft to the second degree, in the hands of RW Br Gunter Schlicht, Worshipful Master of St John Lodge Urania dedicated to Immortality. We are confident', added Brother Fessler, 'that you will not object to being joined on that occasion, by Lord Graves, who was initiated in Oxford, in England. After your receive your third degree on 4th February, in Lodge Frederick William dedicated to Crowned Justice, you will be allowed to select the further Orders beyond the Craft which you may wish to enter' concluded Brother Fessler, with an overt sense of satisfaction at having had all the dates and details at his fingertips. 'I am at your disposal' mumbled the Prince, in a somewhat acquiescent voice . . . images of a reluctant sacrificial lamb fleetingly flashing through his mind.

*   *   *   *   *

Here he was, more than a decade later, about to face the most satisfying day in his relatively brief Masonic career. He glanced at the timepiece on his large velvet-covered desk, and aware that he still had several minutes before his breakfast would be served, he sat on the luxurious sofa chair, laid his head back and once more allowed his mind to drift 14 years back. There he was, at his initiation . . .

The Royal Palace Berlin
20th December 1798

Blindfolded he was led into the lodge by the Most Worshipful Grand Master of the Grand Lodge of Prussia, the Crown Prince Frederick. It is true, part of the ceremony of preparation had been dispensed with, but he now stood in a state of darkness, his breast exposed and properly attired as any other candidate. He repeated his obligation, his large hands resting on the handsome volume of the Sacred Law, with dignity and sensitivity. 'Welcome, newly obligated

Brother among Freemasons' Brother Wolfgang Formey, Worshipful Master of the Lodge, finally intoned as the blindfold was removed.

The occasion of his initiation was not the first time that the Prince attended the Palace. On previous occasions, he was welcomed by a member of the Prussian Royal family and escorted directly to the guest room to join other dignitaries before being formally received. But this time, light restored to his eyes, he was surprised by the sight that greeted him. The candle–lit scene, as he looked around him, took his breath away. He had witnessed many magnificent rooms in his young Royal career. This, however, was utterly stunning: luscious Bordeaux–coloured silk drapes from floor to ceiling and between them, enormous portraits and other masterpieces and the brethren, comfortably seated in plush red cushioned benches, their eyes pinned on him, the newly made initiate, their small decorated aprons and sashes twinkling in the light of the host of candles of the two vast gilt chandeliers.

Brother Formey's words of welcome were warm and sincere and the Prince felt a sense of belonging which he had only experienced in family circles. He was tempted to speak but knew to keep silent until the ceremony was ended. In fact he was not given the opportunity to speak until after he had been made a Master Mason. On 4 February 1799, at the after–proceedings of the meeting and without introduction, he stood up, to the right of the Crown Prince, at the top table in the specially set up dining room in the palace and addressed the crowded gathering. In German, with an accent bordering on perfection, he said: 'Your Highness and my fellow Brethren, I have no words with which to adequately express the warmth in my heart generated by your earnest and cordial welcome. It has been a particular pleasure, in these months leading to this day, to make the acquaintance, indeed to befriend such prominent men now my fellow brothers. I have to thank your Deputy Grand Master, Brother Fessler who has led me by the hand, literally, from the start. His immense knowledge and dedication, not least to the revision of the Rite of Perfection you practice, is commendable. He has been telling me about the introduction of the English system of the three degrees of symbolic Masonry here to Prussia. I fear, from all I am able to understand, that he may be too optimistic to achieve such an ambitious program, as you are all so accustomed to the higher degrees I look to attain in the next months. I can only wish him luck with his proposals. I do really look forward to being bestowed with more light and knowledge. I thank you all.'

Because of what was called his 'healthy curiosity and rapid speed of comprehension', the Prince had soon grasped many of the concepts of the fraternity beyond the third degree, and his incessant and perceptive questions were always clearly and openly answered in detail, within logical reason, by his knowledgeable colleagues. In Prussia, the three Craft degrees were superimposed with six additional degrees known as 'the higher knowledge' and he was eager in his anticipation to gain this 'higher knowledge'.

Induction to other Orders followed rapidly. On 1 March 1799, he was proposed, seconded and approved to take the additional degrees of Scotch Master–Builder, Knight of St Andrews, Knight of the Sepulchre and Knight of the Eagle, all within the authority of his Lodge, which worked all of these high degrees. A week later, 6 March, he was admitted to the degree of Perfect Scottish Master–Builder and on 10 March he was proposed and perfected as a Mason of

Mount Heredom. He had to wait three weeks, an unusually long wait, to be conferred the degree of Knight of the Eagle and finally, on 23 December, he was raised in the Order of the 'Chosen of New Jerusalem'.

He recalled his last appearance at his Lodge in Berlin on Good Friday 11 April 1800. The temple was full in anticipation of his parting speech. 'Worshipful Master and my dear Brethren' he begun, hesitated and repeated 'Worshipful Bro Justus von Taunzien and my dear Brethren, I am about to leave you for good and I feel that I will be tearing myself away from a family.' He was sincere in his tone and demeanour. 'It has been a true privilege to serve you in Lodge as your First Warden since June last year' he continued 'and I am grateful to you all for allowing me to conduct, on so many occasions, the duties of the Master of the Lodge'. In fact he was genuinely not disappointed, even relieved, to have to forego the opportunity of being elected Master, due to his early departure. He had been very active indeed and that was sufficient satisfaction. 'Our Brother Secretary informs me' he continued, addressing his attentive Brethren, 'that I held the Master's gavel on no less than twenty-four occasions. I will also remain ever grateful to you all for introducing me to the additional degrees' he continued 'and I must mention Brother Johann Gottlieb Fichte in particular. It has been truly my privilege to spend so many hours of contemplation with a Brother who is seen as one of Europe's greatest idealist philosophers of our time...'

The thirty-one year old Johann Fichte was made a Mason in Zurich in 1793 and had met the Prince and Fessler in 1799 when he joined their Lodge in Berlin. That very morning Fichte, Fessler, von Taunzien, the Prince and a handful of other select brethren, had discreetly met in a private room of the 'English Coffee House' in Behren Strasse, founded in 1721. It was famous because the now forgotten English owner had received Royal consent from King Frederick William I as the first Coffee house in Berlin, free of all rent. The Coffee House had been frequented by the nobility of the City ever since. 'Gentlemen, permit me to introduce my friend and publisher Johann Fischer. He is here on a short visit as Master of the Inner Orient Lodge in Potsdam'. Brother Fichte appeared tense and uncomfortable, his voice faltering. 'He will attend our meeting this evening'. 'Gentlemen and Brethren, it is my privilege to be a guest amongst you'; Johann Fischer took over abruptly and shook each Brother's hand with unconcealed confidence, as he made his way around the table. 'I am here with excellent news for our Brother Fichte, which I would like to formally announce at this gathering. Our Editorial board of Directors have confirmed that they will publish Brother Fichte's **History of Freemasonry** and I would like to be the first to congratulate him.' concluded Fischer, gently placing his hand on Fichte's soldier in a somewhat patronising gesture reminiscent of a blessing.

As everyone expressed their compliments, the Prince laid his clay pipe on the ashtray, stood up and took Fichte's right hand in both of his: 'Well done my Brother; I know this is an achievement you had not expected so early in your young career, but tell me why you look so concerned?'. Fichte physically led the Prince away from the others, toward the carpeted wall, as he was speaking. 'My dear Prince, this is more troublesome than you will appreciate. I do not trust Fischer as a publisher even though he is a Brother. In all our correspondence on the subject *he has insisted on adding his own comments and interpolation to my text. The publication of this book will be a disaster for me. It will spoil my reputation and now it is too late'. Two years later the Prince was to hear the extent to which Brother Fichte's fears had materialised. The final published volumes in 1802 appeared in a periodical and Fichte's scholarly text had been converted into the story of an imaginary non-Mason to which had been added entries which discussed at length what Masonry was not all about. It had been a sad story.*

'. . . I will take with me memories of you all that will never fade' the Prince was concluding his parting speech. 'You are launching me into my Masonic career and there is no activity I will undertake without recalling the example you have given me. You have taught me that in Freemasonry is to be found true fellowship and brotherhood. I thank you from the bottom of my heart.' He sat down to a roar of applause that long continued.

At the age of 29 he had left Berlin, a well-qualified Mason. On his return to England in 1802, he first joined the Prince of Wales Lodge, and a plethora of Masonic activity thereafter led to where he was today, Grand Master Elect – the first – of the new United Grand Lodge of England, truly the highest accolade any Mason could possibly strive for. And that was really what this day was all about. The installation of him, the Duke of Sussex, as Grand Master of all English Freemasons.

✻ ✻ ✻ ✻ ✻

The loud chiming of the mahogany wall clock brought the Duke abruptly back to the present. He was ready for breakfast and made his way down the carpeted winding staircase to the first floor dining room. 'I was expecting you to appear more stressed than you are.' The Duke was almost startled to hear his brother's voice as he entered the breakfast room. 'Good morning, Edward. What are you still doing here at this time?' asked the Duke, concerned now that his brother would not be ready for the day's events as they progressed. 'Are you not meant to be preparing at St James's? We are to meet in Great Queen Street in just a few hours.' There was a hint of irritation in the Duke's voice. His plans were not being followed in accordance with the strict instructions he had given. 'Come, come my dear Augustus, do not fret. I stayed here overnight and all my regalia are in the safe hands of Brother George Nayler, the Grand Director of Ceremonies. I am as ready as can be. As soon as you are ready, I will gladly travel with you rather than make my own way to Freemasons' Hall.' Edward, Duke of Kent and Strathearn, fourth son of George III, was clearly in high spirits. He viewed the day's events with less concern than his younger brother. In line with many in the family, Edward viewed his brother's intense and dedicated interest in Freemasonry as excessive. The younger Duke had taken all matters into his hands and had persuaded, even cajoled, many close to him to follow and support his determined ambition to bring about Masonic harmony in England.

The Duke on the other hand did not forget that he had to use every ounce of his notorious fiery individuality to bring things to a head. For the past few years, every detail had been planned ahead for this day's events and he was in no mood to be surprised by initiative taken by others, not even his own brother. It had been no mean feat to manipulate events to reach the current state of affairs: two royal brothers each at the head of the two respective Grand Lodges.

Becoming a Freemason in Switzerland in August 1789, Edward too had pursued a Masonic career, though certainly not as intense as that of his younger brother. 'Surely you are persuaded by now that I am totally and wholeheartedly committed to our arrangements.' Edward looked his brother straight in the eye. 'I have no inclination to involve myself in your intrigues with your colleagues, especially in the complicated Royal Arch matters. My interests remain genuinely not with the cause of the Antients – as you once feared – but with a successful and long lasting union. I cannot however deny that the simplicity of the Royal Arch as the fourth degree of the Craft, as practiced by the Antients Lodges, is rational and cannot be dispensed with out of hand.'

This was one of the favourite subjects of debate between the two blood–brothers, and though it was, of course, all too late now to change anything, old habits forced them to continue the dialogue, like actors rehearsing a play. 'Please Edward' retorted the Duke in a condescending tone, as he filled his crested cup with coffee, dismissing the valet who had approached to assist. 'I know of your good intentions, Edward, but as I've said before, I fear the problem that the Royal Arch is causing me has to remain on my shoulders and some aspects are even beyond your comprehension … and they are best left there. In any case, you will not be able to assist.' The Duke sat back on his chair opposite his brother, contemplating the situation, sipping his coffee as he was served his breakfast. 'I had thought the inclusion in the Articles of Union of the Royal Arch as part of pure Ancient Masonry was the end of the matter' suggested the Duke of Kent, somewhat sheepishly, expecting the usual harsh reaction to the candour of his comment. Instead, the Duke of Sussex stood and approached his brother on the other side of the table. He placed his hand firmly on his shoulder and in an overt manifestation of brotherly confidentiality he almost whispered. 'The problem with the Royal Arch is that I am not delivering what I promised' he confessed. 'This Article II you talk of is a compromise but it satisfies nobody. A compromise should satisfy everybody.'

The Duke returned to his seat, his head bent forward, and sat down to continue his breakfast. Edward knew more would follow and remained silent until the Duke of Sussex spoke again: 'Supreme Grand Chapter gave me a free hand to negotiate on their behalf and where are they now? … NOWHERE!' he almost shouted out. 'Nowhere!' he repeated with overt concern, his face expressing the dissatisfaction and disappointment he felt in his heart. 'Our celebrations today are the effective demise of the Supreme Grand Chapter of England. Tomorrow no such entity will exist. What about all the Companions of the Order who trusted in me? I am not sure they are yet aware of the fate I brought on their heads'. This was a very rare display of uncertainty on the part of the Duke, which he only allowed himself because of the intimate family ambiance. He paced the room with deliberate steps, reflecting on the subject, his brother knowing not to interrupt. It took several minutes before the Duke spoke again. 'Edward, I will tell you frankly: I do not know what "part of pure Ancient Masonry" means. What "part" is the Royal Arch to play in future?' He paused. 'Enjoying your breakfast?' he enquired in a deliberate change of his tone, determined not to dwell on the subject anymore.

The Duke had the highest respect and admiration for his elder brother, who was the father of his favourite niece, Princess Victoria. Unlike himself, Edward had had full military training and enormous experience as commander-in-chief of British forces in North America. In joining the Masonic circuit in England after his return from Switzerland, he became a popular figure amongst the Brethren of both opposing jurisdictions. He was honoured as Past Grand Master of the Grand Lodge of England in 1790 whilst he served as Provincial Grand Master of Gibraltar. Thence, in 1792, he was made responsible for the Province of Lower Canada, but now under the jurisdiction of the Antients Grand Lodge. Sussex knew that there was no doubt of his brother's dedication to bring about a union. It was for this very reason that he was elected Grand Master of the Antients on 9 November and installed in a solemn and historic ceremony on 1 December 1813. The Duke of Atholl, whose family had held the Masonic throne of the Antients for two decades, stepped down and Edward took his seat on King Solomon's symbolic throne. Today, in the afternoon's proceedings, he would be proposing, as agreed, that his brother, the Duke of Sussex, be appointed and invested as the Grand Master of the newly founded United Grand Lodge of England: to be proposed in open Lodge and to be seen as a gesture of brotherly love and affection and an ultimate symbol of unity.

Freemasons' Hall
Great Queen Street, London
27 December 1813

At 08:15 precisely, the two brothers sat opposite each other in the imported, two-horse German Landau carriage, and the young coach driver, in a heavy coat and top hat, took off in the direction of Freemasons' Hall. The Duke of Kent had entered the carriage first to ensure that on arrival his brother would be the first to exit the carriage and be greeted. The arrangement worked. On reaching Freemasons' Hall 'Grand Master ... welcome Grand Master' could be heard repeated incessantly from the moment the Duke of Sussex stepped onto the pavement and until he reached the allocated boardroom. His brother had discreetly remained in carriage for a little longer than need be before being escorted to a private lounge room where he was to meet with the senior brethren of his Grand Lodge. The main ceremony was due to start at eleven precisely. This allowed the Duke of Sussex to carry out a number of brief meetings he had promised 'if time permits'. Indeed a queue outside the boardroom had formed before his arrival.

Notwithstanding the approaching hour, the Grand Director of Ceremonies, Sir George Nayler, had generously agreed to manage the Duke's conferences. 'Your Grace, first on the list is the Reverend Dr Neville Coghlan, Grand Chaplain in our Grand Lodge' announced Bro Nayler. 'You will no doubt recall, your Grace, that you have appointed him to conduct the prayers during our ceremonies this afternoon'. The priest entered the room bowing with respect and took the chair offered by the Duke with a gesture of his hand. 'Your Grace, thank you for this brief meeting and I am here at your request and to confirm my total preparedness for this day's ceremonies. I have the three main prayers in hand and will be glad to show them to you.' Reverend Coghlan, an

Irishman of long and respected Masonic lineage, had blurted it all out in one breath and now recovered with a long intake of air. 'I have absolute trust in the selection of your prayers, my dear Reverend' assured him the Duke, a benevolent and patient expression on his face. 'Assure me only' he asked 'that all the prayers are interdenominational, that our Jewish Brethren and others not of the Christian faith who may be present in Grand Lodge will not be excluded by references to the Trinity.'

The Duke of Sussex had long established himself as favouring total religious emancipation. He had had several opportunities to express his views, first in Berlin where he had heard of the exclusion of Jews from Masonic Lodges. He had, at the time, made his views known to King William Frederick III. At one time, while a guest at the Royal Palace in Berlin, he had also noted one of the King's guests, the Swedish Count Le Clerk, commenting with surprise on the existence of English Lodges consisting entirely of Jewish brethren, which would have been an impossible situation in Sweden. The Prince of Prussia had commented and the Duke had again expressed his thoughts on the universality and equality within Freemasonry. His support for those not of the Christian faith was later to manifest itself at the initiation of Abraham Bullais , a candidate of the Jewish faith residing in Tunis, whom the Duke himself had initiated into Royal Alpha Lodge in the Hebrew Language on 20 August 1824".

'I have done as you requested, your Grace.' The Duke was brought back to the present by Reverend Coghlan. There are no references to the Trinity or Jesus Christ in any of the prayers being recited.' The reverend looked distressed. He clearly had something else on his mind, to which the current discussion was just the prelude. He began: 'Your Grace, may I very briefly address you as our First Grand Principal and comment on the rumours I have been hearing amongst the Companions since our November Convocation.' Coghlan was referring to the last meeting of the Supreme Grand Chapter on 30 November, when the Duke had been present. It was at that meeting that freedom was given to the Duke to act at his own discretion on all matters relating to the Royal Arch in the Union negotiations. The Companions are at a loss to understand their standing as Royal Arch masons once the Union has taken place.' Coghlan felt embarrassed at raising what clearly was a delicate subject. They have requested as a group, that I should ask for your clarification of the standing of the Supreme Grand Chapter after the Union. In short: where will they stand tomorrow?'

The minute of silence that followed could be cut with a knife. The Duke walked toward the stained glass windows, his hand on his chin, his eye shut blatantly, as if requesting not to be disturbed. He finally straightened his body and from where he stood, several yards away from the reverend clergyman, he spoke as if making a declaration. 'Today' he almost bellowed the words out 'today we are celebrating the Union of two Grand Lodges. The Supreme Grand Chapter of England is <u>NOT</u> part of these celebrations. The time for the Royal Arch, I promise, will soon come. It is not today. Please inform the Companions of the Order that I have their best interest at heart and will not let them down. They have, however, a duty to allow me time to implement my promise.' The Duke led the Grand Chaplain by the arm to the door and repeated 'I promise' as he gently encouraged him to exit.

The speed with which Coghlan was ushered out of the room was a clear indication to those waiting of their future fate. To the surprise of everyone, there was a knock on the door. The

Director of Ceremonies opened, and having listened for a moment, he shut it and addressed the Grand Master Elect: ' Your Grace, outside the room is M W Brother James Agar, Past Deputy Grand Master of the Antients Grand Lodge, who requests an audience and your kind permission to receive him for just a few moments now, without delay.' James Agar, was the most senior member of the negotiating team present, 'Do please admit him' said Sussex without hesitation. 'My dear Brother, how can I be of assistance to you on this historic morning?', the Duke welcomed his long-standing adversary, now a colleague in a common cause. 'Your Grace, I am here on the relatively minor, though volatile matter of the Royal Arch.' 'Not again.' thought the Duke to himself, outwardly showing concentrated attention to what Agar had to say. 'My brethren in the Antients Grand Lodge who are Royal Arch Masons are concerned even now in these very last moments of preparation, that no attention has been given at all to the Royal Arch in all the complex preparations that have been taking place.' Agar was emphasising that the younger Grand Lodge of the Antients, in perfect opposition to the more senior Premier Grand Lodge, viewed the Royal Arch as the fourth degree of Craft Freemasonry. 'What "exact attention" do your Antient Companions want?' interrupted the Duke, clearly impatient with this matter being raised again now at these very last hours before the final celebrations. 'Please understand me, Grand Master' pleaded Agar, more in search of sympathy than comprehension 'these companions have been used to the presence of Royal Arch symbols in their Craft lodges and their Grand Lodge for the best part of six decades, if not more. In your presence on 1 December when your brother was installed Grand Master, the Royal Arch Banner was prominently carried in the very procession you attended. Now, in these ceremonies, there is absolutely no presence of the Royal Arch in any form or manner whatsoever'. It was an appeal from the heart for something to be done to placate those restless companions who were not all happy with the union as agreed on by their superiors.

The Duke thought for only a moment. He had to resolve this matter which was a persistent theme dominating the day's conversation, not just at his home with his brother, but clearly also in the corridors of Grand Lodge, both among the Moderns and Antients. It was with a sudden sense of shock that he realised the practical truth. 'Allow me to consider the matter, dear Brother Agar. Do return and assure your brethren that it was only expediency and not neglect that brought about this present circumstance.' The Duke of Sussex made sure that he was not promising anything, in spite of his concerns.

The Royal Arch had, in fact, been totally excluded from the ceremonials of the day. It was as if the mention of the Royal Arch as part of pure Ancient Masonry in the Articles of Union had been such a major achievement that that in itself was sufficient to appease all concerned. Nothing more needed to be done for the time being. The amount of work and the time-scale in the events and preparations for the union of the Grand Lodges took priority to the total exclusion of all other matters, including the supposedly 'resolved problem' of the Royal Arch.

'Brother Nayler, I fear this is unacceptable neglect on our part and something needs to be done.' the Duke was seeking suggestions from the small and select band of brethren that surrounded him. 'Can anything be done to include the Royal Arch in the proceedings?' The Duke was well aware that the absence, if not neglect, of the Royal Arch in the day's ceremonies was quite intentional. The Brethren of the Moderns Grand Lodge felt they had been forced into accepting the Royal Arch as part of Ancient Masonry. It was to counter-balance that sense of defeat on the subject that they deliberately excluded the Royal Ach from all events, and the reaction of the Antients was of some satisfaction. Nonetheless, at this last moment, and with Agar's appeal ringing in his ear, the Duke felt that this had been unfair.

As Nayler, the Director of Ceremonies, walked into the corridor to inform the rather disappointed brethren that no further interviews were to take place, Brother James Thomas spoke up: 'Grand Master, could we maybe arrange for a group of Royal Arch Masons to be added to the procession? Or if it is too late for that, there may be some possibility for a group of Royal Arch Masons to be seated together? Their red regalia will be prominent enough to make them stand out.' suggested Thomas. 'Both these suggestion are totally untenable' interceded the Director of Ceremonies, now back in the room. 'The procession is at this very moment being formed and will be in place in the next hour. I can have a look at sitting arrangements but cannot see how we would be able in time to instruct a select number of Companions to wear the appropriate regalia and sit together in one place.' It was clearly an impossible situation, Nayler knew. 'Your Grace. Special arrangements have been made to ensure the intermingling of Antients and Moderns and here we are advocating a separation of Royal Arch Masons' he emphasised. 'But with your permission, Grand Master, let me see if any arrangements to sit a group of Companions separately is achievable.' said the Director of Ceremonies as he made to leave the room hurriedly. 'Consider additional seating in the front rows' suggested the Grand Master as a last proposal. The Director of Ceremonies left on what he knew to be an impossible mission.

The brethren were already beginning to take their seats in the huge hall that had been specially set out and converted to accommodate this very special and unique occasion. Samuel Wesley was playing at the organ, a preamble to his own music composed for the occasion. The most dominant object in the temple was the centrally-placed and elevated throne in the East that was to remain empty during the ceremony until the Duke of Sussex, as newly-elected Grand Master of the United Grand Lodge of England, was due to be seated on it.

Moderns Lodge Room
Freemasons' Hall 10:40 am

Just a few yards away, on either side of the boardroom where the Duke of Sussex and his entourage were discussing Royal Arch events, members of the two formerly rival Grand Lodges were assembled. Through the first entrance on the right, past the two colonnades still under construction, fourteen Grand Officers of the Moderns Grand Lodge, some very senior, had long completed the formality of opening their Grand Lodge. They were dressed in their colourful aprons and collars, their breast jewels scintillating in the light, now waiting for instruction to proceed in file to the Grand Temple. A buzz of excitement could be felt in the room as a dozen topics of conversation were being exchanged among the brethren.

'What about the Royal Arch?' enquired brother Theobold Jones, directing himself to no one in *particular, and taking advantage of the total silence that had for one moment descended on the gathering. 'I am a member of the Order and as far as I can make out, this Union appears to be the end of the Royal Arch as an independent body.' Such a statement from such a senior Mason quickly focused the attention of all present to the thorny subject of the Royal Arch. The Royal Arch had been a persistent theme in every discussion and meeting that took place during the varied and intermittent negotiations leading to this day. Brother Jones's question hung in the air until Right Worshipful Brother Waller Rodwell Wright, a senior diplomat in civilian life and the most senior brother present, rose to his feet. His posture reflected his stature. Clothed in the full regalia of his high rank as the Provincial Grand Master of the Ionian Islands, he looked resplendent in his gilt chain and jewels on his breast, every part of the knowledgeable, authoritative and talented Mason that he was. Among his many other achievements, he had been instrumental in the drafting the Articles of Union and he was the author of the Masonic ode to be recited and sung at the Banquet this very evening, following the ceremonies. The attention of every brother in the room was concentrated on what this respected Mason and personal friend of the Duke of Sussex had to say. 'The matter of the Royal Arch is resolved in the second clause of the Articles of Union. If some of you do not see that as a resolution, it is certainly too late now!'*

A freemason since 1794 and a member of the Lodge of Antiquity No. 1, Waller Wright had been one of the premier Grand Lodge's Commissioners for the Union. This day would be the culmination of his activities. 'I think it a Solomonic solution to have declared that pure Ancient Masonry includes the Holy Royal Arch.' Wright continued calmly, now that he had everyone's attention. 'It satisfies our Premier Grand Lodge's requirements of a three-degree system, as well as those of the Antients, by the inclusion of the mentioning of the Royal Arch. Let us remember Brethren, that without a compromise, we would never have reached a Union.'

Notwithstanding the fact that many senior members of the Premier Grand Lodge were active Royal Arch Masons, the Premier Grand Lodge adamantly refused to acknowledge any degree beyond that of Entered Apprentice, Fellow Craft and Master Mason. The formation of the independent Royal Arch Order as a Supreme body in 1766 had thrown the spanner into the works. The 'Solomonic solution' Wright referred to was the brain-child of the Duke of Sussex. It was the wording of the second paragraph of the Articles of Union, that declared the Royal Arch to be part of pure Ancient Masonry which had finally resolved the last outstanding matter preventing successful negotiation for a Union, removing also any objections Scotland and Ireland might have had on the wordings. Today, 27th December 1813, the three independent bodies were amalgamating — two united and one neglected — to form one single new entity. This was the theme of the discussion going on in the room.

'I cannot understand the need in the first place of having the Royal Arch play any part at all in this Union.' Jones was reflecting the view of a very large number of Masons to whom the situation was far from clear. 'We are two craft Grand Lodges uniting. What has the Royal Arch got to do with anything? Why not let the Royal Arch continue on its own? It is obviously successful. It has, after all, been going on for over 40 years. It has been run by the Supreme Grand Chapter since 1766.' Jones was proud to demonstrate his historic knowledge of Masonic

events. There are two sides to every coin, my dear Brother Jones.' Wright felt obligated to give a balanced view of circumstances. 'An independent Supreme Grand Chapter is certainly sufficient for Royal Arch Masons and such a body is also perfectly acceptable to us, the Moderns, but that is not the way that the Antients see it. To them', continued Wright patiently, 'the Royal Arch has been an integral part of Craft Freemasonry since their foundation. They see it as the fourth degree of their structure. To now suggest that the new United Grand Lodge of England will totally exclude the Royal Arch from its workings is contrary to all their principles.'

Wright was speaking from experience, having been involved in the negotiations leading to his day. He had experienced at first-hand the adamant stand taken by every single Antient Mason he had spoken to. 'It sounds like a victory for the Antients' interceded William Meyrick. 'To threaten total failure in all negotiations unless we accede to their demands borders on blackmail, doesn't it?' Brother Meyrick looked every inch the lawyer that he was. His demeanour generated the kind of impression an attorney presented when appearing in a courtroom. He had a confidence about him that reflected his high Masonic standing. Also a member of Antiquity Lodge, Meyrick was acting as Senior Warden of the Lodge of Reconciliation, and only gave up the office on being appointed the first Grand Registrar of the new United Grand Lodge, the office he was to be invested with this very afternoon. Meyrick was not very sympathetic toward members of the Antients negotiating team. 'Our stand has always been clear. We are a Craft Grand Lodge and we have, since time immemorial, been concerned with Craft degrees and nothing beyond.' Meyrick's voice revealed a trace of anger as he continued: 'You may consider it a perfect 'Solomonic solution' to have pure Ancient Masonry consist of the three degrees including the Royal Arch, but it is a compromise that resolves nothing, except surrender to the whims of the Antients.' He turned away from the group, walked to a distant chair in the room and sat down. 'As a Royal Arch mason, I must agree with Brother Meyrick's views.' The high-pitched, slightly squeaky voice of John Dent was readily recognisable. He was indeed a well-known and senior Royal Arch Mason, until very recently the Most Excellent Zerubbabel of the Supreme Grand Chapter that had last met on 30 November. His comparable seniority in the Craft was manifest in his pending appointment on this day as Deputy Grand Treasurer of the United Grand Lodge of England. This insistence on the inclusion of the Royal Arch in the Articles of Union without definition of its exact standing has placed the Order in a total quandary. The Supreme Grand Chapter is effectively dissolved, as are the two former Grand Lodges. The United Grand Lodge of England is intended to stand supreme and alone. If someone was to ask me 'Where does the Royal Arch fit in?' my answer, even as the most senior member of that Order in this room, would be "I do not know!" Not a happy state of affairs'. John Dent felt a sense of embarrassment rise in his body and turned his face away to avoid the Brethren witnessing the flush on his cheeks. 'How did we reach this situation, sacrificing the Royal Arch for the sake of Unity of the Craft?', the brother asking the obvious question remained almost hidden behind the more portly and senior Masons involved in the conversation.

Meyrick decided to take up the thread and approached the group, now gathered in the centre of the room. He recalled the crucial November meeting almost two months ago. There had been very little discussion and it had been a rather short meeting.The brethren then present were *concerned by the events that had just taken place at the quarterly convocation of the Supreme Grand Chapter on 30 November, a meeting at which all the Royal Arch dignitaries had been present, and during which the forthcoming Union of the two Grand Lodges had been acknowledged. It was also at this meeting that authorisation had been given to the Duke of Sussex to 'Negotiate a Union of the Supreme Grand Chapter with the Premier Grand Lodge'. Though everything may have appeared to run smoothly on the day of the quarterly convocation, it had been far from an easy decision that had been taken by the Companions of the Order.*

In the corridors of Freemasons' Hall preceding the meeting, Brother Samuel Cordigan had expressed his concerns that the Duke had been given total power to do as he pleased without further consultation. 'Let us take an extreme example.' Cordigan had suggested to Meyrick. 'What if, in order to satisfy the other parties' requirements and bring this Union to fruition, the Duke sees fit to dissolve Supreme Grand Chapter? He would have the power to do so just on his own authority.' 'That is rather extreme.' had intervened Brother Gerald Smith 'We are authorising the First Grand Principal to unite the Grand Chapter with the Grand Lodge – nothing more. He will surely adhere to obvious limitations, even if not expressly spoken.' 'We have to rely on trust now.' Meyrick encouraged the Companions to have faith. 'I doubt that the Duke will take any action to the detriment of our Order. He has a handful to contend with and giving him our authority to do his best for us is all we can do. Let us now hope that his best will be ours too.'

Meyrick had to make a concerted effort to bring his mind back to the present. 'Brethren, I must admit that I did not expect to be discussing this issue this late in the course of events. For the clarity of the younger members, however, let me explain that the Companions of the Royal Arch chose by their own free will to have our Grand Master elect, the Duke of Sussex, represent their Royal Arch interest leading to the Union. He received their full authority to negotiate on their behalf – last month, on 30 November to be precise'. 'In that case he has let the Companions down dismally!' Meyrick could not see who had uttered the sentence. Before he could formulate an answer, he heard Dent reply: 'That would not be a fair assessment of the part played by the Grand Master in the protection of our interests.' It was now Companion, rather than Brother, Dent that was responding. 'It may be true that the Companions of Supreme Grand Chapter had visualised a Union of their organisation with the Premier Grand Lodge of England, but how could such a Union possibly take shape? It is clear that the Duke had to compromise to reach his main goal: the Union of the two Craft Grand Lodges. Yes, the Royal Arch missed out this time, but we have to be patient! We have ...' Dent was interrupted in mid–sentence by a loud knock on the door, which opened to allow the Deputy Director of Ceremonies to declare: 'Brethren, please take your allocated places in the procession columns. We will be entering Grand Lodge in just 12 minutes.'

'Brethren!' Dent called out in order to be heard above the commotion that followed. He was determined to conclude his statement. 'It is incumbent on us to secure the continuity of the working of our individual Chapters, no matter what may transpire in the coming days and months.' Satisfied with having said his part, he melted into the group seeking to find their pre–determined places in the two columns that were now being formed, ready for the procession.

Antients Lodge Room
Freemasons' Hall 10:40 am

In the third room to the left of the corridor, two dozen or more qualified Royal Arch members of the Antients Grand Lodge had assembled. The Lodge had been opened in accordance to ancient custom and as required and requested by the organisers. Now, as the brethren awaited being summoned to the Grand Temple, a similar and noisy argument was building up on the same theme as that just taking place in the Moderns lodge room. 'Brethren, silence please!' The dominant voice was that of the highly respected and, until recently, Deputy Grand Master Thomas Harper. The muttering ceased.

The feelings toward Brother Harper, whilst respectful, were ambivalent. He was vilified because of the dual role he had played over the years, alternating in his loyalty between the two camps. He had achieved prominence, both as an Antients and Moderns Mason, and that achievement attracted admiration among many brethren who saw his involvement specially appropriate to help negotiate a union. Harper deliberately delayed his opening words. 'Brethren' he finally resumed 'what we are embarking on is the successful culmination of very long and weary negotiations and the results are undoubtedly in our favour. Let us not forget our immemorial origins', he reminded his brethren, 'the historic ties that our Grand Lodge has with the Royal Arch as the fourth degree of Freemasonry'. Harper spoke with passion and authority. He had unparalleled experience as a freemason. The 'origins' to which he referred was the close link of the Antients with the Grand Lodge of Ireland. All the founder members of the Antients Grand Lodge in 1751 had been Irish, and they had adopted a system that allowed Craft Lodges to confer degrees beyond the Craft. He continued: 'The agreement by the Premier Grand Lodge to incorporate the Royal Arch as part of Ancient Masonry cannot have been an easy pill for the Moderns to swallow. They have forever maintained that only three degrees constitute pure Ancient Masonry. Now they have to contend that our fourth degree, the Royal Arch, is part of Ancient Masonry.' Harper could not hide his glee. 'It is a major achievement for us and it should not be minimised in importance.' he concluded. As assertive as he had been, his comments were not satisfactory to some of the brethren. 'Surely, Brother Harper, this is only a compromise.' James Perry, a journalist and writer by profession and an equally senior and respected Mason picked up the subject. 'All that the signed document, the Articles of Union, state is that the Royal Arch is *included* as part of Ancient Masonry.' He emphasised the word 'included'. 'It does not guarantee that the Royal Arch will be practiced as the fourth degree by the United Grand Lodge after it is formed.' 'But consider what we have achieved!' insisted Harper. 'After all, we are not even a Grand Chapter. We never have been. We are a bunch of individual Antient brethren who have taken the fourth degree, that of a Royal Arch Mason. Now to have the Royal Arch recognised by one and all as part of Ancient Masonry . . .' he stopped in mid-sentence to emphasise his feelings, 'I can promise you, is a major achievement for us.'

Harper wanted to convey in full the true significance of these historic events. 'Does that mean' asked Perry without conviction 'that at my Lodge, meeting Tuesday next, we can conduct

Royal Arch working with impunity?' Harper was forced to think before responding. 'I can think of no impediment, until the full rules and regulations are implemented, that we should not continue and act as in the past.' He considered his words as he spoke, in his mind not totally confident that he was conveying the thinking of his colleagues who had negotiated the Union. 'The only mention of the Royal Arch in the whole of the Articles of Union is the short statement that it is now part of pure Ancient Masonry. In the absence of further guidance, we must presume that we all proceed as before, for the time being.' There was no time for further discussion. The Deputy Director of Ceremonies had made his short way from the Moderns lodge room, and now invited the Antients Brethren to form into their pre-determined processional columns.

*   *   *   *   *

As the Brethren in the adjoining rooms prepared themselves for the procession, the Duke was left alone in his throne-like chair at the end of the otherwise unfurnished room. He had a few minutes to himself. Apart from the issue of the Royal Arch, everything so far had gone like clockwork. He knew he was even seven minutes ahead of schedule. He leaned his head back and reflected once more on the circumstances that had led to this very significant moment. This had been a deeply divided fraternity for the best part of six decades. Royalty and nobility had graced the head of both the contending societies, but never before had two Royal and influential brothers been appointed to lead the respective Grand Lodges. The earliest initiative for peace by the Antients had come to nothing. The Duke felt a sense of satisfaction surge through his body as he contemplated and recalled his own appointment as Grand Master of the Grand Lodge of England, the Premier Lodge, founded in 1717. He had taken over from his brother, the Prince Regent and from the very start had decided that to achieve peace one day between the two antagonistic Masonic bodies was to be his priority. That day had arrived.

Time was running out and the Duke had to gather his thoughts and concentrate on the present. He anticipated the grand entrance he was to make in a few moments, through the massive doors of the Grand Temple in Freemasons' Hall.

Freemasons' Hall
10:55am

'Grand Master!' cried out the Grand Director of Ceremonies in a shrill voice an octave higher than need be. The Grand Director of Ceremonies, Very Worshipful Brother Sir George Nayler, long-standing King's York Herald, had been knighted just a few months earlier. He was clothed in full dress regalia and had every appearance of a senior soldier of the realm. Nayler adjusted the tone of his voice and continued: 'Grand Master, both parties have opened their respective Grand Lodges and now await your pleasure to escort them into the Grand Temple.'

Some minutes earlier, the Temple had been filled with brethren in accordance with the well-laid and detailed plans that had been drawn up. It was clear that any attempts to disrupt the order would be immediately refuted, and the polite request of the Director of Ceremonies to consider the placing a group of Royal Arch Masons was quickly rejected by the senior organisers. The elongated Grand Temple, oriented east–west, was filled to the brim. In the east was a raised platform that was reserved for the Grand Masters, the Grand Officers and distinguished guests of Grand Lodge. Six Grand Stewards were placed on each side, flanking the Grand Master's throne. Also on the stage, at the very back, was the choir from whom sweet choral music, accompanied by the organ, was emanating.

Collegially seated along the north and south walls were Masters, and behind them Wardens and further back still Past Masters of all the Lodges in the Country: Antients and Moderns intermingled. They all wore dinner jackets and bow ties, white aprons and gloves and looked impressive indeed. In front of them were the eighteen empty seats, nine on each side facing each other, for the members of the Lodge of Reconciliation, the 'nine worthies' who were to enter the Grand Lodge in the procession.

In accordance with the Articles of Union, a Lodge of Reconciliation had been warranted on 7 December 1813, consisting of an equal number of representatives of each of the two Grand Lodges, including the respective Grand Secretaries. Dr S. Hemming, a Modern mason, had been elected Master and Brothers Meyrick and Shadbolt as Wardens. Brother W H White was appointed Secretary. It was their agreed ritual and administration that was being implemented as events progressed. In the west were seats for both Senior Grand Wardens, in the south were seats for the Junior Wardens and in the east four seats to accommodate the pair, one from each jurisdiction, of Secretaries and Treasurers.

On the marbled floor of the corridor outside the Temple, flanked by glass–encased dark wood panels, the two processions were formed, ready to enter the Temple. Intended to enter last were the two Grand Masters, preceded by the guest of honour, His Excellency the Count Jacob Gustaf Pontusson De la Gardie, Grand Master of the First Lodge of the North. The presence of this member of the Swedish nobility amongst the guest was totally accidental. On route to Spain to take up an ambassadorial role, the Count had happened to stop over in London and soon found himself a personal guest of the Duke of Sussex, who had been made aware of his presence.

Brother De la Gardie came from a distinguished Swedish military family, and reached the rank of a Lt. Captain by the age of 24. His close relationship with the Royal Court led to a highly successful diplomatic career. As a Mason he had obtained the 11th degree, the highest rank under the Swedish system in the First Lodge of the North, of which the monarch, King Carl XIII, was Master and De la Gardie his deputy. The Count was immaculate in his perfectly–cut high collar and notched black tailcoat and cotton shirt with ribbon ties. When he was within hearing distance, the Duke addressed him: 'Thank you for gracing this important occasion with your presence, my dear Count. I trust your reports to your Grand Master, the King, will reflect the warmth of the welcome we extend to you.' The golden chain collar that sat so comfortably on the Count's shoulders was complemented by the array of jewels on his *left breast. He wore an elaborate though small apron, which on him strangely enough appeared most suited for the occasion. 'I cannot thank you enough for granting me this privilege of attending' the Count hesitated and corrected himself 'of **participating** in your ceremonies on this most solemn and historic occasion.' He had chosen the word 'participating' carefully as the Duke had asked him to be a witness to the proceedings during which facsimile copies of the original Articles of Union would be symbolically signed by the two Grand Masters.*

Right on time, the fifteen-men strong Duke of Kent's Masonic Band, arranged in three columns at the head of the procession, began to play the marching music composed for the occasion by Brother Bernard Kelly. The group led by two Grand Ushers stepped forward. The Antients to the right and the Moderns on the left, reflected mirror-like, their counterpart marching next to them: a Master Mason bearing a cornucopia, duplicated by another that flanked him, two Master Masons in each column carrying two pairs of golden Ewers, nine 'worthy and expert masons' from each of the Lodges of Reconciliation, the Grand Secretaries, the Grand Treasurers, the Wardens, the Deputy Grand Master of the Antients flanked by the Acting Deputy Grand Master of the Moderns followed, on his own, by the honoured guest Count De la Gardie, the sword bearers and the two Grand Masters, finally followed by the two Grand Stewards and the respective Grand Tylers.

As the heavy doors of the Temple shut, the two columns stopped by the throne and the two Grand Masters made their way past the entourage and took their places on either side of the throne. They were followed, in order of seniority, by the remainder of the brethren, each taking his allocated seat. All this time, the band played exhilarating and familiar marching melodies.

The Director of Ceremonies took centre stage, begged for silence and invited the Reverend Dr Barry, Grand Chaplain of the Antients, to commence the proceedings with a prayer. When completed, Sir George Nayler read the Articles of Union in a most solemn manner. This was followed by a sound of a trumpet and the proclamation of the Reverend Dr Coghlan, which he delivered in a clear and loud voice:

> *Hear Ye – this is the Act of Union, engrossed, in confirmation of*
> *Articles solemnly concluded between the two Grand Lodges of Free*
> *and Accepted Masons of England, signed, sealed, and*
> *ratified by the two Grand Lodges respectively; by which they*
> *are to be hereafter and for ever known and acknowledged by the*
> *style and title of The United Grand Lodge of Ancient*
> *Freemasons of England. How say you, Brothers,*
> *Representatives of the two Fraternities? Do you accept of,*
> *ratify, and confirm the same?*

Having received a positive response from the Assembly, the two Grand Masters signed a facsimile copy each of the Articles of Union, followed by the respective Grand Secretaries. Count De la Gardie also witnessed and signed each copy.

After a further trumpet fanfare, the Grand Chaplain of the Antients declared:

*"Be it known to all Men, That the act of Union between the two
Grand Lodges of Free and Accepted Masons of England, is
solemnly signed, sealed, ratified, and confirmed, and the two
fraternities are one, to be from henceforth known and
acknowledged by the style and title of The United Grand Lodge
of Ancient Freemasons of England; and may the great architect
of the universe make their Union eternal"*

*Now there followed the performance of Wesley's symphony, after which the two Grand Masters
left their seats with their wardens and advanced to the superb Ark of the Covenant, a creation
of Sir John Soane, honoured and decorated City Architect and newly appointed Grand
Superintendent of Works. In a symbolic gesture, using the iconic working tools that had been
ceremoniously handed to them, the two Grand Masters sealed the Union with three knocks on
the Ark and declaring in unison:*

*'May the Great Architect of the Universe enable us to uphold the Grand Edifice
of Union of which this Ark of the Covenant is the symbol . . . may we dispose our
hearts to make it perpetual.'*

The Brethren in the room, in one voice, said 'So mote it be'.
*The two Grand Masters now placed their respective facsimile copies of the articles of Union
into the Ark and proceeded with the traditional ceremony of consecration, using the cornucopia,
wine and oil, as directed. The congregation said 'Amen' and the Grand Officers all resumed their
seats.*
*Letters by the Grand Secretaries of the Grand Lodges of Scotland and Ireland, Right
Worshipful Brother Lawrie and Worshipful Brother W. F. Graham (deputy) respectively, were
read aloud by the Director of Ceremonies, both Grand Lodges expressing regrets for their
absence and congratulations and promises of support for the union.*
*At this stage, members of the Lodge of Reconciliation, accompanied by the Count De la
Gardie and Most Worshipful Brother Dr Van Hess, left Grand Lodge to meet in a tiled
apartment adjoining Grand Lodge. Here the members of the Lodge of Reconciliation disclosed and
demonstrated all their conclusions for the correct ceremony to be henceforth conducted and the
group returned to the Grand Temple.*
*His Excellency the Grand Master of the First Lodge of the North loudly announced that the
procedures agreed by the Lodge of Reconciliation were pure and correct and to be adopted by all
Lodges under the jurisdiction of the United Grand Lodge of England.*
*The ceremony was proceeded with, by the two Grand Chaplains laying the Volume of the
Sacred Law on the Ark of the Covenant and placing the square and compass thereupon. The
brethren stood, held hands and repeated aloud the familiar obligation that was being recited by*

the Rev Dr Hemming. They ended by declaring: 'By this solemn obligation we vow to abide, and the Regulations of Ancient Freemasonry now recognised strictly to observe'. The Grand Officers all divested themselves of their chains of office and the Past Grand Master replaced them in their respective seats: Right Worshipful Brother Perry taking the seat of the Deputy Grand Master, Right Worshipful Brother Robert Gill as Senior Grand Warden and Right Worshipful Brother James Deans as Junior Warden.

The Duke of Kent stood up, took a few paces forward, observed the vast crowd of brethren facing him, and stated, in a voice that shook lightly with emotion:

'My dearest Brethren, I became Grand Master of the Antients solely to facilitate the most important object of the Union so happily concluded today. It is my intention now as a culmination to this extraordinary day and proceedings, to propose my illustrious and dear relative to be the Grand Master of the United Grand Lodge of England, for which high office he is in every respect eminently qualified. And I so propose H R H the Duke of Sussex to be Grand Master of the United Grand Lodge of England for the year ensuing.'

The proposition was seconded by Right Worshipful Brother the Honourable Washington Shirley and put to the vote. It was carried with acclamation and unanimously in the affirmative.

The Duke of Kent proceeded to place his brother, the new Grand Master, in King Solomon's Chair, assisted by Count De la Gardie, and the new Grand Master was solemnly obligated. A full and formal Grand Installation ceremony was agreed to take place on St George's Day.

In nominating and appointing his Grand Officers, the Grand Master stated that he was unable to name his Deputy Grand Master who could not be present due to circumstances beyond his control, and that he would be announced at some future date. The Grand Officers having been appointed, it was formally declared and proclaimed that the two Grand Lodges were now incorporated and consolidated into one, and the Grand Lodge was declared open in accordance with ancient custom by the Grand Master.

The Grand Lodge was then called to refreshment but, before exiting, the Grand Master was handed the Cup of Brotherly Love. He lifted the cup high, attracting the attention of the brethren, and before drinking their health, he intoned: 'Peace, Goodwill and Brotherly Love, all over the world.' He drank to the applause of those Brethren who had not yet picked up their glass of wine. He passed the cup to the Warden standing next to him and stepped down from the platform.

The Duke of Sussex, Count De la Gardie, Dr Van Hess and several prominent and senior Masons retired to the boardroom for some light refreshment. De la Gardie's coincidental presence in London was very fortunate. 'It is very gratifying to have everything function perfectly!' volunteered the Duke in the knowledge that chaos and concern had been the order of the day leading up to the events just witnessed. 'A man does not often have the opportunity in his life to witness first-hand history in the making' stated Van Hess, Most Worshipful Grand Master of the Grand Lodge of Hamburg, who was also the guest of the Duke of Sussex.

Deprived of the presence of both Scottish and Irish representatives, the Duke had had to improvise. The presence of these dignitaries — high-ranking Masons and aristocrats in their own respective countries – was an acceptable substitute. 'It is a privilege beyond expression to have spent this unforgettable afternoon with you.' Van Hess was genuinely grateful. A short man and lightly overweight, his delicate state of health was not overtly apparent, neither was his genuine talent as a medical doctor in civilian life. He had entered military life as a youngster but his health had let him down and he opted for academic life at the University of Konigsberg where he befriended the philosopher Emmanuel Kant. He wrote an elaborate history of the City of Hamburg, and had been brought to England on one of his many travels on this auspicious occasion. The Duke, satisfied with these expressions of appreciation by his guests, was now ushered back to the Grand Temple for the conclusion of the afternoon's ceremonies.

On their return, the Grand Lodge was re-called to labour. The first of the resolutions that was passed was quite appropriately and most eloquently proposed by the Duke of Kent. It was a resolution that a presentation be made to H R H the Prince Regent seeking his fraternal patronage. It was seconded by the Honourable Washington Shirley. It was passed unanimously.

Several additional administrative propositions relative to the internal management of the Grand Lodge were made by prominent Masons, seconded and passed with acclamation. A Board of Benevolence consisting of twelve Masters was established, and The Grand Master allowed his private seal of arms to be used on certificates until the great seal of the Grand Lodge should be prepared. The United Grand Lodge of England was closed in ample form and with solemn prayer.

All being now over, arrangements were made for the comfortable transportation of the senior brethren and their guests to the Crown and Anchor Tavern in the Strand, recently rebuilt to accommodate larger events. The historic tavern had associations with the lexicographer, Samuel Johnson, had been the hot-seat for political reform and made famous in James Gilray's caricatures of the period. No such politics this evening, however. It was here that the Grand Banquet of the Freemasons of England was to take place.

At dinner, the Duke of Sussex sat centrally placed to face the several long-table sprigs accommodating the brethren. To his right sat his brother, the Duke of Kent, and to his left his Excellency Count De la Gardie. The food was plentiful and the wine was poured liberally. It was past midnight when the two royal brothers summoned their carriage to the Tavern for the drive back to Kensington Palace. Sitting facing each other, as they had done in the morning on the way to Freemasons' Hall, both were in a far more relaxed state of mind, their cheeks flushed red by the wine and the food they had consumed and much enjoyed. 'I would like to say that "just another day" is over' joked the Duke 'but I do think we have made unparalleled history today, never to be forgotten by the fraternity.' 'You even gave it an international flavour by the presence of De la Gardie and Van Hess' said the Duke of Kent approvingly. He had experienced the value of international relations when stationed in Lower Canada. 'I trust they managed to return to their residences without delays? I heard our Director of Ceremonies was making suitable arrangements for a carriage.'

The idle chat and reminiscences of the day's events continued through the hour-long journey. As the coach approached Kensington Palace, the Duke of Sussex admitted: 'I do have one major concern. We have held the Royal Arch back so far as was practicable, and they have had no part to play in this union. The practical implementation of our union will need my full concentration, and the Royal Arch companions are going to need attention which they will not get.' The Duke clearly had more to say. He thought in silence for a minute. 'What will the future of the Royal Arch be?' This was not a rhetorical question, and his eyes showed that he was seeking an answer that would satisfy his concerns. 'Let things be, Augustus.' The Duke of Kent took his chances, interrupting his brother's thoughts. 'Supreme Grand Chapter may no longer exist, but individual Chapters of the Moderns still exist and the Antients will still be holding 4th degree ...' The Duke of Kent stopped intentionally, to ensure he had the full attention of his brother, before he said: 'Let the Royal Arch be, until you are ready to tackle the subject with your usual vigour and dedication'.

... and so it was until 1817.

THE END

*1. (Shadwell H Clerke *History of 'The Royal Alpha Lodge' No 16* London, 1891.)

* * * * *

Part III

A Chronology: May 1814 - October 2013

Introduction

The following is a continuous 200 year chronology of events of direct or indirect consequence to the Royal Arch, starting from 1814. It is not intended to be a comprehensive list. The years leading to 1817 have a particular emphasis on Craft events which subsequently were to influence the Royal Arch. Selected entries have been included, many of which were reported in the Quarterly Convocations of the United Supreme Grand Chapter until 1821 and Supreme Grand Chapter thereafter. Entries, which are made in the present tense, are representative of more widespread events reflecting Royal Arch activities at the time and/or in the provinces. Each new entry is indicated by a new paragraph and the day and month of the event has been added to the end of the entry, where applicable. The non-Masonic historic data, arbitrarily listed in italics following each year, is intended to place Masonic events in a global context. The lack of Royal Arch-related activity between 1813 and 1817 may be considered to be analogous to the time that it took to publish the first Craft Constitutions in 1723, six years after the foundation of Grand Lodge in June 1717.

The standard format of the report in the minutes of every early Quarterly Convocation has consisted of a heading followed by statistical details and subject headings, as follows:

Supreme Grand Chapter of Royal Arch Masons of England
At A Quarterly Convocation
Situ
Date
Present
Report by Committee of General Purposes:
Accounts
Receipt of Petitions
Grant of Charters
All business being concluded Grand Chapter is closed in Ancient and Solemn Form and adjourned until the next (date provided) meeting

1814 *The Treaty of Paris is signed ending the war between France and the Sixth Coalition, establishing peace between France and the United Kingdom as well as Russia, Austria, and Prussia.*

In 1814 there is still some confusion as to the use of names and numbers by the chapters of both former camps. In general, during the hiatus years of 1814-1817, Royal Arch activity, subdued in the centre and neglected by force of circumstance, nonetheless appears at chapter level to be carried on as usual in all quarters. This is evidenced in various published chapter minutes which record meetings. They show a normal activity of exaltations, lectures, visitations, etc., and exchange of correspondence as well as applications to Grand Chapter in London for certificates and charters . . . and frustrations at delays. (See, for instance, Tokes, John and Flather, David, *The History of Royal Arch Masonry in Sheffield*, Sheffield, 1922).

The revived Restoration Chapter No. 1, the private Chapter of the Duke of Sussex, holds its second meeting (see Part I, p. 26). (28 January).

Article IX of the Articles of Union of 25 November 1813, stated:

> IX. The United Grand Lodge being now constituted, the first proceeding after solemn prayer shall be to read and proclaim the act of Union, as previously executed and sealed with the great seals of the two Grand Lodges; after which the same shall be solemnly accepted by the Members present. <u>A day shall then be appointed for the installation of the Grand Master and other Grand Officers with due solemnity; upon which occasion the Grand Master shall in open Lodge, with his own hand, affix the new great seal to the said instrument,</u> [author's underlining], which shall be deposited in the archives of the United Grand Lodge, and be the bond of union among the Masons of the Grand Lodge of England, and the Lodges dependant thereon, until time shall be no more. The said new great seal shall be made for the occasion, and shall be composed out of both the great seals now in use; after which the present two great seals shall be broken and defaced; and the new seal shall be alone used in all warrants, certificates, and other documents to be issued thereafter.

The Duke of Sussex is installed as Grand Master of the United Grand Lodge of England at Freemasons' Hall, London. The Articles of Union (see above) were intended to be further engrossed by the signature of the Grand Master and the addition of the new seal of the United Grand Lodge of England. No such event or ceremony is recorded as having taken place at this or any other subsequent meetings. (2 May).

The Grand Banquet of the United Grand Lodge of England, following the installation, is held at Freemasons' Hall, London, presided by the Grand Master. (7 May).

The International Compact conference is held at Freemasons' Hall, London, on 27 June and 2 July, attended by the Duke of Sussex, Grand Master of the newly constituted United Grand Lodge of England, the Duke of Leinster, the Grand Master of Ireland, and Lord Kinnaird, Grand Master Mason of the Grand Lodge of Scotland. On 2 July, the revived Restoration Chapter No. 1 also holds its third meeting (see Part I, p. 28).

The agreement reached at this International Compact of 1814 establishes the government of the external relations between the three sister jurisdictions. Clause 1 (of eight clauses) of the International Compact affirms, with one change, article II of the Articles of Union by stating that pure Ancient Masonry consists of three degrees and no more, including the Supreme <u>Chapter</u> of the Holy Royal Arch. By replacing the original word 'Order' with 'Chapter' the compilers are able to accommodate the needs of all three jurisdictions, as explained by John Belton *in extenso* in Chapter 12 of his book (Belton, pp. 102-112). Furthermore, this same Clause 1 excludes references to other Orders of Chivalry, which are included in article II of the Articles of Union. Clause 8 states that the agreement reached will be circulated to all the lodges of all three jurisdictions. This International Compact is seen as laying the foundations for all subsequent Masonic agreements between the three nations. It is quite possible, though without supporting evidence, that an extension to a second day of the conference was necessitated by the subject of the Royal Arch requiring additional discussion.

White's Letter to Scotland

A revealing letter dated 7 September 1814 by William White, Secretary of the United Grand Lodge of England, and addressed to Alexander Deuchar (1777-1844) in Edinburgh, gives an insight into the thinking of the Duke of Sussex regarding the Royal Arch following the union. The following are excerpts from the three-page manuscript letter (LLMF, MS, Letters, 15/C/11C):

'[. . .] circumstances however, have occurred in this country, to prevent our proceeding with the arrangements [. . .] but as the difficulties which existed, are in great measure removed, it is the intention of His Royal Highness [the Duke of Sussex] very shortly to convene a Meeting to consider on the Steps necessary, for placing the Royal Arch upon the footing intended by the Act of Union, and what may be done in consequence of that meeting [. . .].

After this explanation, it is scarcely necessary to state, that there has not been any Meeting of our Grand Chapter since the period of the union, and consequently the subordinate Chapters have been acting under the Old Regulations [. . .].

In this year, the membership of the Lodge of Reconciliation is increased by ten additional Brethren.

1815 *Sunday 18 June the Imperial French army under the command of Emperor Napoleon is defeated by an Anglo-Allied army under the command of the Duke of Wellington combined with a Prussian army under the command of Gebhard von Blücher; this defeat at Waterloo finally ends Napoleon's rule.*

Craft Constitutions

The first post-union constitutions of the United Grand Lodge of England are published: William Williams, *Constitutions of the Antient Fraternity of Free and Accepted Masons. Part the Second. Containing the Charges, Regulations, &c. &c.* (London, W. P. Norris, 1815). Being the first edition of the Craft Constitutions after the Union, as directed by Article XXI of the Articles of Union, the publication contains '*The Charges and Regulations*' (defined as 'Part the Second') but lacks 'Part the First', the 'Historical Section'. Part I was intended to be a revised history but was not ready for publication by 1815. Furthermore, the publication does not include the clause relevant to the Royal Arch pronounced in Article II of *The Articles of Union*, namely that pure Ancient Masonry includes the Supreme Order of the Holy Royal Arch. The exclusion of this clause may be interpreted as a snub at the Royal Arch, an entity ignored by the United Grand Lodge of England from the union until 1817 *(vide* 1817 below*)*. In this context it must be noted, however, that none of the Articles of the Union of 1813 were incorporated into the Constitutions two years later. It may be that the Royal Arch was accepted as part of Ancient Masonry and that it was felt that there was no need for a repetition in the new Book of Constitutions. In fact, the relevant clause was not inserted until the 1853 edition of the constitutions *(vide* 1853 below*)* and even then, by force of circumstance rather than intention.

The revived Restoration Chapter No. 1 holds its fourth and last meeting (see Part I, p. 28). (14 September).

1816 *Abolition of Income Tax formally repealed leading to further expensive government borrowing and a greater burden of "indirect taxes" on the general population.*

It is in this year that the Craft rituals are completely agreed upon by the Lodge of Reconciliation. They remain in effect until the major changes to the Craft regulations in 1843. The lack of formal Royal Arch activity during 1816 reflects the Duke of Sussex being intent on settling complex Craft issues, before focusing his full attention upon the Royal Arch from March 1817.

The Lodge of Reconciliation (see Part I, p. 41) rehearses the opening and the ceremonies of the three degrees of Craft Freemasonry before an Especial Grand Lodge (20 May).

The recommendations of the Lodge of Reconciliation, after two unspecified amendments to the third degree, are adopted by the Grand Lodge. (5 June).

The Lodge of Reconciliation meets for the last time and its minutes record that:

> '…the W Master, Officers and Brethren were awarded the thanks of the Grand Lodge for their unremitting Zeal and Exertion in the cause of Freemasonry.' (4 September).

1817 *The Elgin Marbles, originally part of the Parthenon and other buildings on the Acropolis of Athens, are displayed in the British Museum for the first time; they are brought to England by Thomas Bruce, the 7th Earl of Elgin, British ambassador to the Ottoman Empire; the issue is controversial and debate continues to this day.*

1817 is a crucial year in the history of English Royal Arch Masonry, and thus the following extended and detailed entries.

The last and final meeting of the Supreme Grand Chapter of Royal Arch Masons of England (founded in 1766) takes place on 18 March, immediately followed by the first meeting of the new United Grand Chapter of Royal Arch Masons of England, at Freemasons' Tavern and Hall. The minutes of the last meeting of the Supreme Grand Chapter read:

> The Supreme Grand Chapter of England was opened in ancient and solemn form. John Dent (acting MEZ), John Aldridge (MEH) and William Williams (MEJ) sat as the three Grand Principals. The Rev Dr Hemming (E), read the minutes of the last Grand Chapter meeting, which were confirmed. He then stated that a report had been received from HRH the Duke of Sussex, Most Excellent Zerubbabel stating that by the authority given him at the last meeting on 30 November 1813, he had made arrangements for a Union between this Grand Chapter and the Grand Chapter over which HRH the Duke of Kent formerly presided; those arrangements had been made in such a way as to 'render the connexion between the Grand Chapter and the United Grand Lodge as intimate as the circumstances of the case would permit'.
>
> He further reported that the Duke of Sussex had organised the opening not only of this Chapter but also, in a separate Chamber, the members of the other Chapter had convened and that as soon as business finished both were to meet in a third Chamber to constitute a United Grand Chapter.
>
> It was further resolved that a Committee be formed consisting of the three Grand Principals and eight named members (who were not listed) for purpose of auditing and addressing concerns of the Supreme Grand Chapter.

It was ordered that minutes of this and previous meeting be printed to transmit to all Chapters.

Communication having been received from the members of the other Grand Chapter announcing that they were ready to proceed, Companion Ezra was deputed to go to the other Grand Chapter to inform them that this Grand Chapter would soon meet them.

It should be noted, for purposes of further clarification, as already discussed in Part I, that although the statement above reads: '[. . .] and the Grand Chapter over which HRH the Duke of Kent formerly presided;' no such Grand Chapter of the Antients ever existed and the terminology used in the second paragraph referring to 'the members of the other Chapter' more correctly reflects the standing of the Royal Arch in these two bodies, namely the Supreme Grand Chapter of Royal Arch Masons as an independent body, on the one hand and the Royal Arch companions members of the Antients Grand Lodge, on the other. Further references to an Antients' 'Grand Chapter' are a matter of expediency and 'historic licence'.

The minutes of the United Grand Chapter of Royal Arch Masons of England from the same day, 18 March 1817, read:

> The Members of the two former Grand Chapters having been summoned to meet this Day and the Chapters having been opened, the Members proceeded to the Chamber, where His Royal Highness the Duke of Sussex Most Excellent Zerubbabel was waiting to receive them. The United Grand Chapter was then formed as follows:

> | | |
> |---|---|
> | HRH Prince Augustus Frederick The Duke of Sussex, &c. &c. | MEZ |
> | Companion Thomas Harper, | MEH |
> | Companion John Dent, | MEJ |
> | Companion Dr Hemming, | Ezra etc., etc. |

The Most Excellent Zerubbabel announced that he had called this meeting 'with the purpose of forming a Junction of the Two Grand Chapters, and that laws and regulations might be enacted for the future regulation of the Order'.

It was resolved that the United Grand Chapter will consist of present and past Grand Officers of the Order, a few associate members of either former Grand Chapter, the three Principals of regular Chapters and Past Principals of Chapters who are subscribing members.

Also resolved that the Most Worshipful Grand Master shall be Zerubbabel; the Deputy Grand Master shall be Haggai and that the Most

Excellent Zerubbabel will appoint Joshua. Furthermore that the Grand
Secretaries shall be the Grand Scribe Ezra and that the Most Excellent
Zerubbabel will appoint all other Officers until regulations are in place. The
Grand Officers appointed were:

The Rt Hon Lord Dundas	H
Companion William Williams	J
W H White	E etc.

It was resolved that a committee be formed to consider precedence of
Grand Officers, 'to prepare and digest a code of Laws and Regulations for
the Grand Chapter [. . .]' This committee consisted of the three Grand
Principals and six members (appointed were Agar, Harper; Burckhardt;
Da Costa; Deans; and McCann) with any three members constituting a
quorum.

The events on 18 March 1817 are the culmination of the long-standing efforts of the
Duke of Sussex to bring the two former Royal Arch camps together. However, the
creation of the new 'United Grand Chapter' does not include new rules or regulations,
except for a phrase pronouncing a 'new relationship between the Craft and the Royal
Arch and the indivisible link between the two'. The new officers are only temporarily
appointed as described above.

Though no new rules are adopted or invented at the March meeting, on the 15
April 1817 the Committee appointed at that meeting reports that:

'...having carefully perused the Laws and Regulations, which were in
existence in the two former Grand Chapters, and, after the most mature
deliberation, they had selected such as appeared to them best calculated for
the Government of the Order.'

The report is approved and left in the Grand Secretary's office for inspection by the
companions until the next meeting of Supreme Grand Chapter, thus allowing for
additions and alterations as necessary. The Committee is authorised to continue and
report again.

At the time of writing, some confidential Royal Arch documents deposited
in the Grand Secretary's safe are in the process of being transferred to the
Library and Museum archives. Whilst the particular delicacy and confidentiality
of these documents, many relating to Royal Arch ritual, is not in dispute, there
has never hitherto been an explanation of why or how they may have been
transferred to the Grand Secretary's Office. The entry above clarifies the
circumstances.

Laws and Regulations

At the 20 May 1817 Convocation, presided over by the Duke of Sussex, it was resolved that, some alterations having been made to the laws, these should be confirmed and continue in force until 1 March 1819. A copy of the laws was attached to the 20 May Communication circulated to the Chapters. These 'Abstract Laws and Regulations for the Order of Royal Arch Masons' consisting of sixteen 8vo. pages, were printed as a pamphlet 'for the United Grand Chapter by W. P. Norris in Little Moorgate, London'. The date is given as the AL (Anno Lucis) date IƆƆDCCCXVII (5817) which equates to 1817. This is a change from the previous way of reaching the Anno Lucis date which, according to the old system and until now, was calculated by adding 4004 to the Anno Domini date. Now, in what becomes a simplification for the future, it is just 4000 that is added to the AD year. These first laws for the Royal Arch following the union of 1813, are addressed as follows:

The Supreme Grand and Royal Chapter,

To All the companions of that Exalted and Supreme Degree of Masonry, stiled

The Royal Arch,

Health, Peace and Good-will!

This follows a preamble and un-numerated rules and regulations under various headings:

The 'Regulations of the Order' establish the qualifications for membership of Grand Chapter to which 'are added, on account of their Rank in the Craft, Past Grand Masters, Past Deputy Grand Masters, Provincial Grand Masters [. . .] and Princes of the Blood Royal, and Peers of the Realm, who may be exalted in the Grand Chapter'.

This is followed by the 'Precedence of Officers' which indicate that the designated officers of the Grand Lodge, if properly qualified, automatically hold equivalent office in Grand Chapter.

Other regulations for the conduct of Grand Chapter include the following:

> 'That the Laws and Regulations for the Grand Lodge, while met, shall be adopted for the government of the Grand Chapter as far as the same are applicable, *mutatis mutandis*'.

Laws for the regulation of 'Private Chapters' confirm that all chapters that existed prior to 27 December 1813 are considered regular and qualify, subject to an application being received by Grand Chapter within six months, for a 'free of every expense' Charter of Confirmation to be attached to their Craft Warrants.

The mandatory link between the chapter and a craft lodge is emphasised and other administrative aspects – returns to Grand Chapter, fees payable, election procedures, etc., – are covered. These also include the requirement that no fewer 'than nine registered Royal Arch Masons be present' at the exaltation of a candidate.

As to the candidate, in addition to the requirement of his being a Master Mason of twelve months standing, the pre-union regulation of 1807 is repeated verbatim:

> [. . .] to this Order none ought to be admitted, but Men of the best character and education, open, generous, of liberal sentiment, and real philanthropists, who have passed through the probationary degrees of Masonry, have presided as Masters, been duly proposed and recommended by two or more Companions of the Chapter, balloted for and approved of [. . .].' LLMF,BE 94 GRA (ANC), April 1 1807, p. X)

The post-union laws and regulations of 1817, despite some obvious and necessary changes, are very similar, in parts identical, to the earlier and first nineteen enumerated 'Laws and Regulations of the Grand and Royal Chapter' published on 19 June 1778. Even the title remains the same. Furthermore the requirement for the candidate for exaltation to be a Master or Past Master of a craft lodge is repeated in the 1823 laws and was only removed from the Laws and Regulations published in 1843 (although the regulation had been frequently ignored in the preceding decades).

As already stated, the pre-union Royal Arch regulations of the Moderns were first published in 1778. There was a second revised edition in 1782 (often erroneously believed to be the first), and further editions in 1796 and 1807 (the same year as the publication of the 7th edition of *Ahiman Rezon*). (LLMF Ref: BE 94 GRA. ANC.1813/1807).

The first edition of *Ahiman Rezon* published in 1756 did not include any original Laws and Regulations but copied Spratt's Irish Constitutions of 1751. It continued to do so in later editions. These Constitutions of the Antients are meticulously analysed in Brother Cecil Adams' paper 'Ahiman Rezon, The Book of Constitutions' in *AQC*, 46, 1933, pp.239-306.

Post-union publications covering the laws and regulations of Royal Arch were issued in the following years: 1817; 1823, 1843; 1852; 1864; 1869; 1875; 1879; 1886; 1900; 1907; 1910; 1912; 1913; 1916; 1917; 1926; 1933; 1942; 1949, 1956; 1961; 1970; 1978; 1979; 1984; 1989; 1995; 1999; 2001; 2003; 2005; 2007; 2009; 2012 . Several of these dates are omitted from the listing that appears in the pages of the various Royal Arch regulations.

The Duke of Sussex again presides at the August Convocation. It is agreed that the Committee of 18 March should continue. They are given the power to settle the forms of the Charter of Constitution for Chapters and Grand Chapter certificates. Patterns for the apron are described in detail and illustrated, proposed and approved with some alterations (7 August). (Drawings for new robes for the Principals had been produced, proposed and were approved already in December 1777 by a Committee headed by Bartholomew Ruspini (1728-1813) who is best remembered as the founder of the Royal Masonic School for Girls).

Sussex at the UGLE

On 3 September 1817, The Duke of Sussex sends the following message, read before the United Grand Lodge of England at the Quarterly Communications that day:

> The Grand Master communicates to the Grand Lodge that the Order of the Royal Arch having been recognised and acknowledged by the Act of Union as part of Antient Masonry, he as head of both Grand Chapters [underlined by the author] existing prior to the Union of the Craft caused the members of those two bodies to be convened on the 18th day of March last when after the necessary preliminary arrangements they assembled in one apartment and a Junction was formed under the title of the United Grand Chapter of Royal Arch Masons of England. It being the wish of the members of this Order to render the connection between the Grand Lodge and the Grand Chapter as intimate as circumstances will permit, they have given a vote and rank in their meetings to some Officers of the Grand Lodge and they have as far as possible assimilated their Laws and Regulations to those of the Craft.
>
> The Grand Master derives great satisfaction from being enabled to make this communication and he trusts that the Grand Lodge will be disposed to do whatever may be necessary on their part to establish the connection between the two bodies.

The resolution of the United Grand Lodge of England on the same day confirms:

> 'That the Grand Lodge will, at all times, be disposed to acknowledge the Proceedings of the Grand Chapter, and, so long as their arrangements do not interfere with the Regulations of the Grand Lodge, and are in conformity with the Act of Union, they will be ready to recognise, facilitate, and uphold the same'.

The phrase 'he as head of both Grand Chapters' in line 3 above is curious in the knowledge, as already explained under the heading of 18 March 1817 above, and in Part I of this book, that there was no such body as a Grand Chapter so far as the Antients were concerned. The appointment of equivalent Grand Officers in both the

Craft and Royal Arch is of potential embarrassment to Craft Grand Officers who are not yet Royal Arch Masons and who thus cannot be appointed to an equivalent grand rank in the Royal Arch.

Nine Excellent Masters

The Grand Scribes are ordered to write to lodges whose members were last appointed as one of the 'Nine Excellent Masters' requesting the return forthwith of the jewels to Grand Chapter (5 November).

The Antients Grand Lodge Committee had been created in 1792, consisting of nine 'Excellent Masters' also known as the 'Nine Worthies'. Their function was to promote the uniformity of the ritual and ceremonial amongst the Lodges. Members of the Committee were selected from brethren nominated by lodges in the City of London and Westminster. They were appointed annually and reported on their activities to Grand Lodge on a regular basis. They are not to be confused with any link to the Royal Arch and they were not the representatives of an Antients' Grand Chapter, which, to be emphasised again, never existed.

A Nine Excellent Masters' jewel had been specially minted for presentation to the members of the Antients Grand Lodge Committee and it was these jewels that the Grand Scribes ordered the return of on 5 November 1817. The beautiful 'Nine Worthies' silver jewel depicts a well-engraved scene of a group of operative masons at work on the obverse and a Mason descending into a vault, on the reverse. Frederick Smyth in his *A Reference Book for Freemasons* suggests that the Antients, in selecting the title of 'Nine Worthies', may have been inspired by the nine classic 'Princes', also known by the same collective title, namely: Jeshua, Hector, David, Alexander, Judas Maccabaeus, Julius Caesar, Arthur, Charlemagne and Guy of Warwick. The 'Nine Worthies' ceased their duties at the Union in 1813 (Frederick Henry Smyth, *A Reference Book for Freemasons*, London, QCCC Ltd 1998 p. 204).

A Committee for General Purposes is appointed by the Supreme Grand Chapter to scrutinise and recommend petitions for charters. This committee consists of the three Grand Principals and nine additional members: Thomas Harper; Burckhardt; Da Costa; Meyrick; Deans; McCann; Moore; Broadfoot, and Willis. Any three of these are to constitute a quorum. (5 November).

The Committee of General Purposes is comprised of members appointed by the First Grand Principal and others elected by Grand Chapter from amongst the present and past First Principals. It has no executive powers and is intended to formulate policy and enquire into matters referred to it by either the First Grand Principal or the Grand Chapter. A rough minute book of this committee is housed in the Library and Museum (LLMF, 'Minute Book of the Royal Arch Committee of General Purposes', GBR 1991, SGC 1/1/16) and combines the rough minutes both of the Grand Chapter convocations from 13 May 1818 and those of the Committee of General Purposes on 1 November 1821, 5 February 1822 (there are no minutes taken on this particular occasion but four members are named as being present), 26 February, 1 April, 6 May, 4 and 11 November, 11 December 1822 and 16 January 1823 (though, for some reason, only Thomas Harper is present at this last meeting and consequently no business is conducted).

William Henry White is appointed Grand Scribe Ezra, replacing H J Da Costa (for foreign correspondence) and the Reverend Samuel Hemming, both having been appointed as joint Grand Scribes in 1813.

August 1817 Supreme Grand Royal Arch Chapter of Scotland is founded in Edinburgh, notwithstanding the opposition of the Grand Lodge of Scotland and totally independent of it.

In the Craft this, the Centenary Year of the traditional foundation of the premier Grand Lodge of England, on 24 June 1717, is allowed to pass without note.

1818 *Emily Bronte born in Yorkshire; Netherlands and England sign treaty against illegal slave-handling; Piccadilly Circus is constructed in London.*

Eight companions offer their services as stewards for the Grand Festival of the Order to be held on 13 May 1818. These include Hon W. Shirley of the Restoration Chapter (4 February). (LLMF, GBR 1991 ECM/700 A19882).

More Chapters identify the lodges to which they wish to be attached in order to obtain new charters (4 February).

According to the 12 May minutes, the missing jewel for Lodge 301 was in the hands of Mr Richard Bailey who was expelled from the Craft and promised to send the jewel to Supreme Grand Chapter. Eight of the nine jewels were recovered in 1817and are on display at the Library and Museum of Freemasonry in London. It is not possible to determine whether the missing jewel was the one originally in the hands of Mr Bailey.

The Annual Festival, the first since the union, chaired by HRH the Duke of Sussex, is attended by seventy-two companions. (13 May).

Special Committee consisting of the three Grand Principals and Da Costa; Burckhardt; White; Gill; Moore; Thompson and Cummings, are appointed to conduct 'proper' installation ceremonies of present and past Principals of London chapters that were not already installed, emphasising the importance of the installation ceremony (*vide* 1933 below re standardisation of the installation ritual). (13 May).

All Grand Officers are re-appointed by the Duke of Sussex on the understanding that it is not to be regarded as a precedent. (13 May).

The two Jewels of the 'Nine Excellent Masters' required from Lodges No. 301 and No. 37 have still not been returned. (13 May).

A pattern for the regular meetings of the Supreme Grand Chapter is established and it is decided that the Quarterly Convocations are to be held in February, May, August and November. It is also decided that the Annual Investiture is to take place on the day following that of the Craft. (13 May).

William Finch (1772-1818), a controversial but influential Masonic populist, officially regarded as a charlatan and impostor, dies. Famously associated with the Chapter of St James, London (now No. 2) where three companions were refused joining membership in 1808, because they had been irregularly exalted by Finch.

1819 *Princess Alexandrina Victoria (future Queen Victoria) christened in Kensington Palace; Sir Stamford Raffles founds Singapore; 'Peterloo Massacre' takes place in Manchester.*

The committee formally named as 'the Committee for General Purposes', addresses itself to the 'United Grand Chapter', although Grand Chapter refers to itself as 'Supreme Grand Chapter of Royal Arch Masons'. (3 February).

It is agreed that current Laws and Regulations of 1817 continue in effect until 1 May 1820.

A decision is taken that the installation of the Principals of Chapters not yet installed (as per the resolution taken 13 May 1818) is to be completed by 11 May 1819. (3 February).

Two committees are formed, one for each of the former Grand Chapters, to audit the respective accounts and when completed to unite as one committee. (February 3). The companions nominated to the two committees, which are to meet for the first time on 17 February 1819, are:

Burckhardt	Harper
Hemming	McCann
Rawlins	Willis
Deans	Broadfoot
Thompson	Satterley

In the meeting of 3 February, the Quarterly Convocation of 12 May is declared a Festival. Nine Stewards are stipulated, but only seven offer their services and are appointed.

The Committee of General Purposes is appointed for the ensuing twelve months. It is decided that the Committee is to consist of the three Grand Principals and nine nominated members.

W H White as Scribe E, and Edwards Harper as Scribe N, are re-appointed for another twelve months. It has often been reported that the two companions, who were also joint Grand Secretaries of the United Grand Lodge of England, were frequently at loggerheads. (12 May).

William Williams (1774-1839), Provincial Grand Master for Dorset, resigns as Second Grand Principal. (4 August).

The Committee of the United Grand Chapter of the Royal Arch Masons of England appointed in May makes its first report, consisting mainly of recommendations for Charters to be granted. The report is confirmed at the 3 November Convocation. (29 October).

Several companions offer their services as Stewards for the Grand Festival of the order on 12 May 1819, including William H White citing his membership of the Restoration Chapter No. 1 (see Part I, p.26)

William Williams is replaced as Second Grand Principal by John Aldridge. (3 November).

1820 *Death of George III; accession of The Prince Regent as George IV; the House of Lords passes a bill to grant George IV a divorce from Queen Caroline, but due to public pressure the bill is dropped.*

In the 1820s a number of Chapters in the provinces write to the Supreme Grand Chapter requesting guidance on ritual, which had not been forthcoming since 1817. Initial steps are taken, looking into uniform working for the Royal Arch.

The only Quarterly Convocation meeting of the United Grand Chapter for the year is held in May. Officers of Grand Chapter for the ensuing year are declared. (12 May).

The Committee for General Purposes is re-appointed for twelve months and recommends that 'the office of Director of Ceremonies be added to list of Officers of Grand Chapter'.

The rank and precedence of a Chapter is henceforth to be determined by that of the Lodge to which the Chapter is attached.

No public processions to take place without dispensation from Supreme Grand Chapter.

A decision is taken that the Royal Arch Laws and Regulations are to continue in force until May 1821. (8 May).

1821 *George IV is crowned; Census Year would reveal that half the population enumerated to be under twenty years old; Tories win the General Election; Bank of England, now post-war, returns to the gold standard.*

The Committee of General Purposes is appointed to inspect new applications from chapters to be enrolled in the new Grand Chapter. (5 November).

United Grand Chapter of England meets under that title for the last time. No announcement made on the change of name, created by dropping the word 'United'. (7 November).

Chapters which have conformed to the regulations of the United Grand Chapter, and attached themselves to the Lodges specified by numbers, are listed. The list, which appears at the end of the published minutes, starts with No. 2 St James's Chapter, London and ends with No. 701 Chapter of Original Light, Mansfield. A total of 106 Chapters are registered on the new roll, of which fourteen are in London. By this, for example, Restoration Chapter No.1 in London is thence listed as No. 43. (7 November).

The Committee for General Purposes recommends the following regulations. (7 November):

- A candidate under the age of twenty-three not to be admitted.
- Cost of a Grand Chapter Certificate to be reduced from 10/6 (ten shillings and six pence) to 7/6 (seven shillings and six pence).
- Several motions to reduce fees for exaltation are negated.

1822 *Visit of King George IV to Scotland; William Reading becomes the last person to be hanged for shoplifting; Construction of the Royal Pavilion in Brighton is completed.*

The new title 'Supreme Grand Chapter of Royal Arch Masons of England' is used formally at the Quarterly Convocation. (6 February).

May 1822 is established as the last date by which chapters are to inform Supreme Grand Chapter of the lodge to which they are to be attached. In February there are still ninety chapters that are on record as being in default of informing Grand Chapter. (May).

Drawings for jewels to be worn by officers of private chapters is approved. (8 May).

Accounts, compiled by Samuel Hemming, of the Supreme Grand and Royal Chapter of Royal Arch Masons of England and its successor, the Supreme Grand Chapter of England during the years 1813-14 and later 1818-23, are deposited with the United Grand Lodge of England Library. (23 May).

1823 *George III's personal library of 65,000 volumes etc. offered to the British Museum; the death penalty is abolished.*

Royal Arch Constitutions of 1823 are published, following the end of the period of extension of the Laws and Regulations of 1817. The new *Laws and Regulations* is entitled 'Laws and Regulations for the Order of Royal Arch Masons. Revised and Amended by the Supreme Grand Chapter', (London: Printed for Supreme Grand Chapter by Comp. Laurence Thompson, 1823).

This contains nine regulations in total. It includes rules concerning the work of Provincial Grand Superintendents and private chapters, new candidates, certificates, and regalia such as aprons, collars, sashes and jewels. It contains plates illustrating aprons and officers' jewels. The principal sojourner has the right to appoint the two assistant sojourners (Rule 7 of Private Chapters).

A list of Chapters is also given in the new Rules and Regulations. The last chapter on the list is Chapter of Freedom No. 733, Burnley, Lancashire.

During this year, a rule is established stating that it is not necessary for a companion holding an office in a chapter to have held the same type of office in a Craft lodge.

At the back of the new Rules and Regulations is an 'Index of Chapters', where chapters are grouped according to geographical location, showing:

- London, with 17 Chapters and:
- Provinces, which include: Berkshire 1; Cheshire 9; Lancashire 38; South Wales 1; Scotland 6;
- Chapters in Regiments, include: 17th Light Dragoons No. 36; 81st on Foot No. 406; 14th on Foot No. 432.
- Chapters on 'Foreign Stations', include: Barbados, Jersey, Malta; total 16 Chapters.

The Grand Lodge of Free and Accepted Masons of England According to the Old Institutions is founded in Wigan, as a continuation of the Antients Grand Lodge of 1751. A later endeavour was made to form a Royal Arch Grand Chapter in 1842 (*vide* 1842 below).

The report presented by the Committee of General Purposes on the amendments to the laws, including the requirement for a candidate for exaltation to be a Master Mason of 12 months standing, is confirmed. The requirement for a candidate to have 'presided as Master' of his Craft Lodge is also maintained under the heading 'Candidates &c'. (8 May).

Passing the Chair

The new regulation no longer requiring a candidate for the Royal Arch to have been an Installed Master of a Craft Lodge meant that the custom of 'Passing the Chair', an invented ceremony for such qualification alone first practiced in the second half of the 18th century, could now be dispensed with. This ceremony entailed a mere symbolic installation of a Brother into the Master's chair, giving him no associated benefits other than a salutary lesson and the modes of recognition special to an Installed Master, but allowed him now to become a Royal Arch Mason. Nonetheless, as pointed out in detail in Bernard Jones' article 'Passing the Chair' (*AQC* 70, 1957, pp. 33-53), the ceremony was persistently carried out in Lodges throughout England as late as the 1850s. However, many chapters ignored the ceremony and accepted candidates into the Royal Arch that had not 'passed the chair'.

1824 *The Anglo-Dutch Treaty, resolving issues relevant to the British occupation of Dutch properties during the Napoleonic Wars, is signed in London; the romantic poet George Gordon Byron, 6th Baron Byron (born 1788), dies on 19 April.*

It is ordered that a signature book for Principals in the London district should be provided. (5 May).

It is ordered that a Register of all Principals should be kept. (3 November).

1825 *Cotton Mills Regulation Act establishes a maximum 12-hour day for children under 16; Stockton and Darlington Railway opens with engineer George Stephenson driving; The first horse-drawn omnibuses are established in London.*

Prince Frederick, Duke of York and Albany (d. 1827), is exalted at an Especial Grand Chapter presided over by his brother the Duke of Sussex. The meeting is attended by seventy companions and dignitaries from Ireland and Scotland. Following his exaltation, the Duke of York is made Past Grand Zerubbabel. Robert Dundas, 2nd Viscount Duncan of Camperdown (1785-1859) is exalted at the same ceremony. (19 March).

A vote of thanks by the Supreme Grand Chapter is given to the St James Chapter for use of their robes in the exaltation ceremony. At this ceremony at Freemasons' Hall, Great Queen Street, London, the carpet presented by the Duke of Sussex is also first used. (19 March).

The Rev George Adam Browne (1774-1843), credited with being the creator of the current Royal Arch ritual, is appointed Grand Superintendent for Huntingdonshire and Cambridgeshire.

Richard Carlile (1790 - 1843)

Richard Carlile publishes the first edition of his *Manual of Freemasonry* (Richard Carlile, *Manual of Freemasonry*, London, Reeves & Turner, 1825). This exposure, which dedicates a considerable section to the Royal Arch ritual at the time, had previously appeared in weekly issues in Carlile's 'Republican' magazine between 1819 and 1826. An exposure may be defined as a spurious and unauthorised disclosure of Masonic ritual, usually in the form of a catechism. The most important early exposure was Samuel Prichard's *Masonry Dissected* first published on 20 October 1730.

Although an exposure, namely an unauthorised version of the ritual, Carlile's 'Manual' was used extensively in Masonic circles as a substitute for a ritual book. For this reason, this publication should be placed in context with the later Chapter of Promulgation, formed in 1835 and Claret's Royal Arch ritual of 1845 (*vide* 1845 below).

Richard Carlile, a journalist, radical reformer and champion of free-speech, was born in Devon. Although the author of a multitude of books and pamphlets, his *Manual of Freemasonry* is his only book still readily available to this day. The exposure, which went into many editions, was first written in the format of letters addressed to the leaders of the various Orders. Those detailing the three Craft degrees are addressed to William Williams, the Provincial Grand Master for Dorset at the time, those covering the Royal Arch are addressed to the Duke of York (see above), and those on the subject of the degrees beyond the Craft and Royal Arch, to the Duke of Sussex. Carlile's work included the first published exposures of the ritual of some of the degrees beyond the craft, referred to as the 'Higher degrees of Freemasonry'. The later editions of the exposure begin with 'The Key-Stone of the Royal Arch', an introductory twelve pages that have little to do with the Order. The full title page, however, reveals the scope of the book. It reads:

Manual of Freemasonry;
Part I.
Containing the First Three Degrees-
with an introductory key-stone to the Royal Arch.

Part II.
containing the Royal Arch and Knights Templar Druids,
with an explanatory introduction to the Science.

Part III
containing the Degrees of Mark Man, Mark Master, Architect, Grand
Architect, Scotch Master or Superintendant, Secret Master, Perfect Master,
Intimate Secretary, Intendant of the Buildings, Past Master, Excellent
Masons, Super-Excellent Masons, Nine Elected Knights, Elect of Nine,
Priestly Order of Israel, &c., &c., &c.
With an Explanatory Introduction to the Science and
A Free Translation of some of the Sacred Scripture names.

The many editions of Carlile's exposure appear in a variety of covers, usually green or red gilt decorated with Masonic emblems also on the spine and a variation in the titles.

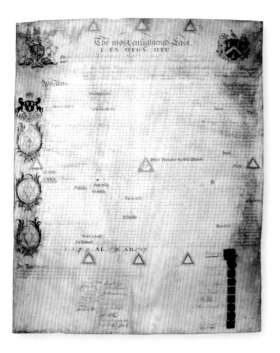

Left **Charter of Compact 1766**
'On 22 July 1766, the Charter of Compact was signed by Cadwallader, 9th Lord Blayney (1720-75) and senior members of the Royal Arch'.

Above **Articles of Union 1813 Page 2**
'The Articles of Union did not provide for the creation of an alternative body to cater for the needs of Royal Arch Masons.'

Below **Articles of Union 1813 Page 1**
'On 25 November 1813, the Grand Masters of both grand lodges met at Kensington Palace with six deputies [...] to sign the Articles of Union'.

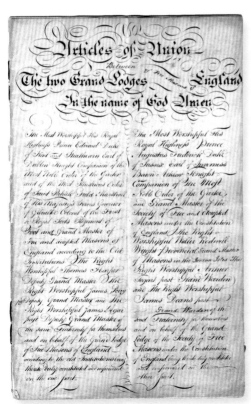

Above **Articles of Union 1813 Page 7**
'The original document [...] is extant in the Library and Museum of Freemasonry in London. It consists of a total of ten pages with text on both sides'

Left: **Grand Registrar's Bag** 'A copy of the Articles of Union [...] until recently, was carried into Grand Lodge at each Quarterly Communication by the Grand Registrar, in the special satchel on display at the Museum of Freemasonry'.

Above **John Harris Royal Arch Tracing Boards [c1890].**
Pair, one depicting layout of a Chapter, the other symbolic. 'The arch of the rainbow, identified in the Royal Arch, is symbolic of the covenant between God and man'.

Top to bottom

Antients Grand Lodge 'Nine Worthies' Jewel 1792
'The beautiful 'Nine Worthies' silver jewel depicts a well-engraved scene of a group of operative masons at work on the obverse and a Mason descending into a vault, on the reverse'.

Antients Royal Arch Jewel (Thomas Harper) 1821
'The same Thomas Harper, London jeweller, was intensely involved with both the Moderns' and the Antients' Grand Lodges leading to the union of 1813'.

Medal with Prince of Wales (Grand Master) & Duke of Clarence (Patron of the HRA) 1802
Relief busts of George Augustus Frederick (1762-1830), later King George IV and William Henry (1765-1837), later King William IV, both wearing Masonic jewels. The medal was commissioned by Birmingham architect and sculptor, W Bro William Hollis (1763-1843) of St Paul's Lodge No 38 (now 43) and made by the medallists Peter Kempson and Samuel Kindon.

Moderns Royal Arch Jewel (Thomas Harper/owned by William Hayes) 1791
'The jewels have Harper's name engraved on them or are identified by the presence of his initials 'T H' (not to be confused with the 'T' placed above the 'H' in the 'triple tau').

Left **Hand painted silk Royal Arch Apron of companion J T Spry c1790** '[...] their small decorated aprons and sashes twinkling in the light of the host of candles of the two vast gilt chandeliers.'

Above **Hand painted rounded leather Royal Arch Apron of companion William Bud c1818**
'Patterns for the apron are described (in the new Royal Arch laws and regulations) in detail and illustrated, proposed and approved with some alterations (7 August 1817)'. Standardisation of Royal Arch aprons took many more years to be fully introduced.

Five standard principal cloth banners of a Royal Arch Chapter
'The first set of five banners are placed in the East behind the thrones of the Principals. They are, are blue, purple, scarlet, and white and depict an ox, a man, a lion and an eagle with the Triple Tau centrally placed as a fifth banner'.

Shield shaped Royal Arch Banners of the Old Union Chapter No 46 c 1880
'Twelve Banners of all the tribes of Israel are represented by Characters figurative of the prophecies of the Patriarch Jacob.'

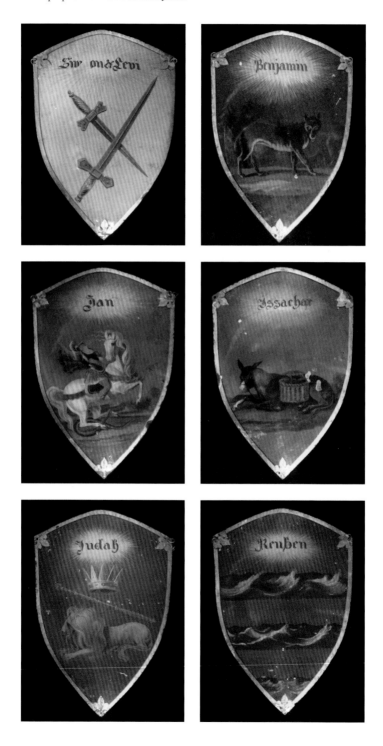

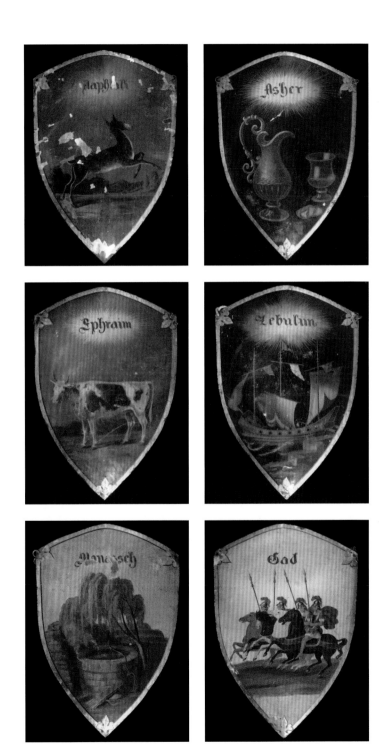

Standard modern cloth banners displayed in Royal Arch Chapters

'The twelve banners in the body of the chapter on either side of the altar, are
derived from ensigns that were borne by the twelve Tribes of Israel [. . .]'

Lau: Dermott, del.

Plan.

A Scale of ten Cubits.

A Scale of ten Cubits: (or, 240 Inches) according to Josephus.

Above **Hand drawn frontis by Laurence Dermott to the Antients Royal Arch Register 1783**
'On 5 November 1783 [. . .] the minutes, all manuscript documents elaborately illuminated with Lawrence Dermott's designs, are attached to the Grand Chapter Register.'

Right **Royal Arch membership certificate of companion George Bailey, Domatic Chapter No 266, 1841**
'The Grand Master allowed his private seal of arms to be used on certificates until the great seal of the Grand Lodge should be prepared (December 1813)'.

Left **Royal Arch Charter of 'Chapter of Charity' No 323, 1824**
'[. . .] all chapters that existed prior to 27 December 1813 are considered regular and qualify for a 'free of every expense' Charter of Confirmation to be attached to their Craft Warrants (May 1817).'

Right **Masonic Offering to HRH The Duke of Sussex M W Grand Master (1813-1843), 1838** Commemorating the Completion of 25 Years as Grand Master. Made by Robert Garrard of London in 1837. Corinthian Columns support a dome crowned with the figure of Apollo surrounded by the twelve signs of the Zodiac. Seated figures represent Astronomy, Geometry, Sculpture and Architecture. Commemorative inscriptions show Solomon receiving the plan of the Temple from his father, King David and the completion of the Temple in Jerusalem with Solomon dedicating it to God's service.

Above **Enlargement of the panel at the back of the 'Sussex Plate' and drawn illustration**
The remaining panel in the back represents the Act of Union. It shows the two fraternities of 1813 headed by the two Grand Masters, (the Dukes of Sussex and Kent) surrounded by their respective Grand Officers.

Above Three Principals of Chapter of Charity No 323, Stockport in full Royal Arch Regalia c1893
'A R Hewitt addresses the Supreme Grand Chapter on 'Early Royal Arch Regalia' (9 February 1970)'.

Above Liverpool earthenware jug with Royal Arch
and Knights Templar printed transfer c1790
'[...] many of the historical aspects of the Royal
Arch, such as, for example, the close association of the
Royal Arch to the Order of the Knights Templar'.

Right First Grand Principal Jewel worn by Albert
Edward, Prince of Wales (later Edward VII)
1874-1901
'Drawings for jewels to be worn by officers is
approved (8 May 1822)'.

Above **Cadwallader, 9th Lord Blayney (1720-75)**
[...] on 22 July 1766, the Charter of Compact was signed by Lord Blayney and senior members of the Royal Arch. At last, members of the premier Grand Lodge could practice Royal Arch masonry openly [...].

Right **Dr Robert Thomas Crucefix (1797-1850)**
[...] Crucefix is exalted in the Naval and Military Royal Arch Chapter No. 40 in Edinburgh in 1830, a year after his initiation into the Craft.'

Left **HRH Prince Augustus Frederick, the Duke of Sussex (1773-1843)**
'[...] Sussex, in establishing single-handedly, so to speak, the standing of the Royal Arch in 1813, is the most manifest aspect of the dependence of the Order on the United Grand Lodge of England'.

Below left **Francis Edward Rawdon-Hastings, Earl of Moira (1754-1826)**
'The Earl of Moira's intervention, as crucial and vital as it was, caused misgivings not least due to his perceptible naiveté, if not ignorance.'

Below **Thomas Dundas, 2nd Earl of Zetland (1795–1873)**
'[...] Zetland is elected and installed First Grand Principal in 1844, having acted as Pro First Grand Principal since 1841. He is to serve until his death in 1870.

The changes to the publisher's address are a guide to the editions, which are normally published undated. The 1843 edition claims on the title page to be a 'new edition, revised and corrected by a Royal Arch Mason'.

1826 *University College London is founded; the first Anglo-Burmese War breaks out; the Zoological Society of London is formed; the Tories win the general election; the first Cowes Regatta on the Isle of Wight takes place.*

The Third Principal of the chapter is required to be an Installed Master of a Craft lodge. (May).

The Second Principal of a Chapter is now required to be an Installed third Principal and the first Principal an Installed Second Principal (August). Due to a shortage of Royal Arch masons, these regulations could not always be observed.

1827 *The Duke of Wellington becomes Commander-in-Chief; George Canning succeeds Lord Liverpool as British Prime Minister; the Treaty of London is signed by France, Britain, and Russia: it demands that the Turks agree to an armistice with Greece.*

The Duke of Sussex issues a warrant for a Lodge or Board of Installed Masters to teach and install those not properly installed. The eleven members include Meyrick, Grand Registrar; W H White, Grand Secretary; John Bott, Junior Grand Deacon; the Worshipful Master of the Grand Stewards Lodge; the Past Master of Lodge No. 1 and other Past Masters. (6 February).

The Province of Lancashire having been split in 1826 following the Wigan debacle, a new Provincial Grand Chapter of East Lancashire is founded with John Crossley as the Grand Superintendent. (7 February).

A letter, signed by W H White and Edwards Harper, joint Grand Secretaries, is circulated to all Masters, with a copy of the warrant for the Lodge of Installed Masters authorised by the Duke of Sussex printed on the reverse, giving the three dates for the meetings of this newly warranted lodge: 17, 22 and 28 December respectively and requesting Past Masters to attend (10 December).

Chapter of Sincerity No. 261, Taunton, Somerset, purchases a tracing board which incorporates a rainbow in its design. The arch of the rainbow, identified in the Royal Arch, is symbolic of the covenant between God and man.

1829 *The Catholic Emancipation Act is passed; Robert Peel's civilian police force is set up in London.*

The Supreme Grand Royal Arch Chapter of Ireland is constituted for its fifty-three chapters. (11 June).

1830 *King George IV dies and is succeeded by his younger brother William IV; Peter Bosse is the last person in England to stand in the pillory for perjury; The Beerhouse Act liberalises regulations on the brewing and sale of beer by individuals.*

Dr Robert Thomas Crucefix (1797-1850) is exalted in the Naval and Military Royal Arch Chapter No. 40 in Edinburgh, a year after his initiation into the Craft.

1832 *The Reform Bill is passed, changing voting from an anachronistic privilege to a much more representative male property-owning right; the electric telegraph is invented by Morse.*

Three Peers of the Realm, James, Marquess of Salisbury, James, Marquis of Abercorn and Frederick John, Lord Monson, are exalted at an emergency meeting of the Grand Chapter by the acting First Grand Principal the Rev. George Adam Brown [sic] . This is the last exaltation ceremony carried out in Grand Chapter. As noted in Part I, Grand Chapter had played a dual role from the start acting both as a regulatory body and as an ordinary chapter undertaking exaltations. It did so intermittently until 1832. (2 May).

1833 *Britain invades the Falkland Islands; The Factory Act forbids employment of children below age of nine.*

Committee for Standardization

Notice is given in the Grand Chapter by E Companion Arthur Thiselton that at the next meeting a motion will be proposed for a committee to be formed to consider 'the necessity of promulgating a form, for the Installation of the Three Principals' in addition to making necessary alterations to the duties of the Principal Sojourner and the traditional Lectures (6 February).

The use of the word 'promulgating' in the minutes quoted has caused some confusion with regard to the date of the establishment of the Chapter of Promulgation. The Chapter of Promulgation was chartered on 6 May 1835 *(vide* 1835 below). All relevant committees and meetings prior to this date are <u>not</u> to be considered as those in or of the Chapter of Promulgation.

It is accordingly resolved in June that a committee consisting of nine members be appointed to consider the standardisation of the installation ceremony of the three Principals and other ceremonies of the Order. The committee is to consist of the three Grand Principals and six companions nominated by the MEZ. Three members are to constitute a quorum. Details are published in the 5 February 1834 report (see below). (15 June).

An amendment to reduce the number of members in the above mentioned committee from nine to seven was rejected. (15 June).

In this year the engraving by Brother John Harris is published of the Duke of Sussex formally seated upon his Grand Master's throne.

1834 *Slavery abolished in British possessions, following on the abolition of the slave trade in 1807; the Hansom Cab is patented by Joseph Hansom, replacing the Hackney Carriage.*

The year sees the publication of the Royal Arch Rules and Regulations that became popularly known as the '1834 Revision'.

The names of the nine members of the committee appointed in June 1833 are now published in the minutes and comprise the three Grand Principals:

The Duke of Sussex,	MEZ,
Lawrence Dundas, 1st Earl of Zetland (1766-1839),	MEH
John Ramsbottom (1810-1845), MP,	MEJ

and six additional companions all nominated by the MEZ, namely

John Lambton, 1st Earl of Durham (1792-1840), Provincial Grand
    Superintendent of Durham;
Colonel Charles Kemeys Kemeys Tynte (1778-1860), Provincial Grand
    Superintendent of Somersetshire;
Rev George Adam Browne, Provincial Grand Superintendent of
    Cambridgeshire;
William Henry White, Grand Scribe Ezra;
John Christian Burckhardt, Past Grand Principal Sojourner; and
Thomas Field Savory, Past Grand Standard Bearer. (5 February).

From now on, decisions taken by the Grand Chapter are communicated to the companions by being published in the annual printed circular, which also incorporates insertions. This is evidenced in the minutes of Grand Chapter on 7 May 1834 when it is resolved that the 'several additions to and alterations in the laws made subsequently to the printing of the Laws of 1823, be inserted in the next circular and forwarded to the respective Chapters'. It should be noted that the next General Regulation for the Government of the Order of Royal Arch Masons was not published until 1843. (7 May).

On the same day, a Committee for General Purposes is elected for the ensuing twelve months, consisting of the Three Grand Principals and nine additional members which, it is resolved, is to 'be regularly summoned to meet one month before each Quarterly Convocation [. . .] and any three be a quorum' (7 May). This was amended at the next meeting to read ' [. . .] on the Wednesday previous to each Quarterly Convocation [. . .]'. (6 August).

Demonstrations

The first report to Grand Chapter by the committee appointed in June of the previous year, 1833, confirms they are 'prepared to communicate the result of their labours which have met with the entire concurrence and approval of His Royal Highness The Duke of Sussex, MEZ'.

It was resolved that the Grand Chapter should be 'summoned in classes to consider separately such portions of the Ceremonies as their qualifications and advancement in the Order and the Craft entitle them to participate in'. (5 November).

The decision not to publish any of the ritualistic details of the conclusions of the committee, but rely on demonstrations of the workings of the various degrees, is undoubtedly a major cause for the variations in the working of the ritual in the various provinces and the many chapters within them. An example is to be found in a rare manuscript text, approved by the Duke of Sussex (LLMF, 'Untitled document', MS, GBR 1991 Supreme Grand Chapter 1/1/3/1/10 *inter alia*) which he signed when visiting the home of Colonel Thomas Wildman in Nottinghamshire. This, which was never circulated or published, reads:

> By a Law of the Grand Chap: no candidate can be received into the R.A. until he shall have been a M.M. of twelve months standing – If then a Candidate presents himself who is qualified in point of time and brings from his Lodge a Certificate to that effect, let the Princ. Sojr: be deputed to examine the Candidate in regard to his knowledge of the M.M. Degree, particularly whether he is conversant in the knowledge of the 5 points (of Fellowship) intimated by the Star in the Signet Ring of King Solomon whom we acknowledge both as the Head of Craft Masonry and the Founder of the R.A. – This examination is to prove the worthiness of the Candidate and it is in strict accordance with a Passage in the 2nd Chap: of the Book of Ezra v. 62 which was pointed out by our Illustrious Grand Principal at Kensington Palace – The passage states that when mustering the Children of the Captivity for their return from Babylon, those who could not find their Registry were excluded from the Priesthood.

> Approved *Augustus GM - Z*
> November 2nd 1834 Newstead
> Abbey Nottingham

At a special convocation of First Principals attended by PZs and Zs only, the recommendations of the Committee, having been read and explained to the companions present, were signed by the Duke of Sussex. (21 November).

Twenty years after its foundation, the Supreme Grand Chapter approves the new opening and closing and exaltation ceremonies in an endeavour to establish some uniformity in the various chapters throughout the Order. These are analysed in some detail by Bernard Jones in his *Freemasons' Book of the Royal Arch* (George Harrap, 1957, pp. 168-172). The five points of fellowship is introduced as the test for the admission of Master Masons to the third degree. A new password for an Installed Masters is established.

The report of the Committee is 'submitted to the Excellent Companions in portions according to their several and respective ranks and fully explained' at a further Special Convocation of Supreme Grand Chapter Presided by the M E Comp Rev G A Brown [sic]. The arrangements are approved and confirmed and thanks are expressed to Most Excellent Companion, 'the Rev G A Brown [sic] for his attention to the welfare and interest of the Order'. (25 November).

George Browne

These appear to be the only two instances where the name 'Browne' is misspelt in the minutes. Harry Mendoza covers in detail both the man and his accomplishment relevant to this period in Royal Arch history ('George Adam Browne - The 1834/5 Revision of the Royal Arch Ritual', *AQC*, 88, 1975, pp. 32-49). The rituals for the Royal Arch after 1834 are often credited to the Rev George Browne, though this is disputed by Mendoza in his article.

George Browne was initiated in 1796 in New Lodge No. 515, Cambridge, and was exalted in 1801 in the Royal Brothers Chapter No. 64. He played a senior role in Supreme Grand Chapter and was, as mentioned above, appointed the first Grand Orator (1813). He was the Provincial Grand Superintendent of Cambridgeshire from 1810 and of Suffolk from 1827. A fellow of Trinity College Cambridge, in 1815 he was appointed Grand Chaplain of the United Grand Lodge of England for one year and acted as the Duke of Sussex's personal Chaplain. He died on 4 July 1843, reportedly from a cold he caught when attending the Duke of Sussex's funeral, ten weeks earlier.

Statistics record a total of eighteen Chapters in London. This was considered to be a sufficient number for the capital and no additional Charters were granted for the next 50 years. (November). An example of a refusal to grant a charter for a new chapter is the petition of the Grand Master's Lodge No. 1, whose petition failed in 1839 and was only finally granted in 1886. This policy of limitation is not restricted to London: records indicate provinces where new Charters are refused from the capital if one or more Chapters already exist in the area.

1835 *Christmas becomes a national holiday; the Municipal Corporations Act is passed this year enabling Manchester, for example, to become a self-governing town; the first railway boom period starts in Britain; Melbourne, Australia, is founded.*

Lawrence Dundas, 1st Earl of Zetland (1766-1839), is appointed Pro First Grand Principal.

Royal Arch Ritual

The term 'lectures', here referring to the catechisms in the ritual and the addresses by the three Principals which follow their Installation, are instituted for the first time in 1835, as is the ceremony of installation itself. As explained in the Peterborough booklet ('Notes for a newly exalted Companion' *QCCC Ltd,* London, 1990), there is no official ritual for the Royal Arch in England to this day. Instead there are several different workings, each developed from two main workings commonly known as 'Domatic' and 'Aldersgate'. Before the union of the two Grand Lodges in 1813 the ritual seems to have been comprised of a short ceremony followed by a catechism. It was only twenty years after the union that the task of revision was seriously tackled. A new ritual was settled in 1835 and all chapters were ordered to use it. The exact wording adopted in 1835 is not known as it was never printed. John Belton suggested, in private correspondence, that this may be due to the fact that the Duke of Sussex knew that he would not be able to impose a written ritual to be followed by all chapters and rather than fighting a losing battle he devised the 'lecture tours' by competent teams throughout the English jurisdiction, demonstrating and teaching the new ritual. Not only does the Royal Arch ritual differ between chapters belonging to the Grand Chapter, the different Royal Arch Associations all have their own version. However, though the detailed wording sponsored by the different Ritual Associations today may vary, the message and legend are the same in all.

In a Grand Chapter meeting, it is resolved that a Special Chapter of Promulgation should be set up. (4 February).

Chapter of Promulgation

A charter is issued by HRH the Duke of Sussex, in his role as the ME Zerubbabel, for a Special Chapter of Promulgation to be 'a Committee or Chapter for Instruction and Promulgation in the several ceremonies of the Order' and 'to establish a conformity of practice and working throughout the Order'. (6 May).

Membership of this 'Committee or Chapter for Instruction and Promulgation' is increased to twenty seven. According to the charter, the following Companions were to be added to the original nine committee members:

Simon McGillivray,		Prov. G. Supt. for Canada
Lord H. John Spencer Churchill		" " " " "
David Pollock,		a G. Assistant Sojourner
William W. Prescott,		G. Treasurer
Richard Percival,		Past G. Assistant Sojourner
William Shadbolt,	/	[Past G. Sword Bearer]
John Bott,	/-	[Past G. Sword Bearer]
Sir Fredk. G. Fowke, Bart.,	/	[Past G. Sword Bearer]
Philip Broadfoot,		Past G Standard Bearer,

being nine Grand Officers and of the Chapter

William R G Key,	No. 7
Benjamin Lawrence,	8
John Fortune,	12
Charles Baumer,	21
Arthur L. Thiselton,	49
Henry Phillips,	109
Lawrence Thompson,	196
Samuel Staples,	218
Samuel M. Briggs,	580

being nine Principals or Past Principals of the Chair
Z. not being Grand Officers

The Chapter of Promulgation, originally chartered for six months, is seen as the culmination of the ritual revision of the Royal Arch that took place 1834-5. As already stated, the ritual and ceremonies of the Royal Arch had been neglected after the union of the two Grand Lodges in 1813 and even after the formation of the United Supreme Grand Chapter in 1817. Over the next decades, Chapters began to diverge in their ceremonies, and complaints were directed at Grand Chapter, asking for guidance. Finally, as described above, a Committee was charged with the task of clarifying and confirming the Royal Arch ceremonies. The final revisions of 1834-5 gave rise to what has been termed 'Sussex Ritual' (named after the Duke and not to be confused with the current ritual of the Provincial Grand Chapter of Sussex). This, *inter alia*, eliminated the ceremony of 'passing the veils' and removed all remaining overtly Christian elements. It also opened the Order to those who had not yet attained the chair of a Craft lodge. Until this year, the Royal Arch had been limited to Past Masters. The 'Sussex Ritual' became the recommended standard ritual. It is the present 'Perfect Ritual' (of which several versions exist!).

It should be noted that the need for a Chapter of Promulgation, which physically demonstrated the new ritual, was necessitated by the refusal of Supreme Grand Chapter to allow the revised rituals for the exaltation and installation ceremonies to be printed. Unlike the Craft, the ceremony of exaltation as practiced by the Chapters was reasonably standardised, which eliminated the need for a Chapter of Reconciliation. The aspect of the union relevant to the Royal Arch, namely the link with the Craft, was further clarified by the formation of the Chapter of Promulgation. Extensive correspondence in the archives of the Library and Museum of Freemasonry shows that there were difficulties to get delegates from cities such as Preston in Lancashire, Leeds in Yorkshire and Stockport in Cheshire to attend meetings in London intended to regulate Royal Arch ritual practice. On the other hand, an undated letter from the Rev George Adam Browne expresses his pleasure of the attendance, at a meeting of the Chapter of Promulgation, of the First Principal of Royal York Chapter, No. 81, Woodbridge, Suffolk (LLMF, 'Letters relating to the administration of the Supreme Grand Chapter', GBR 1991 HC 14/B/9 -15; 41).

At the Quarterly Convocation of the Grand Chapter in November 1835 it is reported that:

> Some misconception having arisen as to what are the ceremonies of our
> Order it is hereby resolved and declared that the ceremonies adopted and
> promulgated by Especial Grand Chapter on the 21st and 25th November,
> 1834, are the ceremonies of our Order, which it is the duty of every Chapter
> to adopt and obey' (4 November).

The 'misconceptions' referred to were the consequence of the objection of Dr Crucefix to the statement made by the Zerubbabel Elect, Companion Goldsworthy, that he was intending to conduct the affairs of Grand Chapter in accordance with the former Athol (or ancient) system, provoking the Grand Chapter to clearly state that it was the duty of every Chapter to conform to the 'Ceremonies of the Order' as agreed on 21 and 25 November 1834. It should be noted that this is contrary to the policy in the Craft, where the Grand Lodge will not interfere in matters of ritual.

1837 *William IV dies and Queen Victoria inherits the throne; compulsory civil registration of births, marriages and deaths in England and Wales commences.*

The Grand Chapter orders that the names of the three Grand Masters and the emblem of the Royal Arch shall be represented on the pedestal in Hebrew or Roman characters but not in Latin (3 May).

Supreme Grand Chapter donates £200 for the rebuilding of the Masonic Temple at Quetta in India following the disastrous earthquake.

Suggestion by George P de Rhe Philipe (Grand Director of Ceremonies in 1837) to invite George Aarons to explain possible changes to Royal Arch ritual to enhance its acceptability by those from all religious beliefs.

Provincial Grand Chapter of Devon conducts a ceremony of installation in Plymouth of several prominent Royal Arch Masons in a Chapter of Promulgation or Instruction in the spirit of the revisions of the ritual and regulations (July).

1838 *The coronation of Queen Victoria takes place in Westminster Abbey (June 28); the first ocean steamer, SS Great Western, departs for the U.S. for a journey of 14½ days.*

St George's Day is the 25th anniversary of the Duke of Sussex as Grand Master. The presentation is made of a massive silver table ornament. (23 April).

The joint Secretarial duties of W H White for the Moderns, and Edwards Harper for the Antients, terminates: W H White continues alone.

1839 *Britain captures Hong Kong; Kirkpatrick MacMillan creates the first true 'bicycle'.*

John George, 1st Earl of Durham (d.1840), is appointed Pro First Grand Principal, only to be replaced by Thomas, 2nd Earl of Zetland following his death.

All members of the Committee 'to form a digest of the Laws' are re-appointed (1 May).

All Chapters are required to make a return of subscribing members to the Grand Scribe Ezra before 1 May each year. (7 August).

1840 *Queen Victoria marries Prince Albert of Saxe-Coburg-Gotha; the last convicts landed in New South Wales, Australia ; 'Can-Can' becomes popular in France.*

The Duke of Sussex writes a letter addressed to the Grand Lodge of Prussia, expressing his gratitude at being made an Honorary Member. (17 January).

The Scottish Royal Arch ritual is standardised following the English '1834 Revision'.

1841 *First full census in Britain completed in which all names are recorded; populations are determined at: Britain: 18.5 million; USA: 17 million; Ireland: 8 million.*

Thomas, 2nd Earl of Zetland (d.1873), is appointed Pro First Grand Principal (until 1844 when he succeeds Sussex as First Grand Principal).

A proposal for quarterage for Charity payable by RA Masons is withdrawn.

Craft Regulation No. 241 permits the wearing of the Royal Arch jewel in Craft lodges (see also 1853 and 1884). This extends to jewels 'as shall appertain to or be consistent with those degrees which are recognised and acknowledged by and under the controul [sic] of the Grand Lodge'.

A patent is issued by Supreme Grand Chapter for the appointment of a Grand Superintendent, Sir Robert Bourchier Clarke, over the District Grand Chapter of Barbados.

1842 *Income Tax is reintroduced in Britain; the British Mines Act is passed, outlawing the employment of women and girls in the mines and supervising boy labour; the Copyright Act is passed.*

Petition to form a Grand Chapter is presented by the Royal Arch Chapter of Temperance, No. 1 to the Wigan Grand Lodge. (16 August).

Wigan Grand Chapter

In 1823 four Lancashire Lodges founded the Grand Lodge of Free and Accepted Masons of England According to the Old Institutions, reminiscent of the title of the Antients Grand Lodge preceding the Union in 1813. These four Lodges, centred in Wigan, had been expelled from the United Grand Lodge of England under circumstances beyond the scope of this book [see Norman Rogers 'The Grand Lodge in Wigan', *AQC*, 61, 1948, pp. 170-210]. The available evidence shows that the Royal Arch was worked in Craft lodges, culminating in a petition being presented to the Wigan Grand Lodge by the Royal Arch Chapter of Temperance, No. 1 on 16 August, 1842. It pleaded the formation of a Wigan Royal Arch Grand Chapter to govern the chapters in the area. Although a month earlier, on 27 July, the Grand Lodge of Wigan discussed the matter there are no further records of any developments or the formation of a Grand Chapter in Wigan. The Grand Lodge in (or of) Wigan ceased to exist in 1913.

This year revised regulations of the Royal Arch are agreed.

The Royal Masonic Benevolent Annuity Fund for men (RMAF) is founded.

1843 *The first Christmas card in England is sent; Euston station opens in London (1st October); the News of the World is first published.*

HRH the Duke of Sussex dies. (21 April).

The seventh edition of *Laws and Regulations* recommended by the Committee of Laws is adopted (1 February).

By the authority of The Grand Chapter, William Henry White, its Grand Scribe, publishes *General Regulations for the Government of the Order of Royal Arch Masons of England* (London: Printed by Thompson and Nias, 1843). (10 May).

The Marquess of Salisbury resigns as Second Grand Principal. (7 February).

The requirement to have been a Past Master of a Craft lodge before exaltation into a Royal Arch Chapter, established in Article II of the Abstracts of Laws for the Society of Royal Arch Masons in 1778, is removed from the regulations. The new Rule 20 states that 'no mason shall be exalted into this sublime degree unless he has been a master mason for twelve calendar months at least, of which satisfactory proof shall be given'.

A patent is issued by Supreme Grand Chapter for the appointment of a Grand Superintendent, Sir George Campbell Anderson, over the District Grand Chapter of the Bahamas (until 1863).

1844 *The Companies Act passed in Britain, stating that companies must register; YMCA is founded in London by Sir George Williams; the Polka dance is introduced to Britain.*

Thomas, 2nd Earl of Zetland, KT, is elected and installed First Grand Principal having acted as Pro First Grand Principal since 1841. He is to serve until his death in 1870.

1845 *The rubber band is patented by Stephen Perry; Tarmac laid for first time (in Nottingham); Kelly's Directories Published for the first time.*

Dr Robert Crucefix asserts in Grand Chapter that the Royal Arch is not a fourth degree but simply the perfection of the third and that any additional dues were unnecessary, causing controversy and extended debate (5 February).

This appears to be the beginning of the long, still on-going debate of the standing of the Royal Arch *vis-à-vis* the third degree. Crucefix had a tendency to be controversial and on more than one occasion found himself at loggerheads with the Masonic authorities; his acrimonious confrontations with the Duke of Sussex are well known and recorded (see 'Robert Thomas Crucefix, 1788-1850' by Richard S E Sandbach, *AQC*, 102, 1989, pp. 134-163).

Publication of George Claret's Royal Arch ritual *The Ceremonies of the Holy Royal Arch also of Passing the Veils* (George Claret, London 1845).

George Claret (1783-1850)

George Claret is immortalised in Masonic literature because he was the author, printer and publisher of the earliest post-union ritual that was not an exposure. He is credited with the standardisation of the Royal Arch ritual, which had previously been practiced in a multitude of versions in the different chapters. Notwithstanding his undoubted achievements, Claret's Masonic career is spotted with dissension and financial embroilments. In his inaugural address as Master of Quatuor Coronati Lodge (*AQC*, 87, 1974, pp. 1-22), Roy A Wells goes into great detail about every aspect of Claret's life and various publications. Claret was the author of a dozen works, including the first official Craft ritual *The Ceremonies of Initiation, Passing and Raising*, published in 1838, popularly referred to as 'The Claret Ritual'. He also published the Royal Arch ritual in 1845, entitled *The Ceremonies of the Holy Royal Arch Also of Passing the Veils*. There is relatively little known of Claret in a Royal Arch context. He was exalted in December 1813 and seems never to have progressed beyond the second Principal's chair.

It is interesting to place his publication on the Royal Arch in the context of the Chapter of Promulgation formed in 1835 and Carlile's exposure of 1825 (see above). Keith Tallon, in his yet unpublished 2013 lectures delivered to various Chapters, has analysed Claret's Royal Arch text in comparison to other rituals currently in use, such as Aldersgate, Domatic, Perfect Ceremonies and the Oxford Ritual. He concludes that we owe more to Claret than to Browne (mentioned above in the context of the Chapter of Promulgation).

Passing the Veils

'Passing the Veils' is a ceremony constituting part of the English Royal Arch ritual in olden days, now practiced only in the Province of Bristol. It is, however, a separate degree in Scotland designated 'the Excellent Master'; attaining the Excellent Master's degree is a prerequisite to exaltation into the Royal Arch. This is also true of jurisdictions that have adopted the Scottish ritual. In this ceremony the three veils, blue, purple and scarlet in colour, hang parallel and at a short distance from each other. An Officer guards each veil. He has to ensure that the candidate is in possession of the necessary proofs of passage for each veil. A fourth white veil hides the three Principals who sit behind it awaiting their participation in the proceedings.

1846 *The saxophone is patented by the Belgian musician Adolphe Sax; the sewing machine is patented by Elias Howe.*

A marble statue of the Duke of Sussex is commissioned by vote of the Grand Lodge and executed by Bro E H Baily, member of the Royal Academy of Arts. It is placed in the apse to the east in Freemasons' Hall, Great Queen street. (At present, the statue is located in the corridor opposite the committee rooms.) (29 April).

1849 *The safety pin is patented by American inventor Walter Hunt; the florin (2 shilling coin) introduced, the first step to decimalisation - achieved in 1971.*

The Provincial Grand Chapter of Staffordshire is founded; Henry Charles Vernon is appointed Grand Superintendent (May).

Provincial Grand Chapter of West Lancashire is founded; Revd Gilmour Robinson is appointed Grand Superintendent.

1850 *American Express is founded by Henry Wells & William Fargo; transportation of British convicts to Western Australia begins; the first settlers for the settlement of Christchurch arrive at the Port of Lyttelton, New Zealand.*

Domatic Chapter of Instruction No. 206 (now No. 177) founded. (15 February).

The Chapter of Judea No. 265 in Keighley, Province of Yorkshire (West Riding), works the ceremony of 'Passing of the Veils' for the last time. (20 January).

Royal Masonic Benevolent Institution (RMBI) is created through the amalgamation of one charity for elderly masons, one for their widows and the Duke of Sussex's 'Royal Masonic Benevolent Annuity Fund for the Relief of Poor, Aged and Infirm Freemasons'. (15 May).

The 'Asylum for Worthy, Aged and Decayed Freemasons', run by the RMBI, is consecrated. (1 August).

The number of London chapters increase to twenty seven following on the death of the Duke of Sussex who had suppressed new chapters in the capital.

1851 *The Great Exhibition is held in 'Crystal Palace'; photography is popularised by the introduction of the 'wet collodion' process; Isaac Singer produces the first sewing machine; gold discovered in Australia.*

The Provincial Grand Chapter of the Channel Islands is founded, and James John Hammond is appointed Grand Superintendent. (25 July).

Patents are issued by Supreme Grand Chapter for the appointments of a Grand Superintendent, Hon Alexander Keith, over the District Grand Chapter of Nova Scotia (until 1870) and Hon William Badgley (d.1888), over Montreal. (5 November).

1852 *Victoria and Albert Museum, first known as The Museum of Manufactures, opens; The Land Survey of Britain completed. Tasmania ceases to be a convict settlement; Wells Fargo is established in USA.*

A patent is issued by Supreme Grand Chapter for the appointment of a Grand Superintendent, Thomas Douglas Harrington, over the District Grand Chapter of Quebec and Three Rivers. (July).

The eighth edition of the *General Regulations for the Government of the Order of Royal Arch Masons of England*, established by the Grand Chapter' is published by the authority of the Grand Chapter by William Henry White in his role as

Grand Scribe E (London: Printed by Thompson and Davidson, 1852). (3 November).

Samuel Rawson (d.1893) is appointed the first Grand Superintendent in and over the Royal Arch District of China. He resigned his post in 1866. China was subsequently divided into two separate Districts of Northern China, and Hong Kong and the Far East.

1853 *Gladstone's first budget: a wide range of duties is abolished, and death duties are introduced; vaccination against smallpox is made compulsory in Britain; Reuters is founded.*

A new Craft book of constitutions is published. Article II of the Articles of Union of 1813 are now introduced for the first time. The Preliminary Declaration, preceding the General Laws and Regulations for the Government of the Craft, reads:

> By the solemn Act of Union between the two Grand Lodges of Free-Masons of England in December 1813, it was 'declared and pronounced, that pure Ancient Masonry consists of three degrees, and no more; *viz.* those of the Entered Apprentice, the Fellow Craft, and the Master Mason, including the Supreme Order of the Holy Royal Arch.

The inclusion of Article II in the Articles of Union in 1813 may have been interpreted as a victory for the Antients, while the lack of further mention of the Royal Arch between 27 December 1813 and the establishment of the 'United' Supreme Grand Chapter of England in 1817, may be seen as a victory for the Moderns. It is erroneous, however, to consider the exclusion of the text of Article II from the 1815 constitutions as a snub at the Antients. None of the articles in the Articles of Union is mentioned in the book of constitutions, and it is clear that Article II of the union was not included in the 1815 constitutions, the first constitutions following the union, or any edition until 1853, simply because it was thought unnecessary.

William Tucker's Demotion

The reason for the inclusion of Article II as the preamble or 'Preliminary Declaration' to the 1853 constitutions and thereafter, is entirely due to force of circumstance. As discussed in great detail in Bro F J Cooper's article 'RW Bro. William Tucker, P Grand Master of Dorsetshire, 1846-1853' (*AQC*, 83, 1970, pp. 124-148), the Grand Master, the Earl of Zetland, became somewhat concerned by the extracurricular activities, so to speak, of RW Bro Tucker, the newly appointed Provincial Grand Master of Dorsetshire.

William Tucker was installed in August 1846 at the same time that he was the Provincial Grand Master of the Knights Templar of Dorset. A few weeks after his installation as Provincial Grand Master, Tucker exalted three new companions into the Royal Arch. The next day he installed the same companions as Knights Templar and Knights of Malta and further perfected them into the Rose Croix and Ne Plus Ultra degrees, all by special dispensation. These activities were of concern to the Grand Master of the United Grand Lodge of England. The culminating event was the appearance of Tucker at his own Provincial Grand Lodge in August 1853, wearing the full regalia of a Sovereign Grand Inspector General of the 33rd Degree of the Ancient and Accepted Rite. In the long speech he then gave, as he had done on several previous occasions, he expressed regret at the limitations of Article II of the union and encouraged the practice of all the many orders beyond the Craft. His removal from office by the Grand Master was not a surprise. The inclusion of Article II in the newly published constitutions of 1853, done at the direction of the Grand Master, was a reaction against a growing interest in diverse side degrees. The inclusion of the Act in the book of constitutions was intended as a reminder to the Brethren of the permitted confines of pure and Antient Masonry.

Craft Regulation No. 241 which permits the wearing of the Royal Arch Jewel in Craft lodges (see 1841 and 1884) is now amended with the following additional words, in italics:

'[...] as shall appertain to or be consistent with those degrees which are recognised and acknowledged by and under the controul [sic] of the Grand Lodge *being part of pure and Antient Masonry*'.

1854 *The start of the Crimean War; cigarettes are introduced into Britain; the Times offers £1,000 for the discovery of an alternative raw material for paper.*

The Provincial Grand Chapter of Yorkshire, established in 1788, is divided into two separate Provinces: North and East Riding with Thomas 2nd Earl of Zetland continuing as Grand Superintendent, and West Riding with Charles Lee appointed as Grand Superintendent.

1856 *The Victoria Cross is created by Royal Warrant, backdated to 1854 to recognise acts during the Crimean War; the treaty of Paris is signed, ending the Crimean War.*

Supreme Grand Chapter donates £500 to the RMBI towards the debt for drainage in the Croydon Homes and £150 toward providing Chandeliers for lighting in the Grand Temple (February).

An amendment is passed reducing the waiting period to be made a Royal Arch Mason from twelve months, as established at union, to four weeks. This reduction date to four weeks only is not confirmed until 1893.

A patent is issued by Supreme Grand Chapter for the appointment of a Grand Superintendent, Sir Samuel Osborne Gibbs (d.1874), over the District Grand Chapter of New South Wales. (May).

The Mark Degree

On the 1 February 1856, a Report is read at the Quarterly Convocation of Supreme Grand Chapter by R W Bro Alexander Dobie, President of the 'Joint Committee' set up by Grand Lodge and Supreme Grand Chapter. His report states, that as 'the Mark Masons' Degree, so called, does not form part of the Royal Arch Degree [...] and it might be considered a graceful addition to the Fellow Craft's Degree'. The Earl of Zetland, First Grand Principal, approved the Committee's report and Grand Chapter resolved that '[...] the question of its introduction into Masonry be left to the Grand Lodge of England.' (J A Grantham *The History of Grand Lodge of Mark Master Masons of England and Wales* London, 1960, p. 41-2). (1 February).

At the Quarterly Communication of Grand Lodge on 5th March 1856, it is proposed, seconded and carried that 'The degree of Mark Mason is not at variance with Craft Masonry, and that it be added thereto, under proper regulations' (Op. cit. p. 42). (5 March).

This decision of the Grand Lodge at first appeared to be momentous, potentially giving way to a remarkable change to the standing of the Mark degree, the existence of which was now recognised and acknowledged for the first time since its inception three generations back. For all practical purposes, the Mark Degree was now part of pure Ancient Masonry.

The members of the Order, however, led by the Mark Lodge Bon Accord had hoped and expected the Mark degree to gain the same status and recognition that had been given by the United Grand Lodge of England to the Supreme Grand Chapter of the Royal Arch. They reacted with horror to the fact that the degree had been relegated to the tail end of the Fellow Craft degree. This, so far as the Mark supporters were concerned, could be the end of the Mark degree, as it was then known. At a special meeting of the Bon Accord Mark Lodge, on 21 May 1856, a marginal note to the minutes states that 'final steps were taken to form a Grand Lodge of Mark Master Masons, and the W M Lord Leigh, was invited to take the position of Grand Master of Mark Masonry in England'. (Op. cit. p. 52).

Thus at the following Quarterly Communication of the Grand Lodge, on 4 June, an amendment to the minutes was proposed by John Henderson, Past President of the Board of General Purposes. He stated that the minutes relating to the Mark degree cannot be confirmed as 'no man, nor body of men, could make such innovation as that now proposed, without endangering the whole stability of the Institution' (Op. cit. p. 45). In the debate that followed, the Earl of Zetland, presiding as Grand Master, declared that he would vote in favour of the non-confirmation of that portion of the minutes relating to the Mark degree. When Henderson's motion to amend the minutes was carried, the response was tumultuous, manifest in enthusiastic clapping and support from those present. This acclaim has been interpreted as being a rejection of the Mark degree, instigated by adherents to the original concepts of the Articles of Union of 1813, which stated that Grand Lodge did not have the power to incorporate a new degree into the structure of Freemasonry. The Mark degree, far from being rejected, however, was saved for posterity. Had it been incorporated as part of the Fellow Craft degree it would have surely soon disappeared and lost as a separate individual degree. Now it was being saved as an independent Order. It was this fact that induced such vociferous response in Grand Lodge to the deletion of the relevant part of the minutes.

Within three weeks of this meeting, the 'Grand Lodge of Mark Master Masons of England and Wales, and the Colonies and Dependencies of the British Crown' was founded on 23 June 1856, with William Henry, 2nd Lord Leigh and Provincial Grand Master for Warwickshire, as its first Grand Master.

1858 *The Great Eastern Railway is launched; The East India Company is dissolved; this year also experiences what was to be referred to as 'The great stink', a smell of the River Thames so unpleasant that it forces Parliament to stop work; The Royal Opera House in Covent Garden, London, opens.*

William Henry White (d.1866), Grand Scribe Ezra, retires. William Gray Clarke is appointed Grand Scribe Ezra (until 1867).
The Grand Lodge of Scotland and the Supreme Grand Chapter of Scotland agree on joint control of the Mark Degree.

1859 *The building of the Suez Canal is started; Blondin crosses the Niagara Falls on a tightrope; Charles Darwin publishes The Origin of Species.*

The Provincial Grand Chapter of North Wales is established and headed by Sir Watkin Williams Wynn as the Grand Superintendent (September).

1860 *Garibaldi's 'Red Shirts' conquer Sicily and Naples; the Prince of Wales (later King Edward VII) visits the United States; the Golf Open Championship begins.*

A protest is launched in Canada because a Chapter under the English Constitution is stated to be illegal notwithstanding Article II of the union, namely that pure Ancient Masonry includes the Royal Arch. Thus, it is argued, all jurisdictions that are in amity with England must accept that under the English Craft Constitution, England will allow a craft Lodge to have a Chapter attached to it. The matter is concluded to the satisfaction of the Canadian Grand Chapter.

External Relations

The earliest reference to external relations in the Grand Chapter minutes dates from 1808. It was then ordered that companions exalted in Scotland and Ireland should be admitted to the Grand Chapters of England and its subordinate chapters. After 1817, uneasiness arose with regard to the growing number of chapters in foreign jurisdictions. Supreme Grand Chapter was sovereign over all aspects of the Royal Arch. It was, however, not wholly independent of the United Grand Lodge of England. Thus the question that arose was: did the Supreme Grand Chapter of England have the authority to grant recognition to other sovereign bodies? The answer is that Grand Chapter does not accord formal recognition to other Grand Chapters, nor does it exchange representatives with other Grand Chapters. If, however, a foreign Grand Chapter consists of membership drawn from a Grand Lodge recognised by the United Grand Lodge of England, then fraternal relations will be seen to exist, allowing for inter-visitation in the respective chapters.

James Henry Legge, 3rd Lord Sherborne was, after a hiatus of many decades, appointed Grand Superintendent of the Provincial Grand Chapter of Gloucestershire and Herefordshire (April 26). The two last Grand Superintendents for that area had been Henry Jenner for Gloucestershire, who resigned in 1807, and Richard Jebb for Herefordshire, who died in 1820. An extended period of interregnum such as this (1820-1860) had been fairly typical after 1820 among the various Provinces in England.

1861 *First steam-powered carousel recorded in Bolton, England; start of American Civil War as the Confederate States of America are formed, comprising the first six break-away States; the Kingdom of Italy is proclaimed by the new Parliament in Italy, with Victor Emmanuel II as King;*

The English Royal Gallovidian Chapter No. 155 chartered in April 1810, meeting in Kirkcudbright, South-west Scotland, is dissolved and surrenders its charter to the Supreme Grand Chapter of England. (Pick, Fred 'The Royal Gallovidian Chapter, Kirkcudbright ' *AQC* 60, 1947 pp. 52-70). This Chapter is the last, with one exception, of the English chapters that remained unattached after the foundation of the United Supreme Grand Chapter of England in 1817, because of their meeting place being in Scotland. The exception is the quaintly named Land of Cakes Chapter No. 15 founded in1787, and meeting regularly under the English jurisdiction, but within the territory of the Province of the Scottish Provincial Grand Chapter of The Border.

1862 *The first pasteurisation test is completed by Louis Pasteur and Claude Bernard; Richard Gatling patents his machine gun; Bismarck becomes first minister in Prussia.*

The Building Committee appoints as their Chairman John Havers (1815-1884), Junior Grand Warden and Past President of the Board of General Purposes (1858-1861), who states that 'it is a disgrace that [this] most ancient Grand Lodge should permit its headquarters to be used as a Tavern' (LLMF 'Minute book of the Building Committee' GBR 1991 FMH MINUTES:/4/3).

1863 *The Football Association is founded in England; the first section of the London Underground Railway opens between Paddington and Farringdon Street; the Battle of Gettysburg takes place in the United States.*

The Hon James Gibbs (d.1886) is appointed the first Grand Superintendent in and over the Royal Arch District of Bombay. (16 January).

Work began on the second Masons' Hall by Frederick Cockerell which incorporated Thomas Sandby's original Grand Hall of 1775. Completed in 1869. Much of John Soane's extensions of 1813 were replaced by Cockerell. (A fire in 1883 destroyed part of the building and the current structure, on the site of the original Freemasons' Tavern of 1775, was begun in 1927 by H V Ashley and Winton Newman, completed in 1933.)

Committee reconsiders the view that Sunday meetings were illegal. (December).

The 'General Grand Chapter for Scotland and the Colonies' is set up by six West Scotland Chapters. It issues charters to eight new chapters before finally fading in 1870.

1864 *The Red Cross is established by twelve nations; the Clifton Suspension Bridge over the River Avon is officially opened.*

The ninth edition of the *General Regulations* is published by the Supreme Grand Chapter for the government of the Order of Royal Arch Masons of England. (William Gray Clarke, *General Regulations*, London: Ford and Tilt, 1864). (3 August).

The Supreme Grand Chapter confirms the ban on Sunday meetings.

1865 *The end of the American Civil War; slavery is abolished in the United States; Abraham Lincoln is assassinated; William Booth founds the Salvation Army; Elizabeth Garrett Anderson becomes the first woman doctor.*

Provincial Grand Chapter of South Wales, Eastern Division, is established and headed by Grand Superintendent Theodore Mansel Talbot.

1867 *The US buys Alaska from Russia; the British North America Act takes effect, creating the Canadian Confederation; the typewriter is invented.*

W J Hughan discovers an original of the first known book to mention the Royal Arch: Fifield D'Assigny's *A Serious and Impartial Enquiry into the cause of the present decay of Free-Masonry in the Kingdom of Ireland* published in Dublin in 1744 by Edward Bate. Now housed in the Masonic Library, Iowa, USA.

The Charity Committee of the Supreme Grand Chapter recommends a £1,000 contribution towards the erection of a new building in Wood Green for the Royal Masonic Institution for Sons of Decayed and Deceased Freemasons.

William Gray Clarke (d. 1868), Grand Scribe Ezra, retires.

In the Craft this, the 150th Anniversary of the foundation of the premier Grand Lodge of England on 24 June 1717, is allowed to pass without note.

1868 *The last British election takes place in which Poll Books (a register of persons entitled to vote at an election) are available; the last convicts land in Australia.*

John Hervey (d.1880), Grand Secretary of the UGLE, is appointed Grand Scribe Ezra (until 1879).

Chapter No. 106 in Exmouth is admonished by Supreme Grand Chapter for exalting a brother on 2 March 1868, who had been raised on 11 March 1867. (5 August).

A new procedure is introduced whereby Chapter documentation and books are confiscated by Supreme Grand Chapter when complaints are investigated and are returned after cases are resolved. (4 November).

Supreme Grand Chapter voted for a £2,000 contribution towards expenses relating to the new building under construction.

One thousand copies of the Royal Arch Constitutions are printed and sold at 1 shilling and sixpence per copy.

1869 *Imprisonment for debt is abolished in Britain; the Suez Canal opens; Cutty Sark is launched in Dumbarton.*

The tenth edition of the *General Regulations of the Royal Arch* is published. (John Hervey, *General Regulations established by Supreme Grand Chapter for the Government of the Order of Royal Arch Masons of England,* London: Harrison & Sons, 1869).

A complaint is made against Companion Ellis, who claimed that a Chapter certificate alone - without one from Grand Chapter - was sufficient evidence of membership of the Royal Arch. He was found not to have been issued with a Grand Chapter certificate and the complaint was upheld. Comp Ellis was suspended. Supreme Grand Chapter stated that a Supreme Grand Chapter certificate is needed to validate Royal Arch membership but that it was not sufficient to let somebody into the order without also carrying out a proper examination. (5 May).

Supreme Grand Chapter refuses to grant a certificate to a companion of Chapter of Concord No. 394 since the companion named was exalted less than four months after he attained the degree of a Master Mason, while commenting that the 'offence being very much in the increase'. (August).

1870 *The unification of Italy is completed; the first British postcard is invented; the halfpenny post is started; Dr Thomas Barnardo opens his first home for destitute children; water closets come into wide use.*

George Frederick Samuel, 1st Marquess of Ripon (d.1909) is elected and installed First Grand Principal (till 1874).

The Supreme Grand Chapter Committee reports that the fine, due from Concord Chapter No. 394, has not been paid. The Chapter is under threat of erasure (2 February).

A petition for a charter for a Chapter to be attached to the Pythagorean Lodge No. 79 in Greenwich concludes with forty-one votes in favour and twenty-four against.

The Concord Chapter convey their apologies to Supreme Grand Chapter who accept the explanation and resolve that Brother Cyprian Wollowicz, who had been made a companion too early, should be re-exalted and a fine of two guineas imposed on the Chapter.

A petition for a new Chapter from the Isle of Man is refused because only two lodges and chapters are active on the island and an additional chapter would be too many.

A decision is taken by the Supreme Grand Chapter stating that for a companion to be eligible to be elected a Principal of an English chapter he must first be, or have been, the Master of an English Craft lodge. (3 August).

The Grand Chapter recommends that a lodge should be at least three years old before a Royal Arch Chapter is attached to it, to ensure that sufficient number of Past Masters is available. It also becomes obligatory for chapters to bear the name of the Craft lodge to which they are attached.

Maj.-Gen. Harvey Tuckett Duncan (d.1900) is appointed the first Grand Superintendent in and over the Royal Arch District of Burma. (8 December).

1871 *The Royal Albert Hall opens; the University Tests Act allows students to enter Oxford, Cambridge and Durham universities without undergoing religious tests; the Trades Unions are legalised in Britain.*

The Provincial Grand Chapter of Jersey is founded with Colonel Edward Charles Malet de Carteret as Grand Superintendent. (19 April).

A motion in Supreme Grand Chapter reads:

> Whilst this Grand Chapter recognises the private right of every companion to belong to any extraneous Masonic organisation he may choose, it firmly

> forbids now, and at any future time, all companions whilst engaged as salaried officials under this Grand Chapter to mix themselves up in any way with such bodies as the Ancient & Accepted Scottish Rite, the 'Rites of Misraim and Memphis', the spurious orders of 'Rome and Constantine', the schismatic body styling itself 'The Grand Mark Lodge of England'; or any other exterior Masonic organisation whatever (even that of the order of the Knights Templar, which alone is recognised), under the pain of immediate dismissal from employment by this Grand Chapter.

The motion, for which Companion Matthew Cooke, Past Zerubbabel from Chapter No. 534, could not find a seconder, was accordingly not proceeded with. (1 November).

Colonel Sir Francis Burdett appointed Grand Superintendent, after a six-decade hiatus, to head the Provincial Grand Chapter of Middlesex. The previous Grand Superintendent had been John Elliot who resigned in 1812. (6 November).

1872 *Secret Ballots are introduced in Britain; the Penny-farthing bicycles are in general use; over 32,000 friendly societies in England are formed.*

The companions in Supreme Grand Chapter are reminded that the Grand Chapter meets in two capacities, both as a legislative assembly and a judicial body or Supreme Court of Appeal. (7 February).

A resolution is passed stating that Supreme Grand Chapter in the future will be responsible for one fifth, instead of one sixth, of the Grand Lodge salaries.

1873 *Remington & Sons start to manufacture typewriters; Glidden invents barbed wire.*

The Provincial Grand Chapter of Monmouthshire is established, headed by Colonel Charles Lyne as Grand Superintendent. (27 January).

The Supreme Grand Chapter, in noting irregularities in the applications for certificates, states that: 'the Principals of the Chapter concerned be severely reprimanded and admonished to be more careful in the future'.

The 2nd Earl of Zetland, former First Grand Principal, dies. (7 May).

A committee reports on the irregular exaltations of Master Masons not yet qualified, which is contrary to Royal Arch Regulation Article 23.

1874 *Disraeli and the Tories come to power in Britain; the first Trades Union MP is elected; the Factory Act introduces the 56-hour working week.*

Albert Edward, Prince of Wales (later King Edward VII, 1841-1910), is elected First Grand Principal (until 1901).

The Supreme Grand Chapter refuses recognition of the Mark Grand Lodge.

A letter from Ireland addressed to John Hervey, Grand Scribe E, dated 13 July 1874 explains why Ireland cannot recognise the Grand Mark Lodge of England, as in Ireland the Mark is a prerequisite to the Royal Arch. The discussion of the letter is deferred to the next meeting because if its seriousness. (4 November).

The last ceremony of the 'Passing the Veil' is worked in the Chapter of Affability No. 308, Yorkshire (West Riding).

1875 *Midland Railway abolishes Second Class passenger facilities, leaving First Class and Third Class; London's main sewage system is completed; the Universal Postal Union is established in Geneva.*

The eleventh edition of the *General Regulations* is issued, size now 32mo (John Hervey, *General Regulations established by the Supreme Grand Chapter for the Government of the Order of Royal Arch Masons of England*. London: Harrison & Sons, 1875). (3 February).

HRH the Prince of Wales is formally invested as the First Grand Principal.

Henry Howard Molyneux, 4th Earl of Carnarvon (d.1890), is appointed Pro First Grand Principal (until 1890).

Col. Marmaduke Ramsay (d.1893) is appointed the first Grand Superintendent in and over the Royal Arch District of Punjab, resigned in 1881 and took up the post of Grand Superintendent of Malta in 1888. (3 June).

1876 *Queen Victoria is proclaimed Empress of India; the Prime Minister Benjamin Disraeli is elevated to the peerage; the Medical Act allows women to be granted medical qualifications.*

Arthur, Duke of Connaught and Strathearn (1850-1942) is exalted in the Apollo University Chapter No. 357. (17 June).

Spencer Compton, 8th Duke of Devonshire, is appointed Grand Superintendent, after a seven-decade hiatus, to head the Provincial Grand Chapter of Derbyshire. The last Grand Superintendent had been Thomas Boothby, 1st Lord Rancliffe, who was appointed in 1793 and died in 1800. (25 February).

1877 *The first cricket Test Match is held between England and Australia, the latter winning by 45 runs; the first tennis championships are held at Wimbledon; Edison invents the microphone and the phonograph.*

W S Gilbert (1836–1911) and Arthur Sullivan (1842–1900), the Victorian-era theatrical duo of librettist and composer, progress through the Royal Arch almost simultaneously: both were exalted into the now erased Friends in Council Chapter No. 1383 in February and July 1877, respectively.

Thomas, Earl of Bective, is appointed Grand Superintendent, after a six decade hiatus, to head the Provincial Grand Chapter of Cumberland and Westmorland. The immediate previous Grand Superintendent was John Losh, appointed in 1803 and who had died in 1814. (30 June).

1879 *The start of the Anglo-Zulu war; Saccharin discovered by Fahlberg and Remsen; the first telephone exchanges opened in London.*

Twelfth edition of the General Regulations for chapters is issued (John Hervey, *General Regulations established by the Supreme Grand Chapter for the Government of the Order of Royal Arch Masons of England*, London: Harrison & Sons, 1879. (16 July).

1880 *An Education Act is passed, causing schooling to be compulsory for five until ten-year-old; Greenwich Mean Time is adopted throughout UK; the mosquito is found to be the carrier of malaria.*

Colonel Shadwell Henry Clerke is appointed Grand Scribe Ezra (until 1891).

John Smallpiece proposes the presence of all companions at the opening of a chapter, instead of the past principals only. The motion is heavily defeated. A rule to this effect was carried out, but only 22 years later, in 1902. (4 February).

The Provincial Grand Chapter of Northamptonshire and Huntingdonshire is established, headed by William, 7th Duke of Manchester, as the Grand Superintendent. (10 March).

1881 *The first public electricity supply is installed in Godalming in Surrey; Postal Orders are introduced; the First Boer War breaks out; flogging is abolished in the Army and Royal Navy.*

Arthur, Duke of Connaught and Strathearn, is elected and invested First Principal of Apollo University Chapter No. 357.

John Bevan (d.1911) is appointed the first Grand Superintendent in and over the Royal Arch District of Westland, New Zealand, South Island. (14 November).

1882 *'The Ashes' is instituted in cricket; the TB bacillus is discovered by Koch; Conan Doyle's Sherlock Holmes makes his first appearance in 'A Study in Scarlet'.*

Grand Scribe Ezra reports to the Grand Chapter that the lost Charter of Compact of 1776 had been located in the muniment room. It was repaired, cleaned and framed. It is now housed in the Library and Museum of Freemasonry, London.

1883 *The Boys' Brigade in Glasgow is founded by William Smith; The Statue of Liberty is presented to the USA by France.*

Freemasons' Hall, London, is partially destroyed by fire. (3 May).

The Supreme Grand Chapter donates £500 for a new organ located in Lodge room No. 1 of the new building.

1884 *John Harvey Kellogg patents corn flakes; the Standard Meridian Conference makes Greenwich the prime meridian of the world.*

Craft Regulation No. 241, reflected in the Grand Chapter Regulation No. 84, is amended to allow the Royal Arch Jewel to be worn in Craft lodges. See below.

Thomas Harper (1735-1832)

Thomas Harper was a London jeweller, based in Fleet Street. He and his family are credited with a large number of very beautiful late eighteenth and early nineteenth century Masonic jewels, in particular ones related to the Royal Arch. This is the same Thomas Harper who was so intensely involved with both the Moderns' and the Antients' Grand Lodges leading to the union of 1813. The jewels are often identified by the presence of the initials 'T H' on the jewel (not to be confused with the T placed above the H in the 'triple tau').

Charles James Egan (d. 1909) is appointed the first Grand Superintendent in and over the Royal Arch District of South Africa, Eastern Division.

1885 *Irish terrorists dynamite Westminster Hall and the Tower of London; Gilbert and Sullivan's comic opera 'The Mikado' opens at the Savoy Theatre; the Statue of Liberty arrives in New York Harbour; Robert Cecil, 3rd Marquess of Salisbury, becomes Prime Minister of the United Kingdom.*

A patent is issued by Supreme Grand Chapter for the appointment of a Grand Superintendent, Sir Henry Burford-Hancock, in and over the District Grand Chapter of Gibraltar. (2 May). He is the first appointment since January 1790 when H R H William Duke of Clarence (d.1837) was appointed to the post.

1886 *The Hockey Association is formed in England; pharmacist John Styth Pemberton invents a carbonated beverage later named 'Coca-Cola'; Putney Bridge opens in London.*

The thirteenth edition, reduced in size to 16 mo, of the General Regulations for Chapters is issued. (Colonel Shadwell H Clerke, *General Regulations for Chapters established by Supreme Grand Chapter for the Government of the Order of Royal Arch Masons of England,* London: Norris & Sons, 1886). (31March).

Inter alia, the right to appoint assistant sojourners reverts from the principal sojourner to the members of the chapter.

The Grand Rank is instituted, and Robert Grey is the first to be so honoured. At this meeting Thomas Fenn, who revised the constitutions up to 1884, is appointed Past President of the General Purposes Committee. (5 May).

1888 *Conan Doyle's first Sherlock Holmes adventure is published; English Football League is established; George Eastman patents "Kodak box camera"; unresolved "Jack the Ripper" murders take place in the East End of London; John J Loud patents the ballpoint pen.*

Col Marmaduke Ramsay (d.1893), formerly in the Punjab, is appointed the first Grand Superintendent in and over the District of Malta. (21 May).

Sir Catchick Paul Chater (d.1926) is appointed the first Grand Superintendent in and over the Royal Arch District of Hong Kong and South China (resigning in 1909). (6 December).

1891 *The first telephone link between London and Paris is established; primary education is made free and compulsory; Thomas Edison patents the motion picture camera.*

Edward, 1st Earl of Lathom (d.1898), is appointed Pro First Grand Principal.

The Provincial Grand Chapter of South Wales, Western Division, is established, headed by William, 4th Lord Kensington. (8 May).

Colonel Shadwell Henry Clerke, Grand Scribe Ezra, dies.

1892 *The electric oven is invented; Alfred Lord Tennyson dies aged 83; the first performance of Tchaikovsky's 'Nutcracker' ballet takes place in St Petersburg.*

Edward Letchworth is appointed Grand Scribe Ezra (until 1917).

The Supreme Grand Chapter approves donation of 100 guineas for the 'Old Peoples Jubilee' appeal.

1893 *Keir Hardy founds the Independent Labour Party; Henry Ford builds the first car; the Liverpool Overhead Railway is officially opened by the Marquess of Salisbury.*

Thomas Fenn, Past President of the General Purposes Committee, again refers the question of the presence of ordinary companions at the opening of a chapter. An attempt to change the rule had failed in 1880. (1 February).

Companion North proposes that a 'Committee of Revision' be appointed to examine the ritual. The motion was negated. (3 May).

The first facsimile edition of Fifield Dassigny's 1744 pamphlet *'A Serious and Impartial Enquiry into the cause of the present decay of Free-Masonry in the Kingdom of*

Ireland' (Dublin: Edward Bate) is published in his *Memorials of the Masonic Union* by W J Hughan, followed by a revised and augmented edition by John Thorp in 1913. (Leicester: Printed by Johnson, Wykes & Paine, 20 unnumbered pages, 1913).

1894 *The Local Government Act is passed; picture postcards are introduced in Britain; Baron Pierre de Coubertin founds the International Olympic Committee; Tower Bridge opens; Alfred Dreyfus convicted of treason in France.*

A ruling by the Grand Scribe Ezra is passed, stating that the ceremony of exaltation may be performed by three Principals, assisted by two or three companions. The ruling is important in the light of the earlier insistence by the Antients Grand Lodge that six companions were needed for the ceremony of exaltation.

A reduction to a four-week qualification period as a Master Mason in the Craft prior to the exaltation to the Royal Arch is confirmed. Since 1822 a twelve-month period had been required, with occasional dispensations granted after four weeks. (7 February).

Robert Isaac Finemore (d.1906) is appointed the first Grand Superintendent in and over the Royal Arch District of Natal (resigning in 1895). (15 May).

Very Revd Charles William Barnett Clarke, Dean of Cape Town (d.1916), is appointed the first Grand Superintendent in and over the Royal Arch District of South Africa, Western Division. (22 October).

1895 *The "Great Frost"; Oscar Wilde is arrested at the Cadogan Hotel, London, for gross indecency; Lord Rosebery resigns as Prime Minister (June) and General election is won by the Conservative Party (August); the last turnpike toll-gates in the UK are removed.*

Ferdinand Jamison Morphy (d. 1904) is appointed the first Grand Superintendent in and over the Royal Arch District of the Argentine Republic. (5 May).

1896 *The zip is patented by Whitcomb L Judson; the first Modern Olympic Games are held in Athens; Guglielmo Marconi receives a British patent (later disputed) for the radio; the term 'psychoanalysis' first comes into use.*

Renewed proposals made in Grand Chapter to allow companions to witness the opening of a chapter fail again (and only succeed in 1902).

1898 *The first photograph using artificial light is taken; the first solo circumnavigation of the globe is completed by Joshua Slocum; Zeppelin builds an airship that carries his name; the Goodyear Tire and Rubber Company is founded.*

William Archer, 3rd Earl Amherst (d.1910), is appointed Pro First Grand Principal (until 1908).

Provincial Grand Chapter of Guernsey and Alderney is founded with Brigadier-Surgeon James Balfour Cockburn (d.1907) appointed Grand Superintendent. (11 May).

George Richards (d.1911) is appointed the first Grand Superintendent in and over the Royal Arch District of Transvaal (resigning in 1905). (1 July).

1899 *The start of the Second Boer War; Winston Churchill captured by Boers; the Board of Education is established in Britain; Valdemar Poulsen invents the tape recorder; Aspirin is marketed for the first time.*

The Supreme Grand Chapter votes in favour of a £2,000 contribution towards alterations to the new building being constructed in Great Queen Street. This is the second contribution, the first having been made in 1868.

Beaufort Chapter No. 103 Bristol restores the ceremony of 'Passing the Veils'.

1900 *The Davis Cup tennis competition is established; the Labour Party is formed; the besieged town of Mafeking under Baden Powell is relieved to wild rejoicing; the underground is electrified; Nobel prizes for Peace are first awarded.*

A new edition of the General Regulations is issued (Edward Letchworth, *General Regulations established by Supreme Grand Chapter for the Government of the Order of Royal Arch Masons of England*, London: Warrington and Co., 1900).

The 25th anniversary of the installation of the Prince of Wales is celebrated with the conferral of Past Grand Rank on nine companions. (2 May).

1901 *The Commonwealth of Australia is founded; Queen Victoria dies and the Prince of Wales becomes King Edward VII; Hubert Cecil Booth patents the vacuum cleaner; Britain's first submarine is launched; Ragtime is introduced into American jazz; the Trans-Siberian Railway opens.*

Arthur, the Duke of Connaught and Strathearn (d.1942), is elected and installed as First Grand Principal (until 1939).

1902 *Empire Day, later renamed Commonwealth Day is first celebrated; the coronation of Edward VII takes place following the end of the Boer War; Arthur Conan Doyle reluctantly accepts a knighthood; Marie Curie discovers radioactivity.*

The Supreme Grand Chapter finally resolves that 'it is expedient that all Royal Arch Masons be permitted to be present at the Opening of Private Chapters'. (LLMF At a quarterly convocation Supreme Grand Chapter of Royal Arch Masons of England. BE 340 SUP fol.).

Three attempts had been made before this resolution was carried through: in 1880, 1893 and 1896 respectively. Prior to this date it was only principals and past principals who could be present at the opening of a chapter, some chapters performing the opening (and closing) ceremony in a side room. (7 May).

1905 *Chelsea Football Club founded; first public protest by suffragettes, led by Emmeline Pankhurst, at Westminster; Ancient Order of Druids initiate neo-druidic rituals at Stonehenge; Irish nationalist Arthur Griffith founds Sinn Féin in Dublin.*

Sir Walter John Napier (d.1947) is appointed the first Grand Superintendent in and over the Royal Arch District of the Eastern Archipelago (resigning in 1909). (13 January).

1907 *English suffragettes storm British Parliament and sixty women are arrested; a derailment in California kills 32 Shriners when their chartered train jumps off the tracks; NZ declares independence from UK; Oklahoma becomes the United States' 46th state.*

A new edition of General Regulations for Chapters is issued (Edward Letchworth, *General Regulations established by Supreme Grand Chapter for the Government of the Order of Royal Arch Masons of England*, London: Warrington and Co., 1907).

1908 *Separate courts for juveniles established in Britain; Lord Baden-Powell starts the Boy Scout movement; SOS becomes effective as an international signal of distress.*

Arthur, 2nd Lord Ampthill (d.1935), is appointed Pro First Grand Principal.

1910 *George V becomes King of the United Kingdom upon the death of his father, Edward VII; William D. Boyce founds the Boy Scouts of America; the Vatican introduces a compulsory oath against modernism to be taken by all priests upon ordination.*

A new edition of General Regulations for Chapters is issued (Edward Letchworth, *General Regulations established by Supreme Grand Chapter for the Government of the Order of Royal Arch Masons of England*, London: Warrington and Co., 1910).

Daniel Johannes Haarhoff (d.1917) is appointed the first Grand Superintendent in and over the Royal Arch District of South Africa, Central Division. (7 September).

1911 *Coronation of King George V and Queen Mary at Westminster Abbey, London; launching of the ocean liner RMS Titanic in Belfast; Suffragettes storm Parliament in London, all are arrested and choose prison terms.*

William James Hughan (1841-1911), foremost Masonic historian, dies. Founder-member of Quatuor Coronati Lodge No. 2076 and author, *inter alia*, of *Origins of the English Rite* (1884) of important relevance to the Royal Arch.

Henry Sadler (1849-1911), remarkable Masonic historian, dies. Served as Grand Tyler of the UGLE (1879-1910), Master of Quatuor Coronati Lodge (1910-11), prolific researcher and author, including the ground-breaking *Masonic Facts and Fictions* (1889).

1912 *The Irish Home Rule crisis breaks out; Captain Scott departs on his last expedition; Albert Berry makes his first parachute jump from an airplane; the 'Titanic' sinks; the telephone system is nationalised.*

A new edition of General Regulations for Chapters is issued (Edward Letchworth, *General Regulations established by Supreme Grand Chapter for the Government of the Order of Royal Arch Masons of England*, London: Warrington and Co., 1912).

1913 *Suffragette demonstrations take place in London and Mrs Pankhurst is imprisoned; the Trade Union Act in Britain establishes the right to use Union funds for political purposes; stainless steel is invented by Harry Brearley of Sheffield.*

A new edition of General Regulations for Chapters is issued (Edward Letchworth, *General Regulations established by Supreme Grand Chapter for the Government of the Order of Royal Arch Masons of England*, London: Warrington and Co., 1913).

The centenary of the union of the two Grand Lodges in 1813 is allowed to pass without note.

Anniversary Celebrations

The only Masonic anniversaries observed by the United Grand Lodge of England were:

a) The 200th birthday of the Premier Grand Lodge at an Especial Communication in the Royal Albert Hall on 23 June 1917, followed by a Masonic Service next day on 24 Jun — 8,000 brethren attended (notwithstanding the pressures of World War I).

b) The 250th birthday of the Premier Grand Lodge at an Especial Communication of Grand Lodge, when 6,500 brethren gathered at the Royal Albert Hall on 27 June 1967. H R H Prince Edward, Duke of Kent was installed Grand Master at this time, in the presence of representatives, the great majority being Grand Masters, of sixty-four guest constitutions.

c) The 275th anniversary was celebrated at the Quarterly Communication at Earls Court Exhibition Centre in London on 10 June 1992, when 11,882 brethren, ladies and guests attended. They included eighty-four sister Grand Lodges, sixty-eight of them represented by their Grand Master. These celebrations included the 25th anniversary of the election of the Duke of Kent as Grand Master, followed two weeks later by an evening Thanksgiving Masonic Service in St Paul's Cathedral.

The formal creation of the Ancients Grand Lodge in 1753 has never been officially commemorated, nor has the union of the two Grand Lodges in 1813. The only anniversary of the Royal Arch that has been celebrated is the bi-centenary of Supreme Grand Chapter on 1 July 1966 (see 1966 below).

The Provincial Grand Chapter of Shropshire is established, headed by Rowland George Venables (d.1920) as the first Grand Superintendent. (15 July).

Bernard E Jones (1880-1965), author of 'Freemasons' Book of the Royal Arch' is exalted in the Savage Club Chapter No. 2190.

1915 *WWI: The Royal Navy battleship 'HMS Formidable' is sunk by an Imperial German Navy U-boat; Charlie Chaplin's film 'The Tramp' released; the last purely Liberal government in the United Kingdom ends (Asquith forms an all party coalition).*

Robert Freke Gould (1836-1915), celebrated Masonic historian, dies. Founder-member and Past Master of Quatuor Coronati Lodge, author (1882-87) *inter alia* of the voluminous and classic *History of Freemasonry*.(Gould, Robert Freke *The History of Freemasonry: Its Antiquities, Symbols, Constitutions, Customs, etc. Embracing an Investigation of the Records of the Organisations of the Fraternity in England, Scotland, Ireland, British Colonies, France, Germany, and the United States. Derived from Official Sources* Volumes I-VI, T C & E C Jack Grange Publishing, Edinburgh [1882-1887]).

1916 *WWI: Paris is bombed by German zeppelins for the first time; the light switch is invented by William J. Newton and Morris Goldberg; Britain initiates daylight saving time; the 'HMS Hampshire' sinks off the Orkney Islands, Scotland, with Lord Kitchener aboard.*

A new edition of General Regulations for Chapters is issued (Edward Letchworth, *General Regulations established by Supreme Grand Chapter for the Government of the Order of Royal Arch Masons of England*, London: Warrington and Co., 1916).

1917 *WWI: President Woodrow Wilson calls for "peace without victory" in Germany before the United States severs diplomatic relations with Germany (February) and declares* *war (April); Mata Hari is arrested for spying; Mexican Revolution: Venustiano Carranza is elected president of Mexico.*

Sir Edward Letchworth, Grand Scribe E of the Supreme Grand Chapter of England and Grand Secretary of the United Grand Lodge of England, dies.

Philip Colville Smith is appointed Grand Scribe Ezra.

A new edition of General Regulations for Chapters is issued (P Colville Smith, *General Regulations established by Supreme Grand Chapter for the Government of the Order of Royal Arch Masons of England*, London: Freemasons' Hall, Great Queen Street, 1917).

1919 *Britain adopts a 48-hour working week; Alcock and Brown complete the first non-stop flight across the Atlantic; the Treaty of Versailles is signed ending the First World War; the first woman sits in the House of Commons (Viscountess Astor).*

The United Grand Lodge of England's Coat of Arms is authorised by the College of Arms. The Supreme Grand Chapter of England does not have its own independent Coat of Arms.

Arthur, 2nd Lord Ampthill, Pro 1st Grand Principal, is appointed Grand Superintendent, after a century-long hiatus, to head the Provincial Grand Chapter of Bedfordshire. The former Grand Superintendent was Edward, 3rd Lord Hawke, who had been appointed in 1811 and died in 1824. (5 November).

1920 *The first roadside petrol filling station in UK opens; Oxford University admits women to degrees for the first time; Thompson patents his 'Tommy' machine gun.*

Appointments in Grand Lodge and Grand Chapter, as well as in Provincial and District Grand Chapters, are limited to active ranks, and appointments to Past Grand Ranks are scarce. At the end of the 19th century, a number of appointments to past ranks was permitted as part of national or Masonic celebrations. Today's habitual practice of awarding past ranks did not begin until 1920.

1921 *The Anglo-Irish Treaty is signed in London, leading to the formation of the Irish Free State and Northern Ireland; Irish Regiments in the British Army are disbanded; the discovery of insulin is announced.*

Prince Albert, Duke of York and later King George VI (1895-1952), is exalted in United Chapter No. 1629 (now United Studholme Chapter No. 1591). (13 February).

1924 *Britain returns to the gold standard; introduction of London's first double decker buses with covered top decks; settlement of last remaining border disputes between the Irish Free State and Northern Ireland.*

Henry J Hyde-Johnson (d.1950) is appointed the first Grand Superintendent in and over the Royal Arch District of Nigeria (resigning in 1925). (6 February).

1926 *Princess Elizabeth is born; the General Strike begins; Harry Houdini, the American stunt-performer, dies; the first public demonstration of television (TV) by John Logie Baird takes place; Kodak produces the 16mm movie film.*

A table of all Lodges on the register of the United Grand Lodge of England is issued, as well as a list of all issued certificates. The table is published in the minutes of the Quarterly Communication of the Grand Lodge and covers a 20-year span. (March).

A new edition of General Regulations for Chapters is issued (Philip Colville Smith, *General Regulations established by Supreme Grand Chapter for the Government of the Order of Royal Arch Masons of England*, London: Freemasons' Hall, Great Queen Street, 1926).

1927 *The first transatlantic telephone call is made; Lindbergh makes a solo flight across the Atlantic; the Menin Gate war memorial is unveiled at Ypres; the first 'talkie' film, 'The Jazz Singer', is released.*

The Prince of Wales, from 1936 to become King Edward VIII and after his abdication later that year to be styled the Duke of Windsor (1894-1972), is exalted in United Chapter No. 1629 (now the United Studholme Chapter No. 1591), then elected and invested as First Principal of the Chapter.

1928 *Women over 21 get to vote in Britain; Madame Tussauds opens; Sir Alexander Fleming discovers penicillin; Turkey adopts the Roman alphabet; Walt Disney launches Mickey Mouse.*

The Duke of York, from 1936 to become King George VI (1895-1952), is exalted in United Chapter No. 1629 (now the United Studholme Chapter No. 1591), then elected and invested as First Principal.

Dr Geoffrey Francis Fisher (1887-1972), later to become Archbishop of Canterbury, is exalted in the Chapter of Justice No. 253 (13 March).

1929 *The United Kingdom general election again returns a hung parliament; Ramsay MacDonald forms the United Kingdom's second Labour government; first appearance of comic strip hero Popeye; the first Academy Awards are presented at the Hollywood Roosevelt Hotel; 'Wall Street Crash'.*

A patent is issued by Supreme Grand Chapter for the appointment of a Grand Superintendent, Stanley Edward Unite, over the District Grand Chapter of Japan.

(6 November). Resigning in 1931, he is to be replaced by Percy Hamilton McKay (d.1934). (August).

1931 *Winston Churchill resigns from Stanley Baldwin's shadow cabinet; Labour Government of Ramsay MacDonald resigns and is replaced by a National Government; Pound sterling comes off the gold standard.*

Grand Lodge of Ireland formally recognises, for the first time, the Royal Arch, This in spite of having been established with Grand Lodge of Ireland's blessing in 1829. (Law No. 2A Irish *Ahiman Rezon*, 1931)

1933 *Hitler becomes the Chancellor of Germany; the last pylon of the initial National Grid is erected; 'Prohibition' ends in USA; only six pennies minted in Britain this year.*

The appointment of a Grand Inspector for Royal Arch Districts Overseas is instituted as a Grand Rank.

The dedication of the Masonic Peace Memorial, the new headquarters of the United Grand Lodge of England at 60, Great Queen Street, is carried out by Arthur, the Duke of Connaught and Strathearn (1850-1942), Grand Master of the United Grand Lodge of England.

The 83rd birthday of Grand Master and First Grand Principal, the Duke of Connaught and Strathearn, is celebrated.

A Special Committee is formed charged with the installation of the Principals of London chapters because of the importance placed on the installation ceremony by Supreme Grand Chapter. (13 May).

The Supreme Grand Chapter makes its first contribution of £750 to the Masonic Peace Memorial fund for special furniture and five new chapter rooms in the new building.

A new edition of General Regulations for Chapters is issued (Philip Colville Smith, *General Regulations established by Supreme Grand Chapter for the Government of the Order of Royal Arch Masons of England*, London: Freemasons' Hall, Great Queen Street, 1933).

Rule 38, requiring dispensation for the Provincial Grand Officers to live outside the Province, is expunged.

The President of the Board of General Purposes makes a statement on the 'Improper Masonic Publications' by members of the Order who had made rituals available to the public.

Cecil Adams addresses the Supreme Grand Chapter with a paper entitled: 'Some notes on the History of United Grand Chapter'. (13 May).

J Heron Lepper (1878-1952) addresses the Supreme Grand Chapter with a paper entitled 'Earliest reference to Royal Arch Masonry in England and Ireland'. (1 November).

1934 *Hitler becomes Fuehrer of Germany; Mao Tse-tung's 'Long March' starts in China; driving tests are introduced in the UK; 'Cats-eyes' are first used on roads in the UK.*

Lewis Edwards addresses the Supreme Grand Chapter with a paper entitled 'Constitutional differences between the Craft and Royal Arch' (2 May).

A patent is issued by Supreme Grand Chapter for the appointment of a Grand Superintendent, Henry James Clark, over the District Grand Chapter of Northern China. (2 May). The new District Grand Chapter of Northern China petitions for the formation of four Royal Arch chapters.

Bernard Harvey addresses the Supreme Grand Chapter with a paper entitled 'The Hebrew Language in the Royal Arch Ritual'. (1 August).

Col Charles Thomas Major (d.1938) is appointed the first Grand Superintendent in and over the Royal Arch District of New Zealand, North Island. (3 October).

H T Cart De Lafontaine addresses the Supreme Grand Chapter with a paper entitled 'Significance of the three Royal Arch lectures' (7 November). The full text of addresses and lectures to the Grand Chapter that are listed are deposited in the London Library and Museum of Freemasonry and available on application.

1935 *Nylon is first produced by Gerard J. Berchet; Hore-Belisha introduces pedestrian crossings; Penguin paperbacks are launched; Malcolm Campbell sets the land-speed record of 301.13 mph on Bonneville Salt Flats.*

The death of Oliver Villiers Russell, 2nd Baron Ampthill, Pro First Grand Principal. (7 August).

The death of Fiennes Stanley Wykeham, 1st Lord Cornwallis. Wykeham was appointed First Grand Principal but died before being invested.

Henry, 6th Earl of Harewood (d.1947), is appointed Pro First Grand Principal (until 1942).

F Fighiera addresses the Supreme Grand Chapter with a paper entitled 'The Relation of the Craft to the Royal Arch'. (6 November).

1936 *George V dies in January; Edward VIII becomes king, but abdicates in December; the Duke of York becomes George VI; the Spitfire takes its first flight; the Spanish Civil War breaks out; the BBC broadcasts the world's first public TV transmission.*

Lord Harewood is installed as Pro First Grand Principal in accordance with Rule 25 of Royal Arch regulations. (5 February).

The Provincial Grand Chapter of the Isle of Man is established and headed by His Honour the Deemster, Sir William Percy Cowley (d.1958), as Grand Superintendent. (4 March).

Arthur Lionel Vibert (1872-1938), Past Master of Quatuor Coronati Lodge (1921), addresses the Supreme Grand Chapter with a paper entitled 'The Interlaced Triangles of the Royal Arch' (5 August).

1937 *The coronation of King George VI and Queen Elizabeth takes place; Neville Chamberlain becomes Prime Minister; the Duke of Windsor marries Wallis Simpson; German planes bomb Guernica in Spain; Japanese forces invade China.*

King George VI (1895-1952) is appointed Past Grand Master of the United Grand Lodge of England (3 March).

May Coronation Honours are conferred on one companion for every seven Chapters plus thirty companions in London, in addition to those under Regulation 36.

Scottish First Grand Principal the Earl of Cassillis visits England.

A Tudor-Craig addresses the Supreme Grand Chapter with a paper entitled 'Rare Prints in the Grand Lodge Museum' (4 August).

The three-volume *Catalogue of Contents of the Museum at Freemasons' Hall in the Possession of the United Grand Lodge of England*, compiled by Major Sir Algernon Tudor-Craig, Librarian and Curator of the United Grand Lodge of England, is published (London: The United Grand Lodge of England, 1938).

Colville Smith resigns as Grand Scribe Ezra due to continued ill health (3 November). Sydney A White is appointed Grand Scribe Ezra.

Lewis Edwards addresses the Supreme Grand Chapter with a paper entitled 'Principal Colours of Royal Arch Masonry'.

1938 *Germany invades and annexes Austria; Chamberlain visits Hitler in Munich and promises 'Peace in our time'.*

Revd Canon W W Covey-Crump addresses the Supreme Grand Chapter with a paper entitled 'History and Allegory in the Royal Arch Ritual'. (2 February).

Arthur Saywell addresses the Supreme Grand Chapter with a paper entitled 'The Sacred and Mysterious Name' (3 August).

1939 *Germany annexes Czechoslovakia and invades Poland; Britain and France declare war on Germany; the evacuation of women and children from London starts; Britain experiences the coldest winter since 1894.*

William John Songhurst (1860-1939), Masonic scholar and long-time editor of *AQC*, the Quatuor Coronati Lodge Transactions, dies. (25 January).

George, Duke of Kent (1909-1942), is elected and installed First Grand Principal. (3 May).

'London Chapter Rank' is given the new altered title 'London Grand Chapter Rank'. (2 August).

1941 *The British population amounts to 48.2 million; Germany invades Russia; the Mount Rushmore sculptures of George Washington, Thomas Jefferson, Theodore Roosevelt and Abraham Lincoln are completed; Japan attacks Pearl Harbour.*

The Complete Workings of the Royal Arch Degree, is published by A Lewis. (Revised editions are issued in 1947, 1957, 1968, 1974 and also 1989, 1990). There is no author or chapter named as being responsible for 'The Complete Workings of the Royal Arch Degree' although A. Lewis was originally the pseudonym of a publisher called John Hogg (1836-1909). During his lifetime, Hogg published books under his own name, including works by John Yarker and Kenneth MacKenzie, but used 'A. Lewis' when publishing rituals. 'A. Lewis' later took wing as a publisher, these days having become well-known across a wide range as 'Lewis Masonic'.

1942 *Montgomery defeats Rommel at the Battle of El Alamein; the Battle of Stalingrad takes place; the first programmable computer is invented by Alan Turin; rationing of soap is introduced; Prince George, Duke of Kent, brother of George VI and First Grand Principal, is killed in an air-crash near Caithness, Scotland.*

Henry, 6th Earl of Harewood (d.1947), is elected First Grand Principal.

Prince Arthur, Duke of Connaught and Strathearn, dies. (16 January).

A new edition of General Regulations for Chapters is issued (Sydney A White, *General Regulations established by Supreme Grand Chapter for the Government of the Order of Royal Arch Masons of England*, London: Freemasons' Hall, Great Queen Street, 1942).

In the interest of war-time economy the list of past grand officers attending Grand Chapter is omitted. (4 February).

1943 *The Allies, under General Sir Bernard Montgomery, invade Italy; Benito Mussolini resigns; the Tehran Conference takes place where Churchill, Roosevelt, and Stalin meet.*

Installation of the new First Grand Principal, the Earl of Harewood. (3 February).

Candidates are exalted in spite of Craft certificates not being issued to them.

Gilbert George Landragin appeals in open Grand Chapter against a decision by the Grand Superintendent over Kent. This is the first such appeal in thirty-eight years.

1944 *D-Day: the invasion of Normandy by 155,000 Allied troops takes place; the Allies enter Germany; PAYE income tax begins; the Butler Education Act is passed, stating that Britain needs to provide secondary education for all children.*

The new District of Ceylon is established, Robert Coleridge Scott (d.1963) is appointed the first Grand Superintendent. (7 June).

A special prayer is given in Grand Chapter by the First Grand Principal the Rt Hon Earl of Harewood, 'to serving brethren, an end to suffering, and safe and victorious return home'.

1945 *Hitler commits suicide; the Channel Islands are liberated; Labour win UK General Election rendering Churchill out of office; a UN Charter is signed in San Francisco; the atomic bomb is dropped on Hiroshima and Nagasaki; the World Bank is established.*

First edition of 'The ritual of the Holy Royal Arch as taught in the Aldersgate Chapter of Improvement No. 1657' is published by 'The Aldersgate Chapter of Improvement No. 1657'

A special prayer is delivered in Grand Chapter by the Third Grand Principal, Seth Smith Somers, Grand Superintendent for Worcester (1 August).

1946 *The Bank of England is nationalised; television broadcasting by the BBC resumes; the first civilian flight from Heathrow Airport takes off; the first Cannes Film Festival.*

A braille version of 'The ritual of the Holy Royal Arch as taught in the Aldersgate Chapter of Improvement No. 1657' is privately printed and published by the Royal National Institute for the Blind.

The wartime emergency regulations are lifted. The year sees a return to normal Royal Arch regulations.

Arthur Alexander Legat (d.1959) is appointed the first Grand Superintendent in and over the Royal Arch District of East Africa (resigning in 1948). (1 May).

1947 *All major British coal mines are nationalised; the first 'Dead Sea Scroll' is found; Princess Elizabeth (later Elizabeth II) marries the Duke of Edinburgh; British military occupation ends in Iraq.*

Edward William Spencer, 10th Duke of Devonshire (d.1950), is elected First Grand Principal.

New regulations stipulate that the office of Almoner should not be applied to a chapter and that the wearing of collars should not be obligatory in Grand Chapter.

The Earl of Harewood, Past First Grand Principal, dies. (6 August).

A new edition of *'The Complete Workings of the Royal Arch Ritual'*, is published. (London, Privately Printed for A Lewis. 1947).

1948 *The twelfth Olympic 'Austerity Games' held in London; private railway companies are nationalised as 'British Railways'; the State of Israel is founded; the first Morris Minor is produced; the British Citizenship Act qualifies all Commonwealth citizens for British passports.*

James Wilfred Stubbs is appointed Assistant Grand Scribe Ezra.

More emphasis is placed by the First Grand Principal on the spiritual aspects of Royal Arch Freemasonry. (28 July).

Hon. Sir Charles William Tachie-Menson (d.1962) is appointed the first Grand Superintendent in and over the Royal Arch District of Ghana. (1 December).

1949 *Clothes rationing ends in Britain; NATO is created by twelve nations; the Russians lift the Berlin blockade.*

A new edition of *General Regulations* is issued. (Sydney A. White, *General Regulations established by Supreme Grand Chapter for the Government of the Order of Royal Arch Masons of England*, London: Freemasons' Hall Great Queen Street. 1949).

The debate about the interchangeable use of the titles Chapter of Instruction and Chapter of Improvement is concluded as per Rule 80 of the Laws and Regulations. (2 February). There had been a continuing debate about the use of the term 'Improvement' i.e. for the purposes of rehearsal of the ritual, as opposed to 'Instruction', namely the teaching of the ritual. The final decision taken in February was that those who used the title 'Chapter of Improvement' could continue to do so but future such entities had to be named 'Chapter of Instruction'.

The Royal Arch is introduced into the Netherlands in accordance with the principles of Supreme Grand Chapter. The 'Order of Freemasons of the Holy Royal Arch under the Grand Chapter of the Netherlands' is consecrated by English companions. (3 February).

The spirituality of the Royal Arch as an Order is again emphasised in Supreme Grand Chapter (4 May).

J Heron Lepper addresses the Supreme Grand Chapter with a paper on 'Legends Popular in Royal Arch Masonry'.

1950 *Petrol rationing ends in Britain; the Korean War starts; soap-rationing ends in Britain; China invades Tibet.*

The Craft records show a total of 6,341 lodges, and 23,229 new registered members are recorded during the previous year.

A change of jurisdiction in India is made since Karachi is now located within the boundaries of Pakistan.

J Heron Lepper addresses the Supreme Grand Chapter with a paper entitled 'The Ceremonies of the Royal Arch'. (26 July).

1951 *The Festival of Britain takes place with the opening of the Royal Festival Hall; 'Zebra crossings' are introduced in Britain starting with the South Bank, London; the first 'Goon Show' is broadcast.*

Lawrence Roger, 11th Earl of Scarbrough (1896-1969), is promoted from Second to First Grand Principal (until 1967). (2 May).

The November Convocation of Supreme Grand Chapter is postponed. Lacking any provision in the book of constitutions for the postponement of a convocation, a decision is taken, on the authority of the Supreme Grand Chapter, to do so.

Ivor Grantham addresses the Supreme Grand Chapter with a lecture entitled 'The Origin of the Legend Communicated to Exaltees'. (7 February).

Hira Lal (d.1959) is appointed the first Grand Superintendent in and over the Royal Arch District of Northern India. (5 December).

1952 *George VI dies; the last tram runs in London; tea-rationing ends in Britain; Eisenhower sweeps to power as US President; the contraceptive pill is invented.*

Prince Philip, the Duke of Edinburgh (b1921) is initiated. (5 December).

Grand Scribe Ezra, Sydney A White (1937-58), KCVO, is knighted. (7 May).

The removal of the Temple Chapter of Jerusalem No. 4611 from the Jerusalem Old City Masonic Hall in Israel to Freemasons' Hall, London, is sanctioned by the Supreme Grand Chapter. (7 May).

The District of Northern China ceases to exist. (30 July).

The New District Grand Chapter of Northern India is established. (5 November).

Heron Lepper addresses the Supreme Grand Chapter with his paper entitled 'Order of the Holy Royal Arch'. (5 November).

1953 *Sugar-rationing ends in Britain; Stalin dies; Winston Churchill is knighted; Mount Everest is conquered by Edmund Hillary and Sherpa Tensing Norgay; the coronation of Elizabeth II takes place; the Playboy Magazine is published for the first time with Marilyn Monroe as a centrefold.*

The death of Heron Lepper, Grand Librarian, is announced in the Supreme Grand Chapter. (4 February).

A declaration of allegiance is made to the Supreme Grand Chapter by companions from other jurisdictions. (6 May).

1954 *Roger Bannister runs a mile in under four minutes; Bill Haley and the Comets release 'Rock Around the Clock'; food-rationing officially ends in Britain; the BBC broadcasts its first television news bulletin.*

An extensive revision of the Regulations is made by James Stubbs, Grand Scribe E, and W G H Browne. The proposals are presented to Supreme Grand Chapter and are confirmed in 1956.

Donald Malcolm Campbell (1921-1967) is exalted in Grand Master's Chapter No. 1. (16 July).

Ivor Grantham addresses the Supreme Grand Chapter with a paper entitled 'The Nature of the Royal Arch ritual in the 18th Century'. (3 November).

1955 *Anthony Eden becomes Prime Minister; the end of the Allies' occupation of Austria following World War II; an anti-polio vaccine is developed by Jonas Salk.*

The Overseas Grand Chapter Rank is instituted.

Thomas Ellis, 1st Lord Robins (d.1962) is appointed the first Grand Superintendent in and over the Royal Arch District of Rhodesia (resigning in 1957). (4 May).

1956 *Premium Bonds are launched; the first Eurovision Song Contest takes place in Lugano, Switzerland; the Hungarian rising against the Soviet occupation is crushed; Israel, Britain and France invade Suez to regain the Canal.*

New revisions of Grand Chapter regulations, placing the Royal Arch in line with the Craft Constitutions, come into force. (1 January). A new edition of *General Regulations* is issued (*General Regulations established by Supreme Grand Chapter for the Government of the Order of Royal Arch Masons of England*, London, Freemasons' Hall Great Queen Street, 1956).

The formal title of the Order is emphasised, namely the 'Supreme Grand Chapter of Royal Arch Masons of England'.

The Committee of General Purposes becomes responsible also for the finances of Supreme Grand Chapter in addition to approving applications for new Charters.

Bernard Jones addresses the Supreme Grand Chapter with a paper entitled 'The Charter of Compact erecting the First Grand Chapter'. (7 November).

Roy A Wells is appointed Scribe Ezra of the Domatic Chapter of Instruction.

1957 *Harold Macmillan becomes Prime Minister; the Treaty of Rome creates the European Economic Community (EEC), consisting of six nations: France, West Germany, Italy, Belgium, Holland and Luxembourg; the first artificial satellite 'Sputnik I' is launched by the Soviet Union.*

The Supreme Grand Chapter decides to issue separate statistics for Chapters every ten years (February).

Publication of first edition of *Freemasons' Book of the Royal Arch* by Bernard E Jones, published by George G. Harrap and Co Ltd, London.

A new edition of the *Complete Workings of the Royal Arch Ritual* is issued (London, Privately Printed for A Lewis, 1957).

Roy A Wells (1908-1990), dedicated Royal Arch author, takes office as First Principal in his own Five Orders Chapter No. 3696 in Southgate.

1958 *The Munich air disaster in which the Manchester United team members are killed; Britain's first parking meters are installed; Charles de Gaulle establishes the Fifth Republic in France.*

Grand Scribe Ezra, Sir Sydney White, dies. (9 March).

James Wilfrid Stubbs, Past Deputy Grand Scribe Ezra, is appointed to be Grand Scribe Ezra and also Grand Secretary of the United Grand Lodge of England (until 1968).

1960 *New £1 notes issued by Bank of England; MOT tests on motor vehicles are introduced; Penguin Books are found not guilty of obscenity in the 'Lady Chatterley's Lover' case; National Service ends in Britain; Hitchcock's 'Psycho' is screened.*

The July convocation of the Supreme Grand Chapter is dispensed with. Afterwards it is agreed that insufficient business is available for four convocations: the custom of having talks, demonstrations and organ recitals at the February and November Convocations had developed markedly during the past decade.

Changes to the Royal Arch ritual are devised, impacting upon the installation ceremony, the penalties, the historical and symbolic lectures, the use of catechism, the exaltation ceremony and the mystical lecture. During the decade permitted variations were introduced regarding the penalties in the obligations, following the lead of Grand Lodge. (A complete removal of the penalties, again following the Craft, took place in 1987.)

1961 *The farthing ceases to be legal tender; John F Kennedy becomes President of the USA; 'White Fivers', £5 notes printed on white paper, cease to be legal tender; Yuri Gagarin becomes the first man in space; betting shops are legalised in Britain.*

A new edition of General Regulations for Chapters is issued (James Wilfrid Stubbs, *General Regulations established by Supreme Grand Chapter for the Government of the Order of Royal Arch Masons of England*, London: Freemasons' Hall, Great Queen Street, 1961).

Changes in the Royal Arch ritual, the so-called Appendix C and Appendix D, are introduced as a permissive variation in the form of the three Installation Ceremonies, providing for the precedence at the Installation of the three Principals of the Chapter in the order of Zerubbabel, Haggai and Joshua. The new changes allow the three Principals Elect to be obligated in open Chapter and in the presence of the companions of the Chapter. (8 November).

1963 *The Secretary of State for War, John Profumo, resigns in a sex scandal; the 'Great Train Robbery' takes place on the Glasgow to London mail train; President Kennedy is assassinated in Dallas, Texas; the Beatles achieve international fame.*

Prince Edward, the Duke of Kent (b. 1935), is initiated in Royal Alpha Lodge No. 16. (16 December).

1966 *The first soft landing on the moon is achieved by the unmanned space shuttle 'Luna 9'; the World Cup is won by England at Wembley; the first Christmas stamps are issued in Britain; eighteen new universities are created in Britain between 1961 and 1966.*

The Bicentenary of the first Supreme Grand Chapter is celebrated at Freemasons' Hall in a Special Convocation. (1 July).

Prince Edward, the Duke of Kent, is exalted in Westminster and Keystone Chapter No. 10, then elected and invested as First Principal of the Chapter.

A R Hewitt addresses the Supreme Grand Chapter: 'The Supreme Grand Chapter of England. A Brief History from Lord Blayney to the Duke of Sussex'. Published as a separate pamphlet and as a paper in *AQC* 78. (1 July).

1967 *Donald Campbell dies attempting the world water-speed record; the 'Six-Day War' in the Middle East breaks out; the first withdrawal from a cash dispenser is made in Britain; colour TV is introduced in Britain; Che Guevara is killed in Bolivia; the first human heart-transplant is successfully carried out by Dr Christian Barnard.*

The Earl of Scarborough, Grand Master and First Grand Principal, resigns. This enables the Duke of Kent to be elected and invested as Grand Master and First Grand Principal. The Earl of Scarborough accepts the office of Pro Grand Master and Pro First Grand Principal.

The Duke of Kent (b. 1935)

Prince Edward George Nicholas Paul Patrick, The Duke of Kent, was born in 1935. He was educated at Eton and Le Rosey, Switzerland. He is a grandson of George V and a cousin of both the Queen and the Duke of Edinburgh. His father, who was Grand Master 1939-42, was the fourth son of King George V, and his mother, Princess Marina, was the daughter of Prince Nicholas of Greece.

A resolution regarding the permissive variations of the penal clause in the Obligations is passed in Supreme Grand Chapter. (27 April).

1968 British Standard Time is introduced; London Bridge is sold; 5p and 10p decimal coins are issued; Manchester United becomes the first English club to win the European Cup; Robert F Kennedy is assassinated.

A new edition of *The Complete Workings of the Royal Arch Degree* is issued. (London, Privately Printed for A Lewis, 1968). The edition is a revision of the edition from 1957, but incorporating the 1967 Permissive Variations. These 'permissive variations' allowed discretion on the part of individual chapters to adopt or reject the new wording for part of the ritual, instituted and recommended by Supreme Grand Chapter. Adoption is officially encouraged, accepted by most chapters.

1969 *Maiden flight of the Concorde; Neil Armstrong and Buzz Aldrin are the first men on the moon; the halfpenny ceases to be legal tender in Britain; the 50p coin is introduced; the death penalty for murder is abolished.*

A R Hewitt addresses the Supreme Grand Chapter with a paper entitled; 'The First Bi-Centenaries of Royal Arch Chapters'. (12 February).

Roy Arthur Wells addresses the Supreme Grand Chapter with a paper entitled 'A Short Study of the Symbols of the Principal Banners' (12 November).

1970 *'Decimal' postage stamps are first issued for sale in Britain; Edward Heath becomes Prime Minister; the ten-shilling note (50p after decimalisation) goes out of circulation in Britain.*

A new edition of *General Regulations* is issued, established by Supreme Grand Chapter for the Government of the Order of Royal Arch Masons of England, Published under the Authority of the Supreme Grand Chapter, London. 1970.

The Senior London Grand Chapter Rank is instituted.

A R Hewitt addresses the Supreme Grand Chapter with a paper entitled 'Grand Chapter Ritual of the Late 18th Century'. (11 November).

1972 *'Bloody Sunday' takes place in Northern Ireland; Ceylon changes its name to Sri Lanka; the last manned moon mission, Apollo 17, is launched; strict anti-hijack measures are introduced at international airports.*

Changes in the use of the R or H signs are approved by the Grand Chapter.

A R Hewitt addresses the Supreme Grand Chapter with a paper entitled 'Early Royal Arch Regalia' (9 February).

1973 *Britain enters the EEC Common Market; the Vietnam ceasefire is agreed; the new London Bridge is opened; the first call is made on a portable cellular phone; 'Concorde' makes its first non-stop crossing of the Atlantic in record-breaking time.*

Terence O Haunch addresses the Supreme Grand Chapter with a paper entitled 'The Royal Arch in England, Ireland and Scotland - Apparent difference within a Basic Identity' (14 February).

1974 *President Nixon resigns over the 'Watergate' scandal; Lord Lucan disappears; the Birmingham pub bombings by the IRA take place; India becomes the sixth nation to explode a nuclear device.*

A new edition of *The Complete Workings of the Royal Arch Ritual* is published, introducing the permissive form of the Obligation and the new form of installing the Three Principals.

A R Hewitt addresses the Supreme Grand Chapter with a paper entitled 'Looking Back 200 years'. (13 February).

1975 *Margaret Thatcher becomes the leader of the Conservative party; Charlie Chaplin is knighted; the 'Yorkshire Ripper' commits his first murder; General Franco dies; Juan Carlos is declared King of Spain; the Sex Discrimination Act comes into force.*

R A Wells addresses the Supreme Grand Chapter with a paper entitled 'Concerning Royal Arch Installations'. (12 February).

1976 *'Mamma Mia' by Abba reaches No.1 in UK; James Callaghan becomes the new Prime Minister; Mao Tse-tung dies; the National Theatre opens in London.*

Terence O Haunch addresses the Supreme Grand Chapter with a paper entitled 'The Royal Arch in Relation to the Scandinavian Rite'. (11 February).

1977 *The Lib-Lab pact is formed; the first personal computer, Apple, goes on sale; the Queen's Silver Jubilee is celebrated; Virginia Wade wins the Ladies Singles at Wimbledon; Elvis Presley dies; the supersonic Concorde service between London and New York is inaugurated.*

E Comp Cyril N Batham, Secretary of Quatuor Coronati Lodge No. 2076 (EC), the Premier Lodge of Masonic Research, arranges for a fund to be set up for a series of official lectures sponsored by Supreme Grand Chapter. The scheme, to follow in the pattern of the Craft's 'Prestonian Lectures', is instituted as the 'Batham Royal Arch Lecture', with two lecturers appointed approximately every five years. The first Batham Royal Arch Lecture is given in 1985. (*vide* 1985 below).

The Supreme Grand Chapter agrees that the Principals' lectures can be given in catechetical form. This format was in practice before 1834 and will, by sharing the ritual, involve more members in the ceremonies.

1978 *The first broadcast of the proceedings in Parliament takes place; the world's first 'test tube' baby, Louise Browne, is born; Pope John Paul II is elected.*

Cyril N Batham addresses the Supreme Grand Chapter with a paper entitled 'Whence Came the Royal Arch?'. (8 February).

Col R T S Kitwood, Grand Superintendent for Hampshire and Isle of Wight addresses the Supreme Grand Chapter with a paper entitled 'The Charter of Compact'. (8 November).

1979 *Ayatollah Khomeini returns to Iran; Margaret Thatcher becomes the first woman Prime Minister of the United Kingdom; Lord Mountbatten is killed in Ireland; corporal punishment is abolished in schools; Southern Rhodesia is given independence.*

Prince Michael of Kent (b.1942) is exalted into the Royal Arch in the Prince of Wales Chapter No. 259. (5 June).

Surgeon-Capt G S Irvine addresses the Supreme Grand Chapter with a paper entitled 'Variations in the Devices on Royal Arch Banners'. (14 February).

Revd Canon Richard Tydeman addresses the Supreme Grand Chapter with a paper entitled 'A New Approach to Mystical Hebrew'. (14 November). This paper by Richard Tydeman leads to the appointment by Supreme Grand Chapter of a committee charged to consider the whole question of the Mystical Lecture. The committee reported on the matter in 1982 *(vide* 1982 below).

1980 *President Tito dies in Yugoslavia; the SAS storm the Iranian London Embassy following a shooting; John Lennon is assassinated in New York; 'Solidarity' formed by unions in Poland.*

K W H Hastwell addresses the Supreme Grand Chapter with a paper entitled 'The Enthusiasm of the Principal Sojourner'. (13 February).

Rev O H Skipwith addresses the Supreme Grand Chapter with a paper entitled 'The Secret Vault - A symbolic Interpretation'. (12 November).

1981 *The Social Democratic Party (SDP) is launched by the 'Gang of Four'; the first London marathon; the first US Space Shuttle; the wedding of Prince Charles and Lady Diana Spencer takes place.*

I Harry Mendoza addresses the Supreme Grand Chapter with a paper entitled 'The Pass Word Leading to the R A'. (11 February).

Roy A Wells addresses the Supreme Grand Chapter with a paper entitled 'Royal Arch in the United States of America'. (11 November).

1982 *Unemployment in England reaches 3 million; Laker Airways collapses; Argentina invades the Falkland Islands; 'HMS Conqueror' sinks the Argentine Navy cruiser 'ARA General Belgrano'; IRA bombings take place in London.*

The committee appointed in 1979 to consider the Mystical Lecture recommends the adoption of one of three options:

- Chapters to continue as before without change.
- The addition to the lecture of a statement pointing out the errors which should be understood in their traditional and historic context.
- The introduction of a modified version explaining the Hebrew characters and the Word on the triangle.

The committee continues its deliberations.

A R W Kent addresses the Supreme Grand Chapter with a paper entitled 'Grand Originals: A Story Behind a Legend'. (10 February).

I Harry Mendoza addresses the Supreme Grand Chapter with a paper entitled 'The Five Signs in Royal Arch Masonry'. (10 November).

1983 *Start of the concept of 'Breakfast TV' in Britain; a seat-belt law comes into force; the £1 coin is introduced into circulation; the first female Lord Mayor of London is elected (Dame Mary Donaldson).*

Harry Carr (1900-83), the leading and prolific Masonic historian, dies, having been Past Master of Quatuor Coronati Lodge (1958-9)and author of one of the most continuingly popular Masonic books: *The Freemason at Work*. (London, Quatuor Coronati Correspondence Circle Ltd., 1976). It contains some 200 questions and answers covering a very wide range of Masonic subjects, all discussed candidly and accurately.

Sir James Stubbs addresses the Supreme Grand Chapter with a paper entitled 'Changes in Grand Chapter 1947-1980 [Part I]'. (9 November).

1984 *The FTSE index exceeds 800; the miners' strike begins; the IRA bomb explodes at a Tory conference in a hotel in Brighton; Indira Gandhi is assassinated; British Telecom is privatised.*

The United Grand Lodge of England begins to pursue a policy of openness on Freemasonry.

T M Greensill MBE addresses the Supreme Grand Chapter with a paper entitled 'The Altar of Incense'. (8 February).

Sir James Stubbs addresses the Supreme Grand Chapter with a paper entitled 'Changes in Grand Chapter 1947-1980 [continued]'. (14 November).

1985 *The Miners agree to call off their strike; Al-Fayed buys Harrods; a European abolition of border controls is agreed between Belgium, France, West Germany, Luxembourg, and the Netherland; the wreckage of the 'Titanic' is found.*

The First Batham Royal Arch Lecture is delivered by B J Bell to Grand Chapter and is entitled 'Ezra - The Scribe'.

Craft Statistics show 8,253 lodges registered in England and Wales of which 1,677 are in London. The number of certificates issued to new Master Masons, 16,126, of which 776 are for overseas brethren, indicate an increase in Craft membership from previous year.

Statistics

There is no precise or accurate information available on the exact number of Freemasons at any one time, because the United Grand Lodge of England does not maintain a continuous record of the death and resignation of its members. Thus the statistical information provided by the UGLE is limited to the registered number of Lodges warranted and the number of membership certificates issued annually.

W W Ruff addresses the Supreme Grand Chapter with a paper entitled 'Reflections on the Royal Arch Jewel'. (13 February).

Rev Canon Richard Tydeman addresses the Supreme Grand Chapter with a paper entitled 'The Words on the Triangle - An Alternative View'. (13 November).

1986 *The Greater London Council is abolished; the Chernobyl nuclear accident occurs, as does the 'Big Bang' of the London Stock Market; M25, the London ring-road, is completed.*

Colin F W Dyer addresses the Supreme Grand Chapter with a paper entitled 'The Royal Arch Words'. (12 February).

Roy A Wells addresses the Supreme Grand Chapter with a paper entitled 'A Brief Study of the Pedestal'. (12 November).

1987 *Terry Waite is kidnapped in Beirut (he is released 17 November 1991); excavations begin for the Channel Tunnel joining Britain and France; the 'Black Monday' Stock Market crash occurs in the City of London; the world's population exceeds 5 billion.*

The penalties of the Royal Arch are transferred from the obligation to the explanation of the signs in harmony with the action taken by the United Grand Lodge of England regarding Craft ritual. (11 February).

I Harry Mendoza addresses the Supreme Grand Chapter on 'The Three Epochs in the History of Freemasonry', as does the Revd Canon R Tydeman on 'History, Mystery and Geometry'. (11 February).

An emergency meeting of Grand Chapter is called to consider and refute accusations by the Anglican General Synod that the Royal Arch is blasphemous. (8 July).

A Special Committee demonstrates the revisions to the Mystical Lecture and ritual in Supreme Grand Chapter. Similar demonstrations are made in the Provinces and continue into 1988.

1989 *A Fatwa is issued against Salman Rushdie for 'The Satanic Verses'; tanks are stopped in Tiananmen Square, Peking, by an unknown protester; the Berlin Wall is torn down; the year sees the start of live TV emissions of the proceedings in the House of Commons.*

Statistics of lodge membership, taken from annual returns, dues and Grand Lodge charity fees, shows a total of over 600,000 registrations of freemasons in the books of the UGLE. This figure includes multiple membership.

Following a lengthy debate (and demonstrations in 1987-8), important obligatory revisions are implemented by the Supreme Grand Chapter. Within twelve months all chapters are required to remove from the ritual the contentious Hebrew characters and tripartite word, and all obligations are to be taken on the Volume of the Sacred Law.

A new version of the Mystical Lecture (now referred to as the Traditional version), in two parts, is introduced. (February).

A revised edition of the *Complete Workings of the Royal Arch Degree* is published by Lewis Masonic, incorporating the changes earlier adopted by Supreme Grand Chapter (*Complete Workings of the Royal Arch Degree*, Shepperton, Surrey, Lewis Masonic. 1989, 2nd Ed 1990).

1990 *Nelson Mandela is released in South Africa; Iraq invades Kuwait; Germany is reunited; Margaret Thatcher resigns as Prime Minister and John Major is elected; the Channel Tunnel excavation teams meet half-way.*

The Peterborough Booklets No. 4, 'Notes for a Newly Exalted Companion', is published by Quatuor Coronati Correspondence Circle Ltd. (London, QCCC Ltd, 1990).

The New Masonic Samaritan Fund is established. (28 November).

John M Hamill addresses the Supreme Grand Chapter with a paper entitled 'Pure Ancient Masonry'. (14 November).

The second edition of *The Complete Workings of the Royal Arch Degree* is published (Shepperton, Surrey. Lewis Masonic. Revised Edition 1990).

Roy A Wells (1908-1990), a dedicated Royal Arch student and notable author, Past Master of Quatuor Coronati Lodge, dies.

1991 *Helen Sharman becomes the first British astronaut in space; the Union of Soviet Socialist Republics is dissolved; Robert Maxwell drowns at sea; the Internet takes off.*

Iain Ross Bryce, Past Deputy Grand Master, is appointed Second Grand Principal (retiring in 2005).

The second Batham Royal Arch Lecture by Anthony R Ough is published, entitled: 'The Origin and Development of English Royal Arch Masonry: a short history of the evolution of the organisation, government and the ritual of the Holy Royal Arch ' (London, Privately Printed, 1991).

Frederick H Smyth addresses the Supreme Grand Chapter with a paper entitled 'Bro Mozart - An Excellent Companion'. (13 February).

John M Hamill addresses the Supreme Grand Chapter with a paper entitled *'225 Years of Grand Chapter'*. (13November).

1992 *Betty Boothroyd is elected the first female Speaker of the House of Commons; the Football Premier League kicks off in England; a great fire ravages Windsor Castle; the Queen, in her Christmas speech to the nation, describes the year as an 'Annus Horribilis'.*

25th Anniversary of the Duke of Kent as First Grand Principal is celebrated at a Regular Convocation of the Grand Chapter in conjunction with the dedication of the new Grand Sojourners' Banners. (11 November).

John M Hamill addresses the Supreme Grand Chapter with a paper entitled 'Royal First Grand Principals'. (11 November).

1993 *The Maastricht Treaty is ratified; the European Union is established; Elizabeth II becomes the first British Monarch to pay Income Tax.*

The third Batham Royal Arch lecture by Douglas W Burford is published: 'The Anomalies of the Royal Arch-Craft Connection'. (London: Privately printed, 1993).

1994 *The Church of England ordains its first female priests; the Channel Tunnel opens to traffic; the National Lottery is introduced.*

Grand Lodge records that the total membership of the Craft is 359,000 brethren. (United Grand Lodge of England, 'International Directory of Registered Masonic Bodies', <http://freemason-international.com/>, accessed 30 March 2013).

John M Hamill addresses the Supreme Grand Chapter with a paper entitled 'The Place of the Royal Arch in English Masonry' (November 9).

1995 *Nick Leeson brings down Baring Brothers; the first item is sold on Amazon.com.; the 'Galileo' spacecraft arrives at Jupiter, having been launched in 1989.*

Statistics indicate the total number of United Grand Lodge of England memberships to be 365,200.

The Revd Peter Hemingway, Third Grand Principal, addresses the Supreme Grand Chapter with a paper entitled 'The Volume of the Sacred Law and the Royal Arch'. (11 February).

Richard A Crane addresses the Supreme Grand Chapter with a paper entitled 'The Spiritual Dimension'. (13 December).

1996 *An IRA bomb explodes in London Docklands; scientists in Scotland clone a sheep (Dolly); Charles, Prince of Wales, and Diana, Princess of Wales, divorce.*

John M Hamill addresses the Supreme Grand Chapter with a paper entitled 'The Revision of the Royal Arch Ritual'. (11 September).

Michael Walker, Grand Scribe Ezra in the Supreme Grand Chapter of Ireland, addresses the Supreme Grand Chapter with a paper entitled: 'Irish Royal Arch Masonry' (11 December).

1997 *'New Labour' wins the election; Tony Blair replaces John Major as Prime Minister; IBM's 'Deep Blue' computer beats chess master Garry Kasparov; Hong Kong is returned to China; Diana, Princess of Wales, is killed in a car crash.*

The fourth Batham Royal Arch Lecture, 'The Zodiac's Path in Past and Present Freemasonry', by the Revd Neville B Cryer is published.

G J Smith, Grand Scribe E, Scotland, addresses the Supreme Grand Chapter with a paper entitled 'Scottish Royal Arch Masonry'. (12 November).

1998 *The Northern Ireland 'Good Friday peace agreement' is signed; the Google search engine is founded; US President Bill Clinton is impeached over the Monica Lewinsky scandal.*

Michael Higham steps down as Grand Scribe Ezra and as Grand Secretary of the UGLE.

James Daniel (b.1941) is appointed Grand Scribe Ezra of the Supreme Grand Chapter of England and Grand Secretary of the UGLE. (June).

Yasha Beresiner addresses the Supreme Grand Chapter with a paper entitled 'A New Look at the Charter of Compact'. (11 February).

1999 *The European Monetary Union comes into force; the Scottish Parliament is officially opened; a total eclipse of the sun is experienced in the UK; the world's population reaches six billion.*

Richard A Crane addresses the Supreme Grand Chapter with a paper entitled 'The Grand Sanhedrin that Sits in the Hall of Hewn Stone' (10 February).

S Fernie addresses the Supreme Grand Chapter with a paper entitled 'Traditional History: The Biblical Background'. (10 November).

2000 The *'London Eye' opens; Ken Livingstone is elected the first Mayor of London; an Air France Concorde crashes on take-off at Paris.*

Statistics from the United Grand Lodge of England indicate total number of UGLE lodges to be 8,656 (1,605 of which are in London). The Craft has reports a total membership of 326,659.

The fifth Batham Royal Arch Lecture by Yasha Beresiner, 'Royal Arch - The Fourth Degree of the Grand Lodge of the Antients', is published. (August).

John M Hamill addresses the Supreme Grand Chapter with a paper entitled 'Some Thoughts on the Origins of the Royal Arch'. (8 November).

2001 *Wikipedia goes on-line; Labour wins the general election; the '9/11' terrorist attack in New York takes place; the Euro is introduced in Austria, Belgium, Holland, the Irish Republic, Italy, Luxembourg, Finland, France, Germany, Greece, Spain and Portugal.*

Rex Thorne addresses the Supreme Grand Chapter with a paper entitled 'London Freemasonry'. (2 February).

Lord Northampton elected and invested Pro Grand Master of the United Grand Lodge of England and Pro First Grand Principal of Supreme Grand Chapter. (14 March).

Lord Northampton (b. 1946)

A British Peer, Spencer "Spenny" Douglas David Compton, 7th Marquess of Northampton, was invested as Pro Grand Master in succession to Lord Farnham. If any individual mason should be singled out for implementing far-reaching changes in Freemasonry during the past 100 years, it would undoubtedly be Lord Northampton. In 1995 he was appointed Assistant Grand Master responsible for London, a position he held for five years. On his appointment as Pro Grand Master in 2000, he had instigated the establishment of a Metropolitan Grand Lodge of London and had seen the fraternity through an intense period of attacks, following the publication of various anti-Masonic books, Stephen Knight's *The Brotherhood - The Secret World of the Freemasons* (London: Granada, 1984) the best known amongst them. His open policies led to a refreshing approach to freemasonry in the eyes of the public and the permanent benefits to the Society are enjoyed to date. He was a popular freemason with whose views and expressions many ordinary brethren in the fraternity identified. Lord Northampton was an innovative Masonic leader and totally dedicated to the Craft and Royal Arch. In March 2008, when he retired as Pro Grand Master and Pro First Grand Principal, he had helped the fraternity come through one of the very difficult periods in its history.

Ronald W Cayless addresses the Supreme Grand Chapter with a paper entitled 'The Grand Temple Organ'. (14 November).

2002 *Introduction of Euro coins and banknotes across the Eurozone – the UK stays out; the Millennium Bridge over the Thames in London is finally opened; the Queen Mother dies aged 101 years.*

The February Convocation is dispensed with. Grand Chapter henceforth meets on the second Wednesday in November and the day following the Annual Investiture of the Craft.

The first Committee of General Purposes, presided over by Anthony Wilson, is appointed. It consists of companions appointed by the First Grand Principal, and others to be elected by the Grand Chapter. The Committee's function is to formulate new policy on matters of ritual; it will have no executive powers.

The prerogative of appointing Grand Superintendents remains personal to the First Grand Principal.

All chapters within a province (in England, outside London) or a district (abroad) are to come under the authority of a Grand Superintendent.

Initial proposals for a Metropolitan Grand Chapter for London are made. (November).

Although a new generic title of 'Metropolitan Grand Chapter Rank', will be established, 'London Grand Chapter Rank' will remain in force. Active 'Metropolitan' officers will revert to the 'London Grand Chapter Rank' after one year of service.

2003 *Last commercial flight of Concorde; England wins the Rugby World Cup; Saddam Hussein is captured.*

Statistics from the Supreme Grand Chapter shows that the number of Chapters on the register is 3,383 (of which 660 are in London, 2,374 in the provinces and 349 in districts and abroad). The number of Grand Chapter certificates presented in 2003 was 4,494.

The Metropolitan Grand Lodge and the Metropolitan Grand Chapter of London are constituted by the Duke of Kent in a ceremony held at the Royal Albert Hall. (1 October).

Lord Millett is appointed Metropolitan Grand Superintendent.

Article II of the Articles of Union of 1813, as it appears in the preamble to the Book of Constitutions and relating to the status of the Royal Arch, is added to by Grand Lodge. The new version of Article II describes the Royal Arch as 'an extension to, but neither a superior nor a subordinate part of the Degrees which precede it'. (10 December).

The First Grand Principal expresses his views that the 2003 declaration as to the status of the Royal Arch is not satisfactory and needs to be replaced with a fresh definition.

A recommendation is issued from Supreme Grand Chapter to Grand Lodge that a Royal Arch representative should be appointed in each Craft Lodge.

2004 *Alistair Cooke, the broadcaster and journalist, dies at the age of 95; Ireland becomes the first country in the world to ban smoking in public places; the enlargement of the European Union now includes 25 members.*

The new and amended Royal Arch Regulations of the Supreme Grand Chapter of England now state:

- A Master Mason may be installed as the Third Principal in a Royal Arch chapter (previously he had to be a Past Master of a Craft lodge).
- A new password is introduced, as the previous password was that of an Installed Master.
- The words 'You may perhaps imagine you have this day taken a fourth degree in Freemasonry: such however is not the case. It is the Master Masons' completed' are mandatorily removed from the ritual.
- The traditional dates attributed to the three Original Grand Lodges are removed from the historical lecture.
- The wording in the Mystical Lecture now reads '[...] it continually reminds us of that great hereafter when we hope to enjoy *eternal life*', instead of '*endless life and everlasting bliss*'.
- A permitted alternative version of the exaltation ceremony is introduced as an option for chapters to adopt.

Recommended changes to the ritual in the exaltation ceremony are demonstrated in Grand Chapter and adopted. (10 November).

After much deliberation by a special working party, the Grand Chapter declares that the Royal Arch is a separate degree in its own right.

10 November 2004 Amendments

The 2004 regulations contain a new updated Metropolitan Working of the Royal Arch Ritual which incorporates the necessary amendments and additions following the convocation of Supreme Grand Chapter mentioned above. The new regulations are seen as crucial to a better understanding and acceptance of the definition of 'pure Ancient Masonry' first mentioned in the Articles of Union in 1813 and the revision of the ritual that took place in 1834. Before this time, the Royal Arch was stated to be the completion of the Master Mason degree, whereas the Master Mason's degree was known to be complete in its own right, as was the exaltation ceremony. In December 2003 the United Grand Lodge resolved to amend the statement to the definition of pure Ancient Masonry (*see above*). Simultaneously, a Ritual Committee was set up to consider the Principals' Lectures. The recommended changes were demonstrated to Grand Chapter in November 2004 and adopted. The Strategic Working Party completed its work and stated that it did not envisage that further changes would be brought before the Grand Chapter in the foreseeable future and that the working of the changes would be kept under regular review: 'It is anticipated that a major assessment will be appropriate in ten years' time to consider the progress and the effects of the present proposals'.

Statistics for the year show a pattern of steadily shrinking membership of the Royal Arch in England and Wales. Membership falls by 2% to 99,000 and there is a 3% reduction in the number of exaltees. Nearly 37% of brethren in the Craft are members of the Royal Arch, a proportion that has remained consistent in recent years.

2005 *Pope John Paul II dies; Pope Benedict XVI is elected – the first German Pope for 1,000 years; suicide bombers attack London; the IRA declare an end to their 'armed struggle'; same-sex civil partnerships become legal.*

George Francis is installed as Second Grand Principal in succession to Iain Ross Bryce. (9 November).

The Supreme Grand Chapter of England website is launched.

Following the amendments and various changes in the ritual approved in November 2004, a letter is sent to the Scribes E of all private chapters summarising the changes and disclosing the new password. All chapters are recommended to bring the new password into use at once, whether or not the Third Principal-elect is an Installed Master. (28 April).

Amendments to the Royal Arch Regulations relating to changing the method of calculating the number of appointments to London Grand Chapter Rank are agreed upon.

New guidance from the Supreme Grand Chapter regarding attendance at the Supreme Grand Chapter recommends that all companions who are subscribing members of a chapter under the Supreme Grand Chapter of England, but not otherwise qualified to attend its convocations, will be permitted to attend Supreme Grand Chapter as non-voting observers. (28 April).

The Supreme Grand Chapter recommends that the 'R or H sign should no longer be given before addressing the Principals for the first time'. It is also stated that the 'changes in the ritual are compelling and apply with equal force to existing versions of the Royal Arch ritual.' It also recommends that 'corresponding changes be made in the traditional version of the Mystical Lecture'. (27 September).

Statistics for the year indicate the total number of registrations within the United Grand Lodge of England to be 279,932.

2006 *Queen Elizabeth II celebrates her 80th birthday; Saddam Hussein is executed; smoking in enclosed public places in Scotland is prohibited.*

Statistics estimate the total membership of the Craft to be 285,000.

A working party under the chairmanship of the Second Grand Principal is set up to look at the recruitment and retention of Royal Arch Masons. (8 November).

As part of a programme agreed upon between the Supreme Grand Chapter of England and the Symbolic Grand Lodge of Hungary, aimed at supporting the expansion of the Royal Arch, two English Chapters (Cockfosters No. 6883 and Heston No. 4888) are given permission to hold future meetings in Budapest.

Andrew Pearmain and the Revd Elkan Levy address the Supreme Grand Chapter with papers respectively entitled 'Mozart - Musician & Mason', to mark the 250th Anniversary of the birth of Wolfgang Amadeus Mozart, and 'The Holy Royal Arch - Enjoyment, Recruiting, Retention'. (8 November).

2007 *Tony Blair resigns as Prime Minister and is replaced by Gordon Brown; smoking is prohibited in enclosed public places in England; the seventh and final 'Harry Potter' book is released.*

C Nigel R Brown is appointed Grand Scribe Ezra of the Supreme Grand Chapter of England and Grand Secretary of the United Grand Lodge of England with effect from 1 February.

Nigel Brown (b. 1948)

Nigel Brown was born in Lusaka, then in Northern Rhodesia and was educated in Southern Rhodesia. From the Royal Military Academy in Sandhurst he was commissioned into the Grenadier Guards, retiring as Captain. He spent the following 15 years in senior management and the last 12 years as a business consultant. Nigel Brown was initiated in the Household Brigade Lodge No. 2614 in 1985. He is married with two adult children. He served as Deputy Grand Director of Ceremonies prior to his current appointment.

A report into the recruitment and retention of Royal Arch Masons is published by the working group set up under the chairmanship of the Second Grand Principal. The report does not cover the Metropolitan Grand Chapter. The report's first suggestion is that there should be a formal Royal Arch representative in each Lodge, possibly as a Lodge officer, who would be responsible for promoting the Order to Master Masons. (14 November).

V Revd Neil Collings addresses the Supreme Grand Chapter with a paper entitled: 'Rebuilding the Temple'. (14 November).

2008 *Barack Obama is elected the 44th President of the United States; surgeons at London's Moorfields Eye Hospital perform the first operations using bionic eyes, implanting them into two blind patients; in the current financial debacle Northern Rock is the first bank in Europe to be taken into state control.*

Statistics show the number of Chapters on the Grand Chapter register to be 3,266 (of which 613 are in London, 2,329 in the Provinces and 324 in Districts and abroad).

Statistics show an increase in Grand Chapter certificates presented in 2008: 3.835 as compared with 3,702 in 2007.

Inauguration of the Supreme Grand Chapter of Estonia. The Supreme Grand Chapter of England is responsible for the introduction of Royal Arch Masonry into that country. (1 May).

2009 *The heaviest snowfall in England in eighteen years disrupts air and road traffic; the Bank of England interest rate is reduced to a record low of 0.5%; England beat Australia in a cricket Test Match at Lord's for the first time in 75 years.*

Lord Northampton steps down as Pro Grand Master of the Craft and as Pro First Grand Principal of the Royal Arch. The Deputy Grand Master Peter Geoffrey Lowndes is appointed to succeed him in both roles. (11 March).

Peter Geoffrey Lowndes (b. 1948)

Peter Geoffrey Lowndes was born in 1948 and educated at Eton. He is a Fellow of the Royal Institution of Chartered Surveyors (FRICS). In 1984 he was appointed Deputy Grand Director of Ceremonies for the United Grand Lodge of England, in which role he served until 1987. In 1992-93 he served as Grand Sword Bearer, after which he became Grand Director of Ceremonies from 1995 to 2003. On 10 March 2004 he was installed Deputy Grand Master and continued as such until his appointment as Pro Grand Master. In the Royal Arch he served as Past Grand Scribe N until 2004 when he was installed Second Grand Principal for the ensuing year. In 2009 he was appointed Pro First Grand Principal.

D W Burford addresses the Supreme Grand Chapter with a paper entitled: 'Lest We Forget'. (11 November).

General Regulations established by the Supreme Grand Chapter for the Government of the order of Royal Arch Masons of England are published on line under the Authority of the Supreme Grand Chapter. (London, Freemasons' Hall Great Queen Street, WC2B 5AZ, 2009).

2010 *The Eyjafjallajökull volcano erupts in Iceland and closes airspace over north-western Europe; thirty-three miners are rescued from a copper mine in Chile.*

Statistics from the United Grand Lodge of England show total memberships in the organisation to be 243,668.

Royal Arch Celebration

The Supreme Grand Chapter, about to celebrate the 'bi-centenary of the declaration of the Royal Arch as the completion of pure Ancient Masonry' in 2013, sets up two committees: the 2013 Royal Arch Committee to be chaired by the Second Grand Principal and the Executive Committee to be run by the Grand Scribe Ezra.

At the Quarterly Communication of Supreme Grand Chapter on 10 November the Second Grand Principal, George Francis, announces:

> The focus of our attention is now moving to the celebration of the Bi-Centenary of the Royal Arch in 2013; to mark the official recognition of the Royal Arch as 'the completion of pure Ancient Freemasonry" at the union of the two great English Grand Lodges in 1813, which also created the United Grand Lodge of England. We therefore celebrate our official birthday, or to put it another way, the full emergence of the Royal Arch as we know it, 200 years ago. (10 November).

As pointed out in Part I, the generally accepted view of the origin of the Royal Arch is that it was 'invented' or introduced into England from abroad in the mid-eighteenth century. On 1 July 1966 Royal Arch Masons from all over the world attended a special convocation at Freemasons' Hall to celebrate the Bi-Centenary of the Supreme Grand Chapter of England founded on 22 July 1766.

'The Royal Arch Masons' 2013 Bicentenary Appeal' for the benefit of the Surgical Research Fellowship Scheme is officially launched by the Second Grand Principal. It is to be run and administered at no extra cost alongside the Craft's 250th Anniversary Fund for the purpose of research by the Royal College.

The Grand Master of the United Grand Lodge of England announces that the recently-introduced Royal Arch tie may be worn in Craft Lodges. (10 November).

2011 *Prince William, Duke of Cambridge, weds Kate Middleton; England wins the Ashes in Australia; the last edition of the 'News of the World' is printed.*

It is proposed in Supreme Grand Chapter to use 2013 as the catalyst to publish new ritual books, which will have all permitted alternatives of the ritual, as well as the main version and the original version printed out separately (April). This is in the process of being implemented.

Six new Grand Superintendents are installed in the Provinces, as well as a new Grand Superintendent for the North Island of New Zealand (9 November).

2012 *The Queen's Diamond Jubilee is celebrated; London hosts the Olympic and Paralympics Games; the findings of the Leveson Inquiry into the British media are announced.*

The number of chapters on the Grand Chapter register is 3,135 (of which 577 are in London, 2,241 in the provinces and 317 abroad).

UGLE withdraws its recognition from the National Grand Lodge of France (GLNF). (12 September).

Royal Arch in Europe

The Royal Arch was not widespread outside England until the second half of the twentieth century. The first European Grand Chapter was attached to the National Grand Lodge of France and dates from the 1930s. Today, Grand Chapters are active – having been erected with the help of the Supreme Grand Chapter of England – in Belgium, Estonia, Finland, Germany, Hungary, Italy, the Netherlands and Switzerland, as well as progressing in various states of development under supervision in some East European countries.

The Research Fellows of the Royal College of Surgeons of England (Dr Martin Birchall, Dr Paul Moxley, Dr Kiran Hussain and Dr John Breze) make a presentation in Supreme Grand Chapter on aspects of their vital research projects funded and supported by the Craft and the Royal Arch. (14 November).

2013 *(or MMXIII), is the year of the publication of this book. It is a common year that started on a Tuesday. In the Gregorian (Western or Christian) calendar, it is the 2013th year of the Christian Era (CE) or Anno Domini (AD), the Year of the Lord. In the Masonic way of measuring time, it is year 6013 of the Year of Light or Anno Lucis (A.L.). It is year 5774 in the Hebrew Calendar and 1435 in the Islamic one. It is the thirteenth year in the third millennium and the 21st century.*

At the Quarterly Communication of the United Grand Lodge of England on 13 March 2013 the Pro Grand Master Peter Lowndes states:

> Brethren,
> In my address to Grand Lodge last December I commented that we should be proud of our history. I therefore have no qualms – indeed I believe it is important – in mentioning that this year marks an important landmark in the history of our Grand Lodge: the two hundredth anniversary of the Union between the Ancients and Modern Grand Lodges. The actual – forming the United Grand Lodge of England – took place at Freemasons' Hall on St John's Day, December 27th 1813.
> It is therefore more appropriate that we mark this major anniversary later in the year at the December Quarterly Communication. At that time I hope that Brothers Hamill and Redman will give us an account of the intriguing story of how this was finally achieved and its importance to English Freemasonry in particular and world-wide Freemasonry in general.
> However, I mention this anniversary today for two main reasons. First, because those of you who are also members of the Royal Arch know that the Order is holding its own celebration in October of this year. It is to mark the decision, achieved during the negotiations leading to the Union, that the Royal Arch be recognised as an essential part of pure ancient Freemasonry, forging an indissoluble link between the Craft and the Royal Arch.
> Secondly, and importantly for us, rather than making major celebrations this year we have decided to concentrate our efforts on 2017 and the celebration of our tercentenary of the formation of Grand Lodge in 1717. This is considered the more important of the two events and a celebration of both would inevitably stretch all recourses beyond any reasonable limit. It is intended that these celebrations will take place throughout the constitution both at home and overseas.

Celebratory Convocation of Supreme Grand Chapter 16 October 2013

The official announcement on the website of the Order, at the time of writing (May 2013), states:

> To mark the bicentenary of the formal recognition of the Holy Royal Arch as part of pure Antient Masonry [...] the Convocation of Supreme Grand Chapter in November 2013 has been moved to the afternoon of the third Wednesday in October to take advantage of what it is hoped will be more clement weather before the clocks go back. Plans are in place for 2013, a significant year for both Supreme Grand Chapter and Metropolitan Grand Chapter. It is the bicentenary of the Act of Union between the Antients and the Moderns, which established Royal Arch masonry as we know it today, and also marks the 10th anniversary of Metropolitan Grand Chapter itself. Supreme Grand Chapter is arranging a celebratory Convocation on the afternoon of 16 October 2013. Additionally there will be a demonstration in the morning of an exaltation using the permitted alternative version of the Aldersgate ritual by the Metropolitan Grand Stewards Chapter. At this planning stage the following provisional program is envisaged:

> 11:00am in the Grand Temple: Convocation of Metropolitan Grand Stewards Chapter No. 9812 in which a demonstration of the Ceremony of Exaltation using the changes authorised in 2004 will be given.

> 1:00pm in the Grand Connaught Rooms: Reception and Luncheon presided over by the ME Pro First Grand Principal.

> 4:30pm in the Grand Temple: Convocation of Supreme Grand Chapter, presided over by the ME The First Grand Principal, HRH The Duke of Kent, KG

> 6:15pm at the Savoy Hotel: Dinner, presided over by the ME The First Grand Principal.

> It is estimated that, after accommodating those whose presence is regarded as essential, there will be space in the Grand Temple for approximately 1,500 at the Demonstration in the morning and approximately 1,500 at the Convocation of Grand Chapter in the afternoon. It is likely that there will be one or more overflow rooms with a video link to the Grand Temple.
> At luncheon in the Grand Connaught Rooms (which will be restricted to those attending the Demonstration and/or the Convocation) approximately 650 places will be available in the Grand Hall and the Balmoral Room and there may also be one or more overflow rooms with a video link. For the

157

dinner in the evening at The Savoy, space will be severely limited and places will be available only to companions attending the Convocation of Grand Chapter in the afternoon.

Post Script Appeal

On 14 November 2012, in addressing the Supreme Grand Chapter, the Pro First Grand Principal, Companion Peter Lowndes, stated:

> I am delighted to say that, with the generosity of so many of you individually and collectively from Chapters, we are well on our way to meeting the target for the Royal Arch Masons 2013 Bicentenary Appeal for the Royal College of Surgeons [. . .] I hope we will be able to exceed our original target [of 1 Million pounds] by a very considerable margin. During the year presenters from the College have attended several Provincial meetings to explain what they do. I am told that these have all been very well received. I would particularly like to highlight an event earlier in the year when the First Grand Principal attended a fascinating presentation at the College in Lincoln's Inn Fields.
>
> Four Freemasons' research Fellows gave talks on their vital research projects that we had funded. These talks dealt with very technical research, but were delivered in such a way that even laymen such as myself could understand them. The importance of their research cannot be over-emphasised and as you know the College receives no NHS funding for research, so this has all to be paid for by voluntary contribution.
>
> We remain justly proud to be the major benefactor and I thank all of you who have, and will be, contributing to this worthwhile Appeal.

*   *   *   *   *

Bibliography

Barlow, C. T., 'H R A Chapter Ensigns and Banners' (Birmingham: Odbury, 1949)

Beckett, D. A., *A talk given to London First Principals Chapter No. 2712 on 31 January 1992*, typescript (LLMF, No. BE 385 BEC)

Belton, John, 'The English Masonic Union of 1813: A Tale Antient and Modern' (Bury St. Edmunds: Arima Publishing, 2012)

Beresiner, Yasha, 'Royal Arch: the 4th Degree of the Antients', *Batham Royal Arch Lecture*, (London: Supreme Grand Chapter of England, Privately printed, 2000)

Brett, Lionel, 'English Royal Arch Masonry Overseas', *AQC*, 96 (1983), pp. 184-189

Brodsky, Michel, 'Some Reflections On The Origins Of The Royal Arch', *AQC*, 102 (1989), pp. 98-133

Burford, Douglas William, 'The Anomalies of the Royal Arch-Craft Connection', *Batham Royal Arch Lecture*, (London: Privately printed, 1993)

Bywater, Witham Matthew, 'Notes on Lau: Dermott G.S. and his Work' (London: Privately printed, 1884)

Carr, Harry, 'More Light on the Royal Arch', *AQC*, 76 (1963), pp. 213-218

    - 'More Light of the Royal Arch', *Masonic Record*, (July 1963), p. 24

    -'The relationship between the Craft and The Royal Arch', *AQC*, 86 (1973), pp. 35-86

Castells, F. de P., 'Antiquity of the Holy Royal Arch: the supreme degree in Freemasonry' (London: A Lewis, 1927)

Clarke, Joseph Ryle, 'The Ritual of the Royal Arch', *AQC*, 75 (1962), pp. 227-231

Cryer, Neville Barker, 'The Master's Part: A re-appraisal', *AQC*, 110 (1997), pp. 21-49

    -'The Royal Arch Journey' (Shepperton, Surrey: Lewis Masonic, 2009)

    - 'What do you Know About The Royal Arch' (Shepperton, Surrey: Lewis Masonic, 2002)

Dashwood, John R., 'Notes on the First Minute Book of the Excellent Grand and Royal Chapter', *AQC*, 62 (1949), pp. 165-185

    -'The Second and Third Minute Books of the Grand Chapter', *AQC*, 72 (1959), pp. 63-74

Draffen, George S., 'The Triple Tau - Supreme Grand Chapter of Scotland' (Edinburgh: Geo Stewart & Co, 1955)

Dyer, Colin, 'William Preston and his Work' (Shepperton, Surrey: Lewis Masonic, 2002)

Edwards, Lewis, 'Augustus Frederick, Duke of Sussex', *AQC*, 52 (1941), pp. 184-222

Gould, Robert Freke, 'Military Lodges 1732-1899' (London: Gale and Polden, 1899)

- 'The History of Freemasonry 1882-7' (Edinburgh: Thomas C Jack, 1887)

Grantham, J. A., *History of the Grand Lodge of Mark Master Masons* (London: A Lewis (Masonic Publishers), 1960)

Hamill, J. M., 'The Duke of Sussex and the Union, 1813. A new document', *AQC*, 86 (1973), pp. 286-290

- 'English Grand Lodge Warrants, Premier and Antients to 1813', *AQC*, 90, (1977) pp. 92-141

- 'English Royal Arch "MS." - Rituals c.1780-1830', *AQC*, 95 (1982), pp. 37-54

Haunch, Terence Osborne, 'The Royal Arch in England, Ireland and Scotland', *AQC*, 86, (1973), pp. 326-327

Hawkyard, W. H. and Worts, F. R., 'The Ceremony of "Passing the Veils"', *AQC*, 62 (1949), pp. 186-193

[Hewitt, A. R.,] 'Bi-centenary, 1766 - 1966, Supreme Grand Chapter of Royal Arch Masons of England: especial convocation, 1st July, 1966' (London: Privately printed, 1966)

Hughan, W. J., 'English Royal Arch Masonry, 1744-1765', *AQC*, 4 (1891), pp. 220-223

- 'Memorials of the Masonic Union of A D 1813 […]' (Leicester: Printed by Johnson, Wykes & Paine, 1913)

- 'Origin of the English Rite of Masonry, especially in Relation to the Royal Arch Degree' (Leicester: Publisher, 1884)

Inman, Herbert F., 'Royal Arch working Ritual Explained: a practical handbook for the guidance of officers' (London: Spencer & Co, 1933)

Johnson, G. Y., 'The York Grand Chapter, Or Grand Chapter of All England', *AQC*, 57 (1944), pp. 196-255

Jones, B. E., 'Freemason's Book of the Royal Arch' (London: George G Harrap & Co, 1957)

- 'Masters Lodges and their place in Pre-Union History', *AQC*, 67 (1954), pp. 13-28

Kelly, William Redfern, 'The Advent of Royal Arch Masonry', *AQC*, 30 (1917), pp. 7-55

Kent, E. A., 'Royal Arch: The Present Day Ritual', *AQC*, 46 (1933), pp. 222-225

Knoop, Douglas, 'Pure Ancient Masonry', *AQC*, 53 (1942), pp. 4-44

Lane, John, 'Masonic Records 1717-1894' (London: Published under the Authority of the United Grand Lodge of England, 1895)

Lepper, J. Heron, 'The Traditioners - A Study of Masonic Ritual in England in the 18th Century', *AQC*, 56 (1943), pp. 138-204

Mandleberg, C. J., 'Promulgation and Reconciliation', *AQC*, 123 (2010), pp. 77-102

Mendoza , I. Harry, 'The Masonic Qualifications for the Royal Arch', *AQC*, 96 (1983), pp. 47-64

Ogilvie, E. E., 'Freemasons' Royal Arch Guide' (Surrey: A Lewis 1978)

Ough, Anthony, 'The Origin and Development of Royal Arch Masonry', *The Batham Royal Arch Lecture* (London: Privately printed, 1991)

Rylands, Richard John, 'The Wakefield Chapter of Royal Arch Masons No. 495' (Wakefield: Privately printed, 1949)

Sadler, Henry, 'Thomas Dunckerley, His Life, Labours and Letters' (London: Diprose & Bateman, 1891)

Sandbach, Richard, 'Understanding The Royal Arch' (Shepperton, Surrey: Lewis Masonic, 1992)

Smyth, Frederick, 'A Reference Book for Freemasons' (London: QCCC Ltd, 1998)

Spencer, Norman Berridge, 'Supreme Grand Chapter, Royal Arch Regalia and Clothing', *AQC*, 73 (1960), pp. 3-9

Stubbs, James Wilfrid, 'Qualification for the Royal Arch', *AQC*, 79 (1966), pp. 195-196

Thomas, Aubrey J. B., 'A Brief History of the Royal Arch in England', *AQC*, 85 (1972), pp. 349-358

Tokes, John, and Flather, David, 'The History of Royal Arch Masonry in Sheffield' (Sheffield: printed by J W Northend Ltd., 1922)

[United Grand Lodge of England] 'Masonic Year Book - Historical Supplement' (London: Freemasons' Hall, 1964)

Vibert, Arthur Lionel, 'The Interlaced Triangles of the Royal Arch', *AQC*, 80 (1967, pp. 328-330

Ward, Eric Dassigny, 'Early Masters' Lodges and their Relation to Degrees', *AQC*, 75 (1962), pp. 124-154

-'Youghal and all that (Royal Arch, Ireland 1744)', *AQC*, 88 (1975), pp. 20-31

Wells, Roy A., 'Royal Arch Matters' (Shepperton, Surrey: Lewis Masonic, 1984)

-'The Premier Grand Lodge and the Delayed Recognition of the Royal Arch', *AQC*, 82 (1969), pp. 74-100

-'Why the Royal Arch? - An Introduction to the Supreme Degree', *AQC*, 78 (1965), pp. 216-221

*Åkerrén, Y., 'London in December 1813: The Place and Time of a Momentous Encounter of English with Swedish Rites', *AQC*, 115 (2002), pp. 184-204

* 'Å' in the Swedish alphabet is the last letter in the alphabet, equivalent to Z.

Appendix I

Select Glossary

ALTAR In the Royal Arch, the altar 'wrought in the form of the double cube' referred to as the pedestal in early minutes, is centrally placed in the chapter with the essential emblems placed on it and the six lights around it in the form of an equilateral triangle.

ANNO INVENTIONIS In relation to the Royal Arch, the words literally translated mean 'The Year of the Discovery', referring to the discovery of the vault at the commencement of the building of the second Temple in Jerusalem in BC 530.

BANNERS Two sets of banners or standards appear as part of the essential furniture of a Royal Arch Chapter in England. Four principal banners, placed in the East behind the thrones of the Principals, are blue, purple, scarlet, and white respectively and have representations of an ox, a man, a lion and an eagle depicted on them. The Triple Tau is usually centrally placed as a fifth banner. The additional twelve banners in the body of the chapter on either side of the altar, are derived from ensigns that were borne by the twelve Tribes of Israel during their encampment in the wilderness, namely Asher, Naphtali, Zebulon, Manasseh, Gad, Reuben, Issachar, Ephraim, Dan, Benjamin, Judah and Simon. "Every man of the children of Israel shall pitch by his own standard."

BATHAM LECTURE This is the Royal Arch equivalent of the Prestonian Lecture in the Craft, the only official Lecture sponsored by the United Grand Lodge of England. It was instituted by Cyril N. Batham in 1977 and is now the only officially sponsored lecture by the Supreme Grand Chapter of England. The appointment is made every few years and five Batham Lecturers have been appointed to date.

CAPITULAR MASONRY The term used when referring to Royal Arch Masonry in the United States under the American system.

CATENARIAN ARCH If a rope is loosely suspended by its two ends, the curve into which it falls is called a Catenarian curve. When inverted this forms the Catenarian arch, considered to be the strongest of all arches. Where a Craft lodge may be seen to take the form of an oblong square, the equivalent in an English Royal Arch chapter is that of a Catenarian arch. The word is derived from the Latin 'catena', meaning a chain. 'The form of a chapter is a "true Catenarian Arch", the three Principals sitting in the Arch and the Companions forming the sides.'

CHAPTER The name now given to the assembly of companions meeting as a body of Royal Arch Masons. It is also used by members of other degrees and orders, notably that of the Ancient and Accepted Rite, popularly denominated 'the Rose Croix' in England. The term Chapter derives from early medieval usage in ecclesiastical contexts. In 'modern' speculative Freemasonry, Lawrence Dermot, Grand Secretary of the Antients Grand Lodge, is the first formally to refer to a chapter in *Ahiman Rezon*, the Constitutions of the Antients, in 1756 when he states: '*a Royal Arch gathering being more sublime and important than any of those which preceded it [. . .] from its pre-eminence is denominated, amongst Masons, a Chapter*'. The earlier references by Anderson in the 1717 Constitutions, to Masters and Wardens of particular '*Lodges*' having the right and authority of congregating in '*Chapters*', are regarded as being a reference to a 'group of brethren' and a 'meeting place', respectively. From the date of the issuing of the Charter of Compact in 1766 the term Chapter is used freely.

COMPANION 'Companion' is the modern term used for a member of a Royal Arch chapter. In the earlier days of Royal Arch Masonry, the term 'Brother' is used for members of the Royal Arch. The term 'companion' starts to be the most common way of referring to a member of a Royal Arch chapter after the signing of the Charter of Compact in 1766 in which the first formal reference to 'companions' occurs.

DATING Royal Arch Masonry uses a system of time measurement that counts as its first year the start of the rebuilding of the second Temple. The rebuilding was begun by Zerubbabel and the year is calculated by adding 2348 to the current year. It is abbreviated A.I., standing for '*Anno Inventionis*', 'Year of the Discovery'.

DOMATIC see GEOMATIC MASTER MASON below

EXALTATION The term is today used for the admission of a brother as a companion in a Royal Arch chapter. 'Initiation' became 'exaltation' for the first time in the Charter of Compact and in some earlier minutes. The source is of Latin origin, and means 'to raise' or 'lift up'. The term 'initiates' is used in a Royal Arch context well into the early nineteenth century. The last recorded use of the word 'initiate' in the sense of admitting a brother as a companion into a chapter is dated c1810.

EXCELLENT MASTER This is a degree no longer practiced under the English Royal Arch ritual. In Scottish freemasonry, however, the degree is essential for a candidate who wishes to be admitted into a Royal Arch Chapter. This is where the ceremony of the 'Passing of the Veils' is conducted, now obsolete in England (with the exception of the Province of Bristol). The term 'Excellent' is applied to the Three Principals and Past Principals of a chapter in the Royal Arch in England, and to their counterparts, the Kings and Past Kings in Ireland.

EZRA See SCRIBE, below

GENERAL GRAND CHAPTER This is, more or less, the American equivalent to the Supreme Grand Chapter of England, being the highest authority for the Royal Arch in the American system. It originated in 1797, since when, because of its scope, it has acted as an administrative body and not a legislative one. Each State in the United States of America has its own Grand Chapter which acknowledges the supremacy of the General Grand Chapter. Several additional Grand Chapters in Europe, Mexico, Canada and the Philippines, do the same.

GEOMATIC MASTER MASON This was the required qualification for a candidate for the Royal Arch under the Antients Grand Lodge prior to 1813. The concept appears to have been equivalent to having served as the Master of a Craft lodge. It is not now part of the Royal Arch system. In the eighteenth century, 'Geomatic' was a term equivalent to 'speculative', as opposed to 'Domatic', which would have equated to 'operative'. These terms were in use in Scotland. They do not occur in the Oxford English Dictionary.

GRAND HIGH PRIEST This title has several connotations. It is the equivalent, in the American system, of the first Principal or Zerubbabel of an English Royal Arch Chapter, namely the presiding officer of a Grand Royal Arch Chapter. Its origins can be traced to the very start of the 19th century. Since 1880, when the Allied Masonic Degrees were established in England, it is one of the five degrees within that Order. All Royal Arch masons are now eligible to attain the degree.

GRAND PRINCIPAL One of the triumvirate that rules the Supreme Grand Chapter of the Royal Arch in England. The peculiar and effectively unique system in England, since 1817, has the *Royal Arch Regulations* prescribing that The Grand Master of the United Grand Lodge of England and his Deputy are the first and second Grand Principals of the Supreme Grand Chapter, provided that they are qualified as installed First Principals of a private chapter. It has also become customary since 1914 for the third Grand Principal to be a clergyman. The Supreme Grand Chapter of England (successor to the Grand and Royal Chapter founded in 1766, and dissolved as part of pure and Ancient Masonry in the union of 1813) had the three Grand Principals named Grand Master Z, H and J, respectively.

HAGGAI This Hebrew prophet at the building of the Second Temple in Jerusalem was one of the twelve minor prophets in the Jewish Bible and the accredited author of the impressive two-chapter Book of Haggai. Zerubbabel, and Joshua the son of Josedech, both appear in that text, and all three, Zerubbabel, Haggai and Joshua, are designated as the names given to the three Principals of an English Royal Arch Chapter.

HIGH PRIEST The High Priest is the presiding officer in an American Royal Arch Chapter, equivalent to Zerubbabel, the first Principal in England. The King (see below) is thus a subordinate. After the rebuilding of the second Temple the High Priest was responsible for the government of the Jews.

HOLY ROYAL ARCH There are several references to the Order as the 'Holy Royal Arch', as it was referred to among the Antients and (as such) the term used in the Articles of Union in 1813. It should be noted that the subsequent official title of the Order does not feature the word 'Holy' and is: 'The Supreme Grand Chapter of Royal Arch Masons of England'.

JANITOR The term is derived from the Roman god Janus who gave his name to the month of January. He was the guardian of gates and thus 'janitor' translates as 'door keeper'. This is indeed the Janitor's duty in a Royal Arch chapter, equivalent to that of the Tyler of a Craft lodge.

JOSHUA Joshua figures as the third Principal in a Royal Arch Chapter, after Zerubbabel and Haggai, as the son of the High Priest Josedech. All three are closely associated with the building of the second Temple in Jerusalem. He is not to be confused with the Joshua who figures in the second degree of the Craft and who became the leader of the Israelite tribes after the death of Moses.

KING The King in a Royal Arch chapter in the United States under the American system is the equivalent of the second Principal in an English chapter. He represents Zerubbabel, the Prince of Judah. The King acts as Senior Warden when the chapter meets in one of the other degrees associated with the Royal Arch, namely as a Mark Lodge or an Excellent Master's Lodge.

MOST EXCELLENT MASTER A degree practiced in the United States, which is a pre-requisite to the Royal Arch. In England it is outside the realm of the Royal Arch and falls within the jurisdiction of the Order of Royal and Select Masters. It is not a degree that is practiced under the Irish or Scottish jurisdictions.

NEHEMIAH See SCRIBE, below

NIL NISI CLAVIS DEEST The literal translation of the Latin is 'Nothing is wanting but the key'. The motto is related to the Royal Arch because it is inscribed on the Royal Arch jewel attached to the double triangle emblem of the Order.

PRINCIPAL The three presiding officers in an English chapter of Royal Arch Masons are called the Three Principals and represent Zerubbabel, Haggai, and Joshua. A companion is not eligible to the First Principal's chair unless he has served twelve months in each of the other two. He must also be the Master or Past Master of a Lodge, except in the case of Joshua, and have served in the office of Scribe, Sojourner, or Assistant Sojourner of the chapter.

RITUAL (the Royal Arch Legend) The present exaltation ceremony is based on the biblical legend in 2 Kings 25, which gives an account of the three sojourners, making their way to Jerusalem after the expulsion of the Jewish people from Persia by Nebuchadnezzar (604 to 562 BC). The candidate acts as one of the sojourners. Their request to the representative of King Solomon and the members of the Sanhedrin to be allowed to participate in the reconstruction of the Second Temple (BC 516 to 70 AD) is conceded. As a result they proceed to work and accidentally discover a vault, within which is a sacred scroll. On reporting back to the Sanhedrin the sojourners are rewarded by being made Royal Arch Masons.

ROYAL ART This is a term that appears some two dozen times in Anderson's Constitutions of 1723 and in one instance it is associated with the words '[. . .] well built Arch.'. These references to the Royal Art are intended to emphasise the patronage of the Craft by monarchs and have no connection whatever with the Royal Arch as a Masonic Order or otherwise.

SASH A sash is worn by a Royal Arch companion as an essential part of his regalia in England and consists of a particularly-coloured and patterned ribbon draping from the left shoulder to the right hip. It may represent the sash that in olden days supported the scabbard of a brother's sword.

SCOTS MASTER This is translated into or from French as 'Maître Écossais'. It has no connection with Scotland. It is seen as an early degree beyond the Craft, possibly practiced by French Prisoners of the Napoleonic War in England (1803–1815), without any detail as to its content and working. Some rites in England and the European continent incorporate the 'Scottish Master' considered to be of the same origin. The appearance of 'Scots Master' lodges in England during the 1730s has given rise to some theories of association with early Royal Arch activity but this speculation lacks evidence as yet.

SCRIBE Scribe is a word with important connotations in the Royal Arch in England in particular, where Scribe Ezra, as Secretary of the Chapter, and Scribe Nehemiah, as the inner guard, are the most senior members of the chapter below the three Principals. This status qualifies them for election to the third Principal's chair. The biblical story of Ezra the Scribe goes back to the time when the Jews had returned from the Babylonian exile, rebuilt the Holy Temple and lived freely in their Holy Land. Jerusalem was the centre of Jewish life. Nehemiah, the son of Hachaliah, is the central figure of the Book of Nehemiah, which describes his work rebuilding Jerusalem.

SPIRITUALITY In freemasonry, spirituality is a personal and private experience. The three Craft degrees are intended as a subjective journey of self-discovery and learning. We are taught, through the ritual and by parables in the lectures, that we are more than practical beings and that by our comportment and by abiding by moral rules we will serve the Lord, no matter what our religious persuasion might be. As my friend and colleague, the Revd Bro Elkan Levy has stated, in the Royal Arch and its interdenominational nature, we are given the opportunity to cultivate that very vital spiritual aspect in the nature of us all. We are here invited to consider the nature of God and our relationship with Him. Spirituality is not to be confused with religion.

TRACING BOARD Royal Arch tracing boards are not a common feature in chapters and most Masonic furnishers do not stock them. Evidence of the nature of the practice of Royal Arch in the early eighteenth century is often attributed to features appearing on early artefacts, which were later incorporated into the Royal Arch ceremony. This applies to some early floor cloths, the predecessors of tracing boards, which appear to display devices recognisable as Royal Arch emblems. There is a design of a Royal Arch tracing board, which is illustrated in the ritual of *The Perfect Ceremonies* since its 1877 edition. (The first edition, entitled *The Perfect Ceremonies of Craft Masonry according to the most approved forms as taught in the Union's Emulation Lodge of Improvement for M. Ms.* [London]), was privately printed for John Hogg under the pseudonym 'A. Lewis', in 1874). This tracing board was based on a 1834 painting by John Harris, who is otherwise best known for his tracing-boards for the Craft degrees. The Royal Arch ritual does not include any lecture on Royal Arch tracing boards. This may be because the layout of a Chapter room displays all elements present in John Harris's painting. In addition, many of the items are dealt with in the course of the ceremony and need no further explanation.

TRIPLE TAU This is the emblem most readily associated with the Royal Arch. It is depicted on the cover of this book. It consists of three taus, the Greek letter 'T', diagrammatically arranged. One early occurrence of its use is in the minutes of the Supreme Grand Chapter of England on 25 December 1766, when Bro [sic]John Maclean is thanked by Bro Dunckerley, just appointed MEZ, as Father and Promoter and is presented with a gold plate with the device on it. The plate also had the following inscription: *'Templum Hierosolymae, or the true Royal Arch Mason's Mark or Badge of Honor, P.S. Pater Societatis, the father of the Society [. . .] &c &c'.*

Until 1817 the simple T over H emblem stood for Templum Hierosolymae (the Temple of Jerusalem). After the re-establishment of the Royal Arch under the jurisdiction of the United Grand Chapter of England, the serifs (the short decorative lines at the finish of the two letters) were removed, creating the three levels now familiar as the emblem of the Royal Arch. The Triple Tau is now altogether differently described and explained in the Lectures that are recited during the ceremony and has no connotation to the Temple of Jerusalem.

During the late eighteenth and early nineteenth centuries, jewels made by the well-known jeweller and freemason, Thomas Harper, often had the triple tau emblem as part of the design of the Royal Arch jewel. This has been erroneously interpreted as being the letters TH identifying the maker by his initials. It is possible to speculate, without evidence, that Harper capitalised on the coincidence of his initials with the Triple Tau and deliberately designed the Royal Arch jewels to include the words 'Tho.s Harper Fecit' imbedded in a ribbon.

VISITING Since the Supreme Grand Chapter of England does not formally recognise other Grand Chapters, all the companions of a Grand Chapter who are recognised by the Grand Lodge in the same territory are deemed to be regular, so long as the Grand Lodge is recognised by the United Grand Lodge of England. Royal Arch Masonic Convention dictates that communications between Grand Chapters be conducted by the Grand Scribes Ezra. English Constitution chapters who wish to host a visit from a companion from an overseas chapter should check with the office of Grand Scribe Ezra to ensure that they are from an recognised and acceptable constitution. Brethren from constitutions that work the Swedish or Scandinavian Rite must have completed their sixth degree to be qualified to attend an English Royal Arch meeting, and reciprocal arrangements apply.

YORK RITE The York Rite is also referred to as the 'American Rite'. It is worked in the United States and, to a lesser extent, in Canada. It incorporates the three Craft degrees, as well as degrees practised in the Royal Arch system, namely the Mark Degree, the Excellent Master's and the Royal Arch Degree itself and the Orders of the Red Cross, Malta and the Temple (abbreviated titles). The candidate for the York Rite must pass through each of these degrees in turn. After becoming a Royal Arch mason a companion may also take the degrees of the Order of Royal and Select Masters, but these are not normally regarded as essential. In each State of the United States there is a close relationship between the Grand Lodge, the Grand Chapter, the Grand Council and the Grand Commandery of the respective Orders.

ZERUBBABEL (there are many variations in the spelling of the name). Zerubbabel is a Biblical figure. He was the Prince of Judah at the time of the return of the two tribes to Jerusalem from the Babylonian captivity. It is generally agreed that he was the lineal descendant of Nathan, son of King David. After the decree of Cyrus, King of the Persians, Zerubbabel led the returning colony to Jerusalem, accompanied by Joshua (or Jeshua) the son of Josedech, and accompanied by Haggai and Zechariah. In the Holy City he supervised the rebuilding of the Temple. Zerubbabel's most important role in Freemasonry is in the Royal Arch. In England he is represented as the first of the three Principals of a Royal Arch Chapter, with kingly power and office, and is denominated 'Most Excellent'.

Appendix II

Administration of Supreme Grand Chapter

The Supreme Grand Chapter of England is the governing body of Royal Arch Masons in England, Wales and the Channel Islands. Its headquarters is situated at:

Supreme Grand Chapter
Freemasons' Hall
60 Great Queen Street
London WC2B 5AZ
Tel: +44 (0) 20 7831 9811
Fax: +44 (0) 20 7831 6021

Convocations of the Supreme Grand Chapter of England are held each year on the second Wednesday in November and on the day following the Grand Festival of Grand Lodge. It has 107,167 members (as of April 2013) grouped in 3,484 chapters. Chapters in London (an area within a ten-mile radius of Freemasons' Hall), are organised into groups administered by the Metropolitan Grand Chapter of London. Chapters outside London and within England, Wales and the Channel Islands are grouped into forty-seven provinces, based on the old counties, each headed by a Provincial Grand Superintendent. Chapters meeting abroad are grouped in thirty-two districts, each headed by a District Grand Superintendent, and seven groups each headed by a Grand Inspector, with seven chapters being administered from Freemasons' Hall.

Appendix III

Titles of Grand Chapter

In 1765 an 'Excellent Grand and Royal Chapter' was established by members of the Moderns (or premier) Grand Lodge. Its existence was ratified by a Charter of Compact dated 22 July 1766 that constituted this new body as the 'Grand and Royal Chapter of the Royal Arch of Jerusalem'. This entity changed its title on several occasions before it became the 'Supreme Grand Chapter of England', the governing body of Royal Arch freemasonry that was formed on 18 March 1817 (dropping the appellation 'United', without ceremony or formality, in 1822). The following is a listing in **alphabetic** order of the headings in the Minute Books of Supreme Grand Chapter, between 1765 and 1813. The date following each entry indicates the first time that a new title was used. 'The' has been omitted from the titles.

Chapter – Minutes: 2 Feb to 13 Dec 1776

Excellent Grand and Royal Chapter - [First named body meeting in 1765]

General Chapter - Minutes: Dec 1797

General Chapter of Communication Royal Arch – 1 May 1798

General Chapter of Communication of Royal Arch Masons – Minutes: 22 Mar 1803

General Chapter of Communication Royal Arch Masons under the authority of the Supreme Grand & Royal Chapter of England - Minutes: 25 Jan 1803

General Chapter of Convocation – Minutes: 13 May 1797

General Chapter of Convocation Royal Arch - 20 Dec 1798

General Chapter of Convocation of Royal Arch Masons – Minutes: 7 May 1807

Grand & Royal Arch Chapter of General Communication – Minutes: 10 May 1793

Grand & Royal Arch Chapter of Jerusalem – Minutes: 28 Nov 1793

Grand & Royal Chapter – Minutes: 8 May 1778

Grand & Royal Chapter – Minutes: 25 May 1781

Grand & Royal Chapter of Communication - Minutes: 4 May 1792

Grand & Royal Chapter of England – Minutes: 25 Jan 1803

Grand & Royal Chapter of General Communication – Minutes: 20 Dec 1792

Grand & Royal Chapter of Jerusalem – Minutes: 28 Mar 1793

Grand & Royal Chapter of the Royal Arch of Jerusalem – Charter of Compact 1766 and Minutes: from 27 Mar 1794

Grand & Royal Chapter of The Royal Arch of Jerusalem – Minutes: 25 Apr 1793

Grand Communication of Royal Arch Masons – Minutes: 18 Dec 1794

Grand Convention – Minutes: 27 Feb 1794

Grand Convention of Royal Arch Masonry - Minutes: 10 May 1793

Grand Convocation – Minutes: 19 Dec 1793

Grand Convocation Communication - Minutes: 9 May 1794

Most Excellent Grand Royal Chapter – Minutes: 12 Jan 1776

Royal Arch Grand Chapter – Minutes: 26 Jan 1808

Royal Arch Grand Chapter of Communication – Minutes: 16 Dec 1802

Royal Arch Grand Lodge - Minutes: 12 Jan to 11 May 1781

Supreme Grand & Royal Chapter of England - Minutes: 7 May 1807

Supreme Grand & Royal Chapter of Royal Arch Masons of England – Minutes: 22 Feb 1803 & Union 1813

Supreme Grand & Royal Chapter of Royal Arch Masons of England Grand Chapter of Convocation - Minutes: 24 Jan 1809

Supreme Grand & Royal Chapter of Royal Arch Masons of England - Grand Chapter of Communication – Minutes: 2 Apr 1808

Supreme Grand Chapter – Minutes: 23 Apr 1801

Supreme Grand Chapter of England – Minutes: 18 March 1817

United Supreme Grand Chapter of England – Minutes: March 1817

Index

H

Z